Professional Music-Making in London

Professional Music-Making in London

Ethnography and Experience

STEPHEN COTTRELL

SOAS Musicology Series

ASHGATE

Published by
Ashgate Publishing Limited
Gower House
Croft Road
Aldershot
Hampshire GU11 3HR
England

Ashgate Publishing Company
Suite 420
101 Cherry Street
Burlington, VT 05401-4405
USA

Ashgate website: http://www.ashgate.com

British Library Cataloguing in Publication Data
Cottrell, Stephen
    Professional music-making in London : ethnography and experience. - (SOAS musicology series)
    1.Musicians - England - London 2.Music - Performance - England - London
    I.Title II.University of London. School of Oriental and African Studies
    780.9'421

Library of Congress Cataloging-in-Publication Data
Cottrell, Stephen, 1962-
  Professional music-making in London : ethnography and experience / Stephen Cottrell.
    p. cm. -- (SOAS musicology series)
  Includes bibliographical references.
  ISBN 0-7546-0887-5
    1. Music--England--London. 2. Ethnomusicology. I. Title. II. Series.

ML286.8.L5C68 2004
780'.9421--dc22

2003063997

ISBN 0 7546 0887 5 (Hbk)
     0 7546 0889 1 (Pbk)

Typeset by DC Graphic Design Ltd, Swanley, Kent
Printed and bound in Great Britain by TJ International Ltd, Padstow, Cornwall

For Eva

'What do you mean by that?' said the Caterpillar sternly. 'Explain yourself!'

'I can't explain myself, I'm afraid, sir,' said Alice, 'because I'm not myself, you see.'

Lewis Carroll, *Alice in Wonderland*

Contents

Preface

Given that much of what follows is already written in my own voice it seems unnecessarily narcissistic to include any more of it at this point. Instead it is incumbent upon me to thank those others who have provided a counterpoint to my voice (be it dissonant or consonant) or have chided and challenged it when it has become too voluble, too assertive or just plain wrong.

Most importantly, I have drawn upon the knowledge, expertise and time of a great number of musicians, either through formal interviews, informal discussions or as a result of the influence they have had upon me in those experiences of my own which lie embedded in the text. The protocol I have chosen to adopt here prevents me from naming even those who have been most directly involved, and although they must remain unidentified I thank them all now, while also hoping – paradoxically – that the anonymity I have worked hard to create will ensure that their efforts, so generously given, will never be duly credited.

Others are less fortunate in this respect. Much of this work has evolved within the stimulating environment of the music department of Goldsmiths College, London, and many of its inhabitants, staff and students alike, have provided helpful criticism of one sort or another, as parts of it have surfaced in seminars and conferences: Simon McVeigh, Colin Lawson (now at Thames Valley University) and Anthony Pryer have all furnished me with valuable feedback which has caused me to reflect on certain issues. Elsewhere Ruth Finnegan and Keith Howard read an earlier version of this work, and provided much constructive criticism upon it. My thanks to all of these, and to any others who may have now slipped my mind during the rather long gestation period of this study. I am also indebted to the Humanities Research Board of the British Academy for their award of a postgraduate studentship; this facilitated the doctoral studies which provided the foundation for the work.

Several parts of the book appeared in embryonic form as conference papers, and I am grateful for the comments and observations of delegates too numerous to mention, in these most congenial of surroundings. Chapter Three appeared as 'Music as Capital: Deputizing among London's Freelance Musicians' in the *British Journal of Ethnomusicology*, 11(2), 2002; my thanks to the editors for permission to reproduce it here, and to my anonymous readers for their insightful and stimulating comments.

Two final names remain, both of whom have, in their own way, overseen my transformation from poaching musician to gamekeeping ethnomusicologist: first, my erstwhile supervisor and now colleague, John Baily, who proved a master of both stick and carrot when needed, and who supported me in so many ways in my fledgling steps in the world of academe as well as providing numerous hours of convivial company outside it; also my wife, Eva Mantzourani, who met and married a musician but who has continued to offer her love and support throughout these most 'unmusical' of endeavours, and whose own enthusiasm for scholarship has been the inspiration for my paler attempts.

All remaining errors and inadequacies are mine alone.

Stephen Cottrell, London, July 2004

CHAPTER ONE

Points of Departure

Introduction

In the early 1990s, having worked for nearly a decade as a professional musician in London, I returned to academia part-time and enrolled for a Masters qualification. Although my chosen vocation was very hard work, and not especially financially rewarding, it did contain roughly equal proportions of both stimulating and disheartening employment: a perfectly normal mix for Western musicians and, no doubt, others besides. I did feel ready, however, for new intellectual challenges so, being fortuitously close to a college of the University of London, I scoured the prospectus of the music department for a suitable course. Since my 'day job' was as a performer and since like many musicians I had been studying musical performance for most of my life, I was disinclined to enrol for another predominantly performance-based qualification; nor did I feel drawn to the more historical approaches of traditional musicology, or the nuts and bolts of advanced Western music theory. This left one option, ethnomusicology, a word I could barely spell and knew nothing whatsoever about. It seemed the ideal choice.

There were only two of us at the first class of the course and to begin the proceedings the lecturer asked us how we might define the word 'ethnomusicology' to others. My new colleague answered first, and gave what appeared to me a learned and extensive response outlining a brief history of the discipline, various ways in which the word might be considered and, I think, ending up with Alan Merriam's now well-rehearsed definition of 'the study of music as culture' (Merriam, 1977:204). During this peroration my stomach sank slightly, and I had time to consider whether this course had been an entirely wise choice on my part. Naturally I had done some preliminary reading, particularly *The Anthropology of Music* (Merriam, 1964), and although my head was full of new ideas and concepts I was by no means able to put them forward in the same authoritative manner. However, bearing in mind that musicians like to joke that they can 'bluff at any speed', it was perhaps drawing on this ability that encouraged me to reply, when asked, that ethnomusicology was 'the study of people through their music'.

I am still rather fond of this definition, although I am perhaps now able to consider its limitations more clearly than I was then; it does at least avoid the ideological skid-pan of defining exactly what culture is.[1] But it remains true that people and their relationship to what they construe as music lie at the heart of ethnomusicology, as well as being more than occasionally significant within its two cognate disciplines, anthropology and musicology. The Greek etymology of the former illustrates this clearly enough, combining *anthropos* (human being) and *logos* (word, reason). But we are also dependent on people to define for us what music is, at least for them. In Western society (although not always elsewhere)[2] we generally incorporate the idea that musical sound originates with human beings in our definitions of what we consider music to be:[3] John Blacking's (1976) 'patterns of humanly organised sound' is one good example. Yet I am not the first to point out that traditional musicology has, until very recently, often treated the study of Western music in a rather abstracted, 'dehumanized' way, frequently divorcing musical texts, and the recreations of them, from the cultural environments in which they have arisen.[4]

Two significant points arise from this preamble: first, that I consider this study of professional musicians and music-making in London to be in some way ethnomusicological, and second, that, as my rather autobiographical introduction reveals, I intend to give myself a particular role within it. With regard to the first point there seems little to be gained here by continuing the debate as to what ethnomusicology is or should be. Merriam (1977) provides a comprehensive listing showing how the definition of the discipline has been manipulated over the years, and I have already added my ha'pence worth above. But I am mindful not only of John Morgan O'Connell's (1998) distinction between ethno-musicology and eth-no-musicology, but also of Laurence Picken's (1998) admonition that what most people are doing in the discipline these days should be described as the anthropology of music, *not* ethnomusicology: something that might be described perhaps, following O'Connell's morphological musings, as eth-'no music'-ology. Personally I am untroubled by these rather fine distinctions, and like many others I am prepared to consider these various terms as essentially synonymous, while remaining conscious of the differences that might be inferred from them. However the present work remains a cultural study of the work and lives of musicians in a particular context, and there is little reference to specific musical structures in what follows, and no musical examples or analysis. And although Picken and those of a similar inclination might wish to describe this work as essentially anthropological (and I could not argue with them for that) I shall continue to describe it as fundamentally ethnomusicological, representing an approach to the study of Western art music-making which draws to a considerable degree on the percepts and concepts of that notoriously hard-to-define discipline. As for the autobiographical nature of parts of the study, this is a significant point which I will deal with at length below.

Ethnomusicology and Western art music

Just as anthropology has sometimes been criticized as being ahistorical or overly synchronic, of providing us with ethnographies in which the experiential histories of individuals and groups have been subsumed among large-scale statements of social structures and cultural patterns, so one might criticize traditional musicology for just the opposite, of being unduly concerned with historical 'facts' and biographical details of individuals as apparently necessary prerequisites for illuminating or justifying the significance of this or that particular masterwork. Such musicology has seldom considered the way in which individuals and groups use music, or how the meanings with which they endow it might change according to context. Some have argued that such approaches are incompatible with Western music, that it is 'just too different from other musics, and its cultural contexts too different from other cultural contexts' (Kerman, 1985:174). Recently, however, traditional musicology has broadened its horizons and, like anthropology before it, has taken something of an 'interpretive turn', with the evolution of various trends such as Critical Musicology or New Musicology. The former has been influenced not only by the ideas of critical theory from which it takes its name, but also by sociological approaches to Western pop music.[5] The latter term covers a wide variety of approaches which in some way seek to move musicological discourse away from its traditional positivist path by drawing (in true postmodernist fashion) on a wide variety of disciplines, including psychoanalysis, semiotics, gender studies and so on.[6] Some of these studies seek to make connections between musical patterns and cultural contexts in an analogous fashion to the way in which ethnomusicologists have sought to explicate the music of other cultures.

What is clear, then, is that the traditional boundaries between various musicological approaches are becoming eroded; or to put it another way, the methodological holes which ethnomusicologists alone might previously have sought to plug are becoming fewer. This has a number of ramifications. It means that ethnomusicological approaches to Western music must compete not only with a newly invigorated musicology, but also with studies by sociologists,[7] psychologists[8] and social psychologists,[9] perhaps inevitably, given the inherent ethnocentricity of all these disciplines. Furthermore a conundrum arises from the fact that the majority of these academics are themselves Western, and many care passionately about, and identify with, the Western art music tradition which is also the object of their study; consequently theirs is also 'a native's point of view', which they are not slow to defend. Thus the 'happy-go-lucky liberal ethnomusicologist', as I was once memorably described by a fellow academic in a convivial post-dinner discussion on the merits and demerits of the Glyndebourne opera audience, treads warily in such company.

However, as Jonathan Stock (1998) has pointed out, there remain significant differences between these 'new' musicological approaches and those advocated by ethnomusicologists. In particular, the relationship between the writer/observer and the subject remains fundamentally different in these two areas. Musicologists cast themselves in the role of informed experts, providing readings or interpretations of musical practice *which remain subjective*, notwithstanding that their interpretations or readings of given artworks may attempt to establish links with other social or cultural practices in a manner analogous to ethnomusicological method. There is seldom room in their texts for other voices, except those fellow academics who are deemed worthy of inclusion for the purpose of theoretical engagement or as an obligation arising out of academic convention. Ethnomusicologists also cast themselves in the role of informed experts, but they attempt in their texts to make room for the folk view: interpretations of events or practices by those others for whom the music may be equally important or meaningful (and often more so), and whose view of it may be slightly different from that of the expert, or may give the latter's opinion more depth or resonance. It is this aggregation of the views of others which is a defining characteristic of musical ethnographies (and indeed modern ethnographies in general) and which, I suggest, distinguishes ethnomusicological approaches to Western art music from those mentioned above, no matter how new or critical they may be. This is not to suggest that ethnomusicologists promote an entirely objective perspective, a point to which I shall return below. But what ethnomusicologists *can* bring to the study of Western art music is an approach which draws more heavily on anthropological principles and which makes room for the voices of all those who consider the music to be theirs; in short, an approach which seeks, however imperfectly, to promote a more generalized, collective view, even though this view may be elucidated and edited by a single ethnographer and scaffolded by the framework of his or her own theorizing. But there is, I believe, a clear distinction between the long-term immersion in fieldwork which is necessary for this, and the frequently more subjective approaches advocated elsewhere.

Another feature which ethnomusicology has inherited from its alliance with matters anthropological is an approach which frequently foregrounds local rather than global perspectives. The discipline's focus on understanding the emic (insider's) point of view has often resulted in studies which emphasize the roles and meanings of musical sound within particular locales, or for relatively clearly-defined groups, rather than theorizing about global or even national trends. This is not entirely the case, of course, and there are enough examples which contradict this statement to reveal it as a generalization. For example, Mark Slobin's *Subcultural Sounds* (1993) is in part concerned with the relationships between locally grounded musics (subcultures) and the more overarching, umbrella-like forces (supercultures) with which they have symbiotic and sometimes tense relationships. Alan Lomax's well-known cantometrics project (Lomax, 1968) sought to establish comparative relationships between vocal style and social structure across a wide range of cultures. Yet, however flawed the observation may be, the characterization of ethnomusicology as being preoccupied with 'the folk view' appears sufficiently widespread for one recent critique of the discipline to be able to observe that 'it seems that the idea of the emic is so sacred ... that it is one of few theoretical and methodological approaches that not only form part of the field but almost define it' (Nercessian, 2002:12).

For present purposes, however, this thumbnail characterization of ethnomusicological practice suggests a significant potential benefit in applying ethnomusicological methodology to Western art music, and a notable contrast to approaches often taken by those musicologists who normally concern themselves with this tradition. For not only have such writers usually advanced interpretations of musical artworks which are highly subjective, frequently uncontested by any voices in their texts other than their own, they have also implicitly argued – in the absence of any suggestion to the contrary – that their readings of these works are equally relevant in all areas where such art works are propagated. This strikes me as improbable. As I argue at the beginning of Chapter Seven, it seems unlikely that a performance of, say, Elgar's *Pomp and Circumstance* marches or Wagner's *Siegfried* can mean the same to audiences in London, Dresden, Delhi and Hong Kong, yet the readings of such works provided by musicologists usually assume that they do. If an ethnomusicological investigation of locally grounded resonances and nuances can reveal different layers of meaning in such works as they are appropriated by different societies around the globe, this would seem to provide, at the very least, a useful adjunct to the appropriation practised by a small group of usually white, usually male, Western academics, however honourable their intentions.

However, while library shelves need continual lengthening to accommodate those approaches – 'new' or otherwise – advocated by various musicologists, the number of studies of Western art music by ethnomusicologists, or which we may cautiously describe as being in some way ethnomusicological, remains disconcertingly small. These would appear to fall into three discrete categories. The first encompasses those papers which consider the relationship between ethnomusicology and Western art music from a variety of theoretical perspectives. For example, Bruno Nettl (1963) suggests that paying attention to folk music taxonomies, an established methodology in ethnomusicology, might prove equally illuminating in the case of Western art music; Klaus Wachsmann (1981) reviews exoticism in Western art music composition and argues that 'the time has come for an Easterner or an African to be asked to give us an analysis of Western music in an Eastern or African way' (85); and both Kay Kaufman Shelemay (1996) and Jonathan Stock (1998) consider the nature of the overlap between ethnomusicology and 'conventional' musicological discourse.

A second category comprises those monographs and papers which apply ethnomusicological methodologies to Western institutions of one sort or another. Marcia Herndon's (1988) work on the demise of the Oakland Symphony Orchestra examines the degree of cultural fit between the orchestra and the community it nominally serves, and shows how the breakdown of this relationship reveals certain discrepancies which were not otherwise apparent. Her paper, although brief, is significant as an early practical application of ethnomusicological thinking to a Western art music ensemble. Two other studies scrutinize institutions of musical learning in the United States: Henry Kingsbury's (1988) *Music, Talent, and Performance* and Nettl's (1995) *Heartland Excursions*. In the former, Kingsbury examines the workings of an American music conservatoire and suggests that both music and talent are flexible concepts, defined by the way they are perceived and negotiated in a variety of contexts. He observes that music, particularly, cannot be defined without reference to 'a cultural system, a system of various and yet interdependent representations ... music is a cultural integument of social activity' (180–81). Nettl's subtitle (*Ethnomusicological reflections ...*) betrays his somewhat broader approach to a paradigmatic 'Heartland U.' music school, where he examines the nature of myth-making in the Western art music tradition and, as with Kingsbury, certain value systems arising within the institution itself. Both of these make occasional appearances in my own text. Perhaps more substantial is Georgina Born's (1995) *Rationalizing Culture*, a detailed ethnomusicological study (my description, not hers) of IRCAM,[10] Pierre Boulez's subterranean Parisian hideaway for advanced research into electro-acoustic music. Born's work has a very specific focus: to examine the usually antagonistic relationship between musical modernism, as represented by the technological boundary pushing which was IRCAM's *raison d'être*, and postmodernism, represented as a musical 'other' within this particular institution. It is a significant study which has perhaps not had the consideration in ethnomusicological circles it deserves, but I have been influenced by several of the approaches Born has taken, notably her introduction of certain elements of psychoanalytic theory, which have stimulated my own searches for appropriate theoretical frameworks.

Thus these four studies, and indeed a number of studies emanating from other disciplines,[11] all deal with bounded entities, fixed musical institutions of one sort or another. In three of the above four cases these entities are physically embodied in the buildings within which their work occurs, although of course they do have influences beyond this. The fourth, the symphony orchestra, does not really reside within a particular building in quite the same way (although it may have a concert hall which it uses regularly and an orchestral office), but it is of course delimited by its regular players and full-time administrators; it is relatively straightforward to decide where the orchestra begins and ends.

This is in noticeable contrast to ethnomusicological studies of musicians elsewhere, notwithstanding that it is also a natural consequence of the different social structures prevailing in Western society. Daniel Neuman (1980), for example, examines the lives and work of musicians in the Hindustani culture of North India (principally Delhi), the social structures existing among musicians, the relationship of such musicians to the larger society, and the strategies and concepts which underpin their work. Lorraine Sakata (1983) examines (among other things) the ethnosemantics surrounding the word 'musician' in certain parts of Afghanistan, while John Baily (1988) builds on her work to give a more complete picture of music in the city of Herat in western Afghanistan; his study, like Neuman's, also considers the social organization of musicians and their conceptualizations of its underlying structure. Thomas Turino (1993) has offered a comparative study of different Peruvian groups, from the older, rural generations of the Peruvian Altiplano, in both their original context and their regional clubs in Lima, to their children who have migrated to the urban centres, all of whom are involved with the same panpipe and flute traditions, notwithstanding that their participation is grounded on very different terms. In all of these musical ethnographies (and there are numerous similar studies which might equally have been cited) the perspective offered is one of musicians more fluidly integrated into and contextualized within the larger social whole, not necessarily perceived as belonging to institutions or ensembles, but perhaps identified through familial association, social rank, hereditary ascription or simply through shared practices and concepts.

Such approaches offer a third potential interface between ethnomusicology and Western art music, albeit one which has been infrequently adopted thus far. Shelemay's (2001) consideration of the early music scene in Boston, and the insights her ethnography provides into both the organization of that scene and the claims made by its various participants for the music they perform, is a rather isolated example. Faulkner's (1971) earlier study of Hollywood studio musicians, albeit that its roots are more sociological than anthropological, concentrates on musicians who are technically freelance, yet usually employed within a particular fixed orbit: the Hollywood recording studios which provide the majority of their work. As such these musicians lie somewhere between the 'institutionalized' orchestral musician or college student, and the free association of independent musicians elsewhere. Yet these rather more fluid models, of loose networks of musicians integrated within society at large but in some ways separately identifiable from it by virtue of their specialism, more accurately represent the musicians who form the focus of this study. With the exception of a handful of orchestral musicians, the majority of professional musicians in London are not tied to one particular ensemble or conservatoire, but exist within a matrix of personal and professional relationships whose nodal points may be said to be the groups, institutions and performance events in which they come together.

In short, then, this study is about the way such a matrix is conceived and created by this community of professional, classically trained musicians in

London, the strategies and negotiations they employ to sustain it, and the ideologies and performance events which constitute such important parts of it. Within this last sentence, however, there are three concepts which require further examination: 'classically trained', 'professional' and 'community'. Although we may feel that their meaning is clear enough and we may use them in everyday conversation without complaint, on closer inspection they reveal a rather more slippery nature, and it is necessary and appropriate to consider the wider ramifications of these three seemingly innocuous terms.

A community of professional musicians

London is, unquestionably, one of the busiest musical centres in the world; indeed it is often thought of by those musicians who work in it to be the musical capital of the world. There are, I suspect, a greater number of musicians in the city than anywhere else, who feed into a plethora of different types of musical performance events. Some of these musicians will have had, like myself, what I would describe as a conventional Western musical education: learning an instrument from an early age, and gradually specializing more and more in music as one progresses through the educational system, often finishing with a university degree or equivalent conservatoire qualification. This is the system which I describe as 'classically trained', in which the basic principles of Western art music theory and practice furnish the core of the various educational curricula, notwithstanding that most students will also have had the opportunity to study or play other musical styles or genres. Allied to this will be an extensive period of instrumental tuition with one or more specialist teachers.

Certain professional musicians in London, however, have not arrived by exactly this route. Some may have studied other subjects at tertiary level, while continuing to take part in large amounts of classically oriented practical music-making, before pursuing a career in music; many others have worked their way up, particularly in the jazz and pop fields, where conventional musical qualifications count even less than elsewhere; still others may provide music to ethnic groups in this multicultural city, and for them the system of Western music education may be almost completely irrelevant; and there are no doubt others besides. In certain situations – musicals, commercial sessions, even, occasionally, in art music concerts – these different types of musician may well sit side by side, contributing to the same musical end result and effectively being treated as the same; but they are not the same, and their perceptions of what they do are likely to be very different, as will become clearer later. This is not to privilege one type of musician over another (often a rather spurious distinction anyway), which I am emphatically not doing. My reasons for concentrating on what I describe as 'classically trained' musicians are simply pragmatic: some limitations must be set, however ill-defined, on the group of people I claim to be dealing with; and, moreover, this group most closely approximates to my own particular situation in this world, which is a necessary precondition if I am to include my own experience within the limits of this study, or if I am to make any claims which may have a wider validity beyond my own subjective perception.

The concept of 'professional' is equally thorny. While we may superficially make the distinction between the professional who is paid for his or her work and the amateur who is not, the situation on the ground is more ambiguous. Both Baily (1979) and Sakata (1983) have shown the conceptual malleability of the term in the Afghan context, with Sakata suggesting that the distinction there is made 'on the basis of exchange, that is, whether the negotiations for the musical performance are business or social in context' (76), although she points out that even this does not allow for hereditary musicians or amateurs who become professionals. Merriam (1964:125) suggests that 'professionalism seems to run along a continuum from payment in occasional gifts at one end to complete economic support through music at the other'. Ruth Finnegan takes up this theme in her study of amateur music-making in Milton Keynes, and I would agree with her observation that:

> The ... 'obvious' amateur/professional distinction turns out to be a complex continuum with many different possible variations. Indeed, even the same people could be placed at different points along this line in different contexts or different stages of their lives. (Finnegan, 1989:14)

Finnegan herself was interested in those who lie towards the amateur end of this continuum, while my concern is with the opposite pole. But much of what she writes concerning the way aspiring professionals use amateur music events as a springboard to a professional career (17) resonates comfortably with my own observations and experience. For those who do successfully make the transition from one to the other, the ambiguity between the two states is frequently at its most acute while at the London music colleges (or equivalent), and in the often difficult years immediately afterwards. At this stage the most important thing for the young professional, and the thing which makes the greatest impact on your peers, is to be paid to play. Of course, the nature of employment is also significant. Those who are fortunate enough to be doing 'real' professional work, with the major orchestras or in professional shows, immediately gain increased respect: they have already made it, and have proved their ability to translate their fledgling musical skills into a money-making enterprise, the ultimate goal of the aspiring professional. The even more fortunate few who perhaps get an orchestral position before they leave college, or are already established enough as freelancers to leave without completing their courses, are regarded with a mixture of envy and awe by those they leave behind. But everybody at this stage wants to be paid for their performances, and the concept of gaining valuable experience, although significant, comes a poor second. I was reminded of this only recently when one of my 18-year-old students, just about to embark on a music degree, enthusiastically described to me how she had been invited to play at a wedding during the school holidays: *'And guess what? I got paid for it!'* Indeed, I have my own memories of traipsing around various often dilapidated London halls, and beyond, playing in the pit band of amateur musicals or Gilbert and Sullivan operettas, for notably less than the professional rates for the job. But I was at least consoled by the fact that I was 'getting there', I was 'on the way up'.

Finnegan's point about positions on the continuum changing according to time or context is also well made. There are many who would think of themselves as professional musicians even though they may have incomes from other sources; I know a musician who also sells paintings, another who writes, another with a small private income, several who rent property, and so on. But I have no doubt that they (and I) would describe themselves as 'professional' musicians. Nearly all the musicians I know do some form or other of teaching, but occasionally the balance between such teaching and paid musical performance is tilted very strongly in favour of the former; and since teaching is generally regarded as something qualitatively different to paid musical employment this does create difficulties in the use of the term 'professional'. While completing this research I have also done fewer performances than previously as well as undertaking more paid academic work, so my own position in this continuum has changed; but I would still describe myself as a 'professional' musician. Indeed one of my university students prefaced an email to me with the observation *'As a professional musician yourself...'*, notwithstanding that my salaried employment provided the context for our relationship.

It is also clear that whereas in current usage the term 'professional' connotes essentially positive values and is used to underpin certain desirable qualities of musical performance, it was not always so positively employed. Paula Gillett (2000) has shown how in late nineteenth-century London the term might be used quite disparagingly, to illustrate a distinction in social class between those amateurs of independent means who were keen (and sometimes proficient) performers, and those who were professional, with the implications of servitude this adjective often conveyed at the time. So the description 'professional' is a flexible, negotiable term whose meaning inheres through use rather than through unambiguous definition.

In the amateur world, as Finnegan also notes, the word 'professional' might be applied to a musician of a good standard even if he earned his living elsewhere (15); similarly, among professional musicians, the reverse is true. Whereas student musicians implicitly acknowledge their amateur status in striving to be regarded as professionals, so professionals will derogatorily refer to social behaviour or musical standards of which they disapprove as 'amateur'. One musician who played several times with a small ensemble in another city, a group which most people would describe as professional, told me: *'They were ok, but it was all a bit semi-pro, really'*, by which he meant not only that their playing was not of the highest standard but also that their general attitude to music-making did not meet with his approval. Again he did not mean that they were not paid for their performances, or that they had other jobs as bank managers or policemen, but that their social and musical behaviour did not conform to his perceptions of what 'professional' music-making demanded. And there is a further piece of linguistic behaviour by which musicians affirm to themselves and others their status as paid professionals, and this is in their concept of 'work'.

'Work' is the term given by professional musicians to their paid musical production, be it giving concerts, paid rehearsals, recordings or other similar ventures. It does not include unpaid activities such as charity performances, unpaid rehearsals or practice; and it definitely does not include teaching, even at the London conservatoires, notwithstanding that many performers of significant rank might teach there. Thus musicians frequently ask each other 'Do you have much work on?', 'Are you busy?', which might elicit various answers including 'I don't have much in the diary next week, only teaching'. This was reinforced to me by a conversation with a university lecturer who maintains a significant performing career. Having moved from a university in the Midlands to one in London he explained the convenience of this move, *'because of course this is where most of my work is'*. For him there was nothing incongruous about this statement; despite having had a full-time job and accompanying salary for many years elsewhere, he still saw himself as a professional musician whose 'work' was based largely in London.

So the concept of 'work', being paid for one's musical production, becomes a significant symbol through which individuals partially refract their self-conception as professional musicians; and, quite apart from the economic necessity of needing work to survive, it is also a symbol through which they reinforce to themselves and others their sense of group identity: 'we are professional musicians and being paid to play music is our job'. Sharing this concept with others both sustains this sense of group identity and differentiates this group not only from non-professional musicians but also from society at large; and it is because musicians share and process symbols in this way that we can consider this group as a 'community'.

The word 'community', like 'society', 'culture' and other seemingly innocuous nouns, has provided grist for many anthropological mills.[12] But its usefulness here lies not in treating it as some conveniently bounded unit which can be circumscribed in terms of physical structures, geography or ethnicity, and so on, but rather, as Anthony Cohen suggests, by regarding notions of community as being largely in the mind. He writes:

> As a mental construct, [community] condenses symbolically, and adeptly, its
> bearers' social theories of similarity and difference. It becomes an eloquent and
> collective emblem of their social selves. (Cohen, 1985:114)

Cohen shows how this mental construct, the coming together of individuals' ideas into a shared yet largely internalized conception of belonging, is sustained by symbols which, while sharing outwardly similar forms, are capable of multiple interpretations by members of the community, according to their individual perceptions of what it means to them to be a member. He writes that 'the reality of community in people's experience thus inheres in their attachment or commitment to a common body of symbols' (1985:16), and yet 'symbols do not so much express meaning as give us the capacity to make meaning' (15). Elsewhere he suggests that 'the distinction to be made ... [is] between the socially propagated *forms* of symbols, and their *meanings* which are the products of individuals' aspirations' (Cohen, 1994:73).

It is in this sense that I describe the concept of 'work' as being a symbol shared by professional musicians which binds them together into what might reasonably be construed as a community. It can be subject to a number of different inflections. For the musician in a long-running West End show, 'work' might be a relatively stable occupation occurring at fixed times and which has become something of a habit, if not a chore; for the permanent orchestral musician, 'work' takes place largely with the same group of people, frequently involving much the same repertoire and governed by the orchestra schedule given out each month; for the aspiring professional, 'work' is any kind of paid musical employment, however bad, and so on. For all of them, however, it is their perception that being paid to perform is not only central to their economic well-being but also a significant component of their own self-conception, one which distinguishes them both from other musicians further down Finnegan's continuum and also from non-musicians. Moreover, 'work' is conceived not only in terms of what it is, but also what it is not: teaching, practice, unpaid rehearsals, and so forth.

But there are other, perhaps more tangible, symbols which musicians can employ to reinforce their sense of belonging. For many years, until the trade union closed shop was outlawed by Thatcherism in the 1980s, all professional musicians had to belong to the Musicians' Union, and the vast majority of employers, orchestras, broadcasters and so on had agreements with the union only to employ its members. Musicians themselves had to agree not to work with non-union members as a condition of membership, and could in theory be penalized or expelled if they did so. Thus membership of the union, and particularly the card which came with it, became a symbol of one's involvement with professional music-making. Many musicians would also use the union diary, supplied to them free every year and quickly recognized by other musicians, which was a rather more subtle way of asserting status, especially when discussing with other musicians one's availability for a particular engagement. These were not infallible signs, because anybody who paid the union subscriptions could become a member, and there were, and are, many semi-professional or amateur musicians who are members; but the overwhelming majority of professional musicians were members, and not only did non-union performers run the risk of being found out, and thus not offered employment, but there was also a definite stigma attached to not having joined, or not having paid your subscription. This has changed today and union membership is less widespread; but most professionals remain members, and their membership continues to be a symbol which may be interpreted reflexively, if not always objectively, as an indicator of professional status.

The advent of mobile communications technology (phones, pagers) is also significant, and these have become very popular with musicians. The widespread use and availability of these technologies has perhaps diminished their significance in this context now, but my perception (and I offer no empirical evidence for this) is that they were initially far more widespread among my musician colleagues than among the general population. There is, of course, a very practical reason for this, in that musicians tend to live very peripatetic lives, and the ease of communication which such technology offers is a valuable asset in a profession where messages (especially those involving 'work') often need to travel swiftly. So mobile phones, particularly, quickly became *de rigueur,* implying that you were a busy musician, often on the move, who needed to be easily available to deal with offers of work. This led to a perception in some quarters that if you did not have a mobile phone then the opposite was true, that you were not a busy musician, or not frequently contacted, somehow 'second class'. I have myself experienced this on several occasions. Having been a late arrival to the mobile phone party I occasionally felt that I detected a degree of surprise when people who were dealing with me as a musician discovered that I did not have one: an implied subtext which says, 'How can you be a musician and not have a mobile? You can't be much good.' It is possible, however, that this represented a degree of hypersensitivity on my part.

One final symbol of professional musicianship is the diary service, a small company which keeps a copy of a musician's diary, allowing potential employers to know quickly if the musician is available for work at a particular time without needing to speak to the musician themselves. Again, although there are many practical advantages for a musician in having such an arrangement, it does also transmit messages about being busy and in demand. Most of these companies simply take a monthly fee from any musician who cares to use the services they provide; some are a little more selective, and will only accept musicians whose work is in a particular field or is largely with specific ensembles, notably the major orchestras. Thus using one of these latter companies also carries metamessages about importance and social rank.

Cohen argues that another characteristic of communities is their resistance to change, and he suggests:

> One often finds in ... communities the prospect of change being regarded ominously, as if change inevitably means loss. A frequent and glib description of what is feared may be lost is 'way of life'; part of what is meant is the sense of self. (Cohen, 1985:109)

Here we might recall the BBC musicians' strike of 1980, which was provoked by the Corporation's proposal to disband four of its regional orchestras, plus a smaller London group called the London Studio Players. In response, all BBC musicians went on strike, and they were supported by musicians from a range of musical organizations as well as other freelancers, whether or not they worked frequently for the BBC. It was noticeable that the picket lines outside Broadcasting House in London (the BBC headquarters) were manned by many different musicians and not just those whose jobs were immediately under threat. The potential consequences of the BBC's plan, and the prospect of significant structural change to the whole community, were clearly issues in this dispute.

So I am suggesting here that for professional London musicians a sense of community inheres through their use of a variety of different symbols. Some of these, such as the concept of 'work', are mental constructs; others, such as union cards and diaries, are more concrete. All may be inflected differently by those who use them to assert not only their sense of what it is to be part of this larger group, but also their own individual position within and relationship to the group as a whole. Furthermore this community reacts defensively when threatened, in order to preserve the status quo with which it feels comfortable. Naturally this is an anthropological model and it is not how most musicians would describe their sense of community. But it is not difficult to find examples of musicians demonstrating patterns of communal behaviour which might be more widely recognized as such: looking after each other or helping each other out. I shall finish my discussion of community with just two instances of this.

The first occurred in 1997, when Clarence Adoo, a widely known and well-liked trumpeter, was involved in a car accident which left him severely injured, needing constant supervision and unable to care for himself, much less ever play again. Many musicians, and trumpet players particularly, were shocked and saddened by this, and a trust was formed by his former colleagues to help meet the costs of his nursing needs. Since then, numerous different events, not only benefit concerts but sponsored runs, climbs and so on, organized largely by other musicians, have attempted to raise money for the Clarence Adoo Trust; in July 1998, for example, six trumpeters set out to climb the highest peaks in each of England, Scotland and Wales, raising £20000 for the Clarence Adoo Trust fund in the process.[13] A second example is offered by a scheme run by certain freelance London woodwind players, which is designed to provide mutual support for any member of the group who is ill and unable to work. Once a musician joins this scheme they need pay nothing until somebody makes a claim, at which point everybody in the group agrees to make a small contribution for a set period of time. It is a small-scale, self-administered form of health insurance, and not only provides an economic safety net for its members but, again, may be considered a symbol of professional musicianship for the players involved in the group.

I suggest that the anthropological model above, together with these rather more obvious community-oriented patterns of behaviour, demonstrate that there is a social grouping of professional musicians here which we may reasonably construe as a community, within the terms I have outlined. It is in the context of my own involvement in this community that I now seek to objectify particular traits, beliefs and relationships occurring within it which, as a member, I have previously taken at face value, without reflecting on the hows and whys that the anthropologist in me now demands. This methodological liminality, 'betwixt and between' the natural familiarity of the insider and the mitigated familiarity of an incoming participant–observer, requires some consideration.

The native ethnomusicologist

Ethnographies have traditionally taken a form in which the anthropologist spends an extensive but fixed period of time immersed among a particular group of people, usually in cultures which might loosely be described as 'traditional' or 'rural', even 'exotic' from the Western perspective. After this period (or periods) of fieldwork, in which the fieldworker frequently becomes overwhelmed by potential data, these data are brought home, where they are then analysed, filtered, reworked and otherwise manipulated into one or more ethnographic texts. It would not be entirely inappropriate to describe this approach as 'classical' ethnography; indeed, given the frequent emphasis on abstracted social structures, cultural rules and ethnographic models, we may also consider such approaches as being in some ways modernist. In recent years, however, the scope and aims of anthropology have changed somewhat, and a broader range of studies have appeared, including a number dealing with urban groups much closer, geographically speaking, to the Western centres of learning where anthropologists themselves most frequently (but not always) reside. These approaches may be subsumed under the description 'anthropology at home', and Anthony Jackson, writing in a book which takes this phrase as its title, has suggested a number of possible reasons for the growth of these studies, not least of which are reductions in academic funding, ease of access to these areas, a general perception that there are large areas of one's own society of which we are relatively ignorant, and a growing interest in anthropology generally (see Jackson 1987:8). Jackson's book provides many examples of this kind of work; Judith Okely's (1983) study of British traveller-gypsies provides another.

Furthermore the nature of anthropological enquiry has changed. Through the influence of writers such as, famously, Clifford Geertz, anthropologists have taken a more interpretive approach, seeking cultural meaning through the explanation of a particular body of symbols, for example, or through ethnomethodology, utilizing more fully other cultures' theories about their own cultural patterns. We might describe this as a rather more postmodern approach to anthropology, one which rejects the overarching, occasionally ethnocentric approach of the grand narrative in favour of a more pluralist, less hierarchically differentiated view of the world's cultures. Within these overall changes there are two particular developments which are significant in the present context. The first is the rise of the native anthropologist, a group into which I must inevitably place myself, and the second is a heightened awareness of the way anthropological texts are constructed.

The term 'native anthropologist' describes those who study a particular group or culture to which they themselves already belong, rather than one to which the anthropologist is attached in the traditional anthropological sense that I outlined above. Examples would include Jean Ablon's (1977) study of middle-class American women or Stella Mascarenhas-Keyes' (1979) study of her own Goan community in London. Ethnomusicological examples might include Nazir Ali Jairazbhoy's (1971) study of North Indian ragas, and J.H. Kwabena Nketia's (1963, 1974) or Kofi Agawu's (1984, 1987) work on African music. To some extent such approaches render invalid the traditional anthropological distinction between, on the one hand, the 'emic', insider's or subjective viewpoint and, on the other, the 'etic', outsider's perspective, since the native anthropologist must deal with both at the same time, perhaps giving more or less emphasis to one or the other as the occasion demands, but necessarily having always to reconcile the differences between the two. This leads to what Mascarenhas-Keyes (1987:180) calls 'professionally induced schizophrenia between the "native self" and "professional self"', a necessary consequence, perhaps, of the attempt to see one's own culture as strange. Such an approach inevitably suggests a rather contrasting perspective to that given by traditional ethnographies, although this is not to suggest that it is by definition better, merely different. These differences arise from native anthropologists having to deal with a number of advantages and disadvantages over their more 'conventional' cousins.

Perhaps the most obvious advantage is that native anthropologists, being already immersed within the cultural system they wish to explore, 'understand' (in Wittgenstein's sense of possessing the ability to use them correctly) the language, conventions, customs, symbols and so on which they seek to interpret for anthropological purposes. This has a number of positive consequences, such as obviating the need for interpreters and perhaps being more receptive to linguistic nuances, running less risk of upsetting people through inappropriate behaviour, having a better idea of when and where to be, and so on. But, for the sensitive ethnographer, all of these come with attendant drawbacks. Not having to learn a language might make one think less about exactly what words mean, how they are used and what this might reveal about underlying concepts. Being familiar with certain customs excludes the learning process that comes with *not* being familiar and the insights which may arise from this learning, since such learning has generally been left far behind in a time when it was most likely unconscious. I can relate to this from my own experience of having married into a Greek family. Kissing both cheeks on greeting and parting is a ubiquitous part of Greek culture, but this is not the case in England. I have had to learn who to kiss, when to kiss and, just as important, who and when *not* to kiss, a learning curve which has been accompanied by much dance-like gyration on my part as I look for clues in the demeanour of those for whom it is natural.

Another advantage is that one already has access to a number of potential informants in the shape of one's own network of friends, colleagues and other contacts, all of whom may well have interesting views on the issues at hand. This undoubtedly makes the process of formal interviews easier, but it also carries methodological difficulties. Do you choose to ask for information from people simply because they are easy to approach, even though there may be better placed sources elsewhere who might have notably different opinions? (Ideally, of course, you contact both.) How can one ensure a proper cross-section of informants, relative to a particular anthropological approach, if one is only choosing the people to whom access is easy? And so on.

Of course, one does have a considerable amount of personal experience within the culture on which to draw, and this can be a rich source of data. In this sense the fieldwork has less of a clearly definable time span than usual and, perhaps, a greater historical dimension. And although personal introspection and autobiographical detail clearly cannot be a complete substitute for data or evidence acquired through conventional anthropological approaches, I would argue that all of these various components have a role to play in the proper construction of a thoughtful ethnographic text. It would not be true, therefore, to suggest that the native anthropologist need not indulge in the normal anthropological practices of keeping a diary (during periods of intensive fieldwork), conducting interviews, collecting data and so on. Equally, it would be absurd not to draw on one's own experience where appropriate. But I have done so warily, knowing that memory can play tricks with the facts when they are not recorded in some form or other. Timothy Garton-Ash, an historian who has also drawn on his own experience (in East Germany) in his work, notes the danger of this when he recalls Thomas Hobbes's line that 'imagination and memory are but one thing' (Garton-Ash, 1997:97). Thus research methodology, while still recognizably anthropological, is perhaps a little different for the native anthropologist, and a note about my own methods of data collection is in order here.

Although I have had recourse to incidents and experiences stretching back many years, my own intensive fieldwork took place between September 1996 and July 1997, a timescale which approximates to one London music season. During this time I kept a fieldwork diary, attempting to relate as accurately as possible the details of conversations, rehearsals, concerts or other significant events which I thought might be relevant to my research. I would usually contribute to this diary on a weekly basis, although sometimes more frequently if there was a particular conversation or event which seemed deserving of immediate note. I was generally unable to take down specific conversations immediately after they occurred, for a variety of reasons. First, I was always keen to present myself just as another working musician, and did not want to be seen rushing off to dark corners of rehearsal spaces or concert venues in order to write notes on what had just been said. Second, it was in those breaks during rehearsals or performances when such note-taking might have been undertaken that potentially valuable conversations would occur, and I did not want to extricate myself from these occasions for fear of missing something useful or important. Third, the professional role which I was obliged to play inevitably demanded from me (as with all musicians) significant amounts of concentration; I could not risk jeopardizing my responsibilities or concentration levels by seeking to disappear every so often to record verbatim conversations. Thus recording personal experience in this kind of professional field presents its own particular problems where one has a specific professional role to play. There were many situations when I wanted, mentally, to withdraw from a performing situation and allow the anthropologist in me to take over, to observe and perhaps take notes – another aspect of the 'professional schizophrenia' referred to above. But the concentration required for rehearsals and performing, the professional demands made upon me, seldom allowed this, and I often had to wait until much later before I could reflect on what had been said and done, and note down what I could remember of it. During performances, particularly, any 'lapses of concentration' (an odd way of conceiving ethnographic reflection, I admit) also made me feel rather nervous. My colleagues were unlikely to have been impressed by an excuse such as 'I'm sorry about that wrong note – I was thinking too hard about what we were all doing'! Although this may be seen as a drawback for the native anthropologist in such professional fields, the possible detrimental effects of this situation are, I suggest, outweighed by the proximity, not to say intimacy, the ethnographer can achieve with the subject(s) of study, and the rich sources of data which become available through being taken as 'one of us' rather than 'one of them'. Such pros and cons are certainly inevitable consequences of participation on these terms.

Mascarenhas-Keyes (1987:184) notes how she suffered a certain amount of negativity from others in Goa who wanted 'to challenge my claim to special expertise, the implication being that any Goan with time on their hands and the ability to inveigle funds from an agency could do the "research"'. My experiences, however, were almost entirely positive; most musicians were interested in what I was doing, although I usually made no mention of it unless requesting time for an interview, presenting myself just as another working musician and without my hidden ethnomusicological agenda. Many of them seemed to enjoy undertaking the formal interviews, several even claiming that they had found it quite a cathartic experience. Only on two occasions did I experience a more negative reaction. On the first, very early, occasion I was reading *The Anthropology of Music* on a band bus between concerts (in retrospect this was perhaps rather ostentatious, and a practice I quickly abandoned). One of the other musicians saw the title of the book and remarked, 'Huh! Reading about music? Get a life, will you?'; to which I rather curtly replied, 'You call this a life?' Perhaps his most revealing remark came next: 'That's true,' he said, before taking his seat. The second occasion was rather more disturbing to me, since it involved a musician with whom, at the time, I was personally and professionally closer. He had a permanent orchestral job, and I asked him several times if he might arrange for me to have some contact with the orchestra as part of my research. I knew this would be a problem, since all the major orchestras in London are under tremendous pressure and seldom like hangers-on of any description. We had a number of long discussions about this, and although he was willing to give me some of his own (valuable) time I could sense that he was unwilling to take it any further than that (I later learned that he felt I was being very presumptuous in asking). During one of these discussions he said: 'You do realise that some of these people in the orchestra are very intelligent, easily capable of a PhD, and they'll give you a very hard time if you're not up to the mark?' Although I did not doubt his assessment of his colleagues (nor do I now), like Mascarenhas-Keyes I was made aware of the underlying implication that 'any of us could be doing this, what makes you so special?' Relationships in the field, therefore, even when the field is in fact one's own back yard, are never entirely straightforward, and need to be considered and contextualized for the sake of ethnographic validity. This is particularly true when the ethnographer is part of the plot, since my relationship with those I have studied and whose lives and views I seek in part to represent necessarily determines the perspective my work takes.

Furthermore, these established anthropological techniques of interview, observation and so forth can also be supplemented in a literate culture such as our own by a variety of different media used for the dissemination of information. Such media offer us a number of other potential data sources, and so I have also availed myself of newspaper and magazine articles, as well as television documentaries and books written by and about musicians, certain parts of which are incorporated into my own text. Such resources not only provide information about what musicians themselves think and do, but also tell us something of the way in which their work is received and perceived within society at large, and these considerations also form part of this study. I am conscious, however, that this kind of material must be handled with care; it is one thing to have a musician tell you directly what they believe they do (which itself may be quite different from what they actually do) and quite another thing to have information relayed, inevitably filtered and edited, by a third party.

Because of the particular role played by the native anthropologist both in the collection of information and in the refashioning of it for the ethnographic text, it is at this point that I feel compelled to present something of my own autobiography; not for the sake of any self-aggrandisement, nor indeed because my 'pathway' (Finnegan, 1989:297ff) has been noticeably different from that of other professional musicians (and therein lies any value in relating it), but so that I may position myself as distinctly as possible within the ethnographic frame, allowing others to judge more clearly the veracity of my work.

I have mentioned above the bare outline of what it means to be classically trained. I started learning the clarinet when I was about eight years old and continued throughout my secondary school years, along the way learning some piano and guitar, and playing in various musical ensembles – orchestras, jazz bands and pop groups – until the age of eighteen. I was an active but in no way exceptional musician, notwithstanding that I had reached a relatively high standard (Grade VIII) in the system of exams which underpins instrumental music education in Britain. Most of my musical activities were based around my school and, unusually, I did not even play in the local county youth orchestra, which was a significant point of contact for my musical peers. It did not occur to me at this stage to apply for one of the London conservatoires because I was simply not good enough. I elected instead to study music at a provincial university, where then, as now, rather more importance was attached to academic competence and rather less to performing expertise than is the case at the conservatoires.

My university department was quite small, and I had the 'misfortune' to arrive when there were three other, rather good, clarinettists in the department, so it became quickly apparent that I was unlikely to secure many performing opportunities. At this stage, however, I was studying music not with a view to becoming a professional musician but because it had provided me with a passport to getting to university. Just before going up I had purchased a rather old and dilapidated saxophone and, after some persistence on my part, the department agreed that I could study the saxophone rather than the clarinet; in the classical music world at this time (the early 1980s) the saxophone was still regarded as something clarinettists played when they were bored. I was duly despatched to a teacher in London, who I suspect was rather shocked by what he saw; if I was poor on the clarinet I knew nothing at all about the saxophone. Rather to my surprise, however, I worked very hard on my playing at university, and at the end of my course I was given a place on a one-year postgraduate course at a London conservatoire.

The transition from a provincial university to the London metropolis was difficult, as it is for many, not least because the playing standards were so much higher than I was used to, and I was no longer the only saxophone player in the vicinity. Furthermore, I was on what was described as a 'postgraduate orchestral training course' which, given the relative dearth of saxophone parts in the orchestral canon, meant I was rather on the periphery of this particular institution. I set about organizing performances where I could, and put together a saxophone quartet as a means of playing with others. After a year of this, however, I had decided that a professional music career was not for me, and I made a conscious decision on the way home from a trip abroad that I would take some time out to travel, before pursuing some other vocation. That night, on arriving back at my London flat, I discovered that I had been awarded a grant to study for a year with the professor of saxophone at the Paris Conservatoire, which caused me to reverse, or at least (so I thought) postpone my somewhat short-lived resolution.

From this point on, however, I drifted into a freelance musical career, establishing contacts where I could, meeting other musicians, trying to generate concerts for myself and the quartet, and teaching. I cultivated an interest in contemporary music, something that has remained with me and which has developed into a specialism. Slowly I have worked my way up, undertaking in the process, like most freelancers, a wide variety of work to make ends meet: shows, ensemble work, occasional solo concerts, a little orchestral work, some studio work, and continuing work with the quartet. In the last few years, as my interest in academic matters has grown, I have done slightly less playing, much of which at the moment is self-generated, by which I mean that I am contacting promoters and getting them to book myself or the quartet, rather than waiting for the phone to ring.

There is nothing in this potted autobiography which is, I think, particularly different from the routes most other musicians have taken, although the details would naturally differ, with the exception that many musicians go to music conservatoires at the age of eighteen, either in London or elsewhere, and a few may have been to specialist music schools before that. There are a few points worth making, however. First, to revert to ethnomusicological parlance, my position would be described as being achieved rather than ascribed (Merriam, 1964:131). I was not born into a family of hereditary musicians as in India, or a caste of musicians as in parts of Africa. I have become a musician of my own volition and, like most others in this community, I have had to work hard for whatever success I have had. Yet, although I would agree with this description of 'achieved musicianship', I would not describe myself as a driven musician, one whose entire life has been aimed at pursuing a career in music, and for whom that is the ultimate goal. By contrast, I feel almost as though I have arrived here by accident, as a product of a particular set of circumstances. This is also the case with regard to my choice of principal instrument, the saxophone. In other circumstances I might have continued as a clarinet player, or something else entirely. I see this apparent fortuitousness reflected in other musicians; a number of viola players have said how they ended up on the viola having started on the violin because they were quite big for their age, and the larger size of the former instrument suited them; one of my colleagues, who specializes in the baritone saxophone, started learning this instrument at school because when he got to the instrument cupboard that was all that was left. So although the term 'achieved musician' may imply somebody consciously striving to attain clearly definable ends, this is not the whole story, and we should allow room within this description for what I shall call, warily, coincidence.

Second, a point which I think is more applicable to myself than to others is that I frequently find myself not, perhaps, marginalized but certainly contrary to mainstream activity. As a classical musician I am, unusually, a saxophone player; I am also interested in contemporary music, unlike many of my fellow musicians whose musical feet are anchored in much more traditional waters; as a saxophone player, however, I am a *classical* musician and I play very little jazz, again putting me slightly out of kilter with the majority of saxophonists; even as an ethnomusicologist my interest lies with Western art music, so once again I find myself out of step from the majority, whose interests lie with the music of other cultures. I mention this because much of what follows in other chapters concerns questions of identity at one level or another, and it is perhaps this contrariness, a continually ambivalent relationship on my part with the mainstream and the questions it raises about my own musical identity, which provokes my interest in the way identities are constructed and maintained elsewhere. It also begins to show the limits of my work and how my position within it necessarily changes according to context: in certain parts my role is more central and my viewpoint subjective, or at least 'emic', within the constraints that I believe good anthropological practice allows; elsewhere I feel more like an observer, less able to draw on my own experience as a starting point. For example, whereas I feel comfortable in using my experience to underpin my assertions on the lives of freelance musicians in general, I cannot claim any intimate knowledge of life in a symphony orchestra, working day after day with the same group of musicians. It is possible, but not a foregone conclusion, that this ambivalent position facilitates my scholarly dance between various 'emic' or 'etic' postures; this is not sleight of hand but a necessary piece of ethnographic gymnastics, necessitated by the 'professional schizophrenia' induced by my long-time immersion in, followed by my objective appraisal of, professional musical life in London.

I have also included this short autobiography because another of the threads running through this work involves conceptualizing the self, and the relationship between self (including myself) and the larger social group of which the individual self forms a part; and the dynamic equilibrium, not to say antagonism, which often inheres between the two. Cohen, in his book *Self Consciousness,* suggests:

> Instead of conceptualising the self as a replicate in miniature of society, we could begin by paying attention to the ways in which people reflect on themselves, and then see in what ways these reflections are indicative of social and cultural context, or require such contextualisation to be intelligible to us. (Cohen, 1994:29)

I had unwittingly been adopting this approach before I read Cohen's book, and much of what he has written resonates comfortably with my own viewpoint.

Cohen's principal argument is that anthropologists have for too long generalized about groups of people (cultures, societies, communities and so on), and have not sufficiently considered the role of individual experience within these groups, particularly where such experience might be seen to cast a different light on the more overarching assertions made by the ethnographer. To illustrate this point he reviews the anthropological literature on Greek marriage (of understandable interest to this particular self, of course) and suggests that there are contradictions between those studies which take into account people's consciousness of themselves as individuals, in which they are seen as having choices within their culture through which they express their own sense of self, and those which, by contrast, see individuals as fulfilling prescribed roles within society, over which they have little or no control (ibid.: 80–92). Furthermore he suggests that anthropologists are wrong when they deny self consciousness[14] to others but happily ascribe it to themselves, and that in order to fully appreciate others' sense of self the anthropologist must reflexively consider his or her own self in relation to the people studied. He suggests:

> To understand the thinking selves who we observe we have to invoke our personal experience as thinking selves, in as controlled a manner as our discipline will allow ... [this] simply requires that we admit personal reflection explicitly into our anthropological work. (Ibid.:154)

He also observes:

> Our interpretations of what we witness around us proceed from our own experience, our consciousness, of ourselves, even though we may not be conscious of its peculiarity to ourselves. Anthropologists have to qualify their self-experience by subjecting it to the disciplines of comparison and of theoretical and methodological rigour. But they subvert their own enterprise if they permit their science to obscure the primacy of the self. (Ibid.:191)

The penultimate sentence, of course, reminds us that simple autobiography will not suffice. The mere description of patterns and events from the perspective of the individual who experiences them is not anthropology *per se,* but Cohen's point is that such self conscious experience, both of the anthropologist and of the 'other', must necessarily be incorporated or fed back into the essentially objective anthropological model, to assess its validity.

This position is also resonant with Pierre Bourdieu's idea of 'the objectification of objectification', a theoretical posture in which he suggests that not only should we take a metaphoric step back, to gain an objective vantage point of the subject under study, but we should accompany this with a further step back, to consider our own relationship with the assertions we make about what we study. Like Cohen, Bourdieu speaks of incorporating experience, but he also talks of strategies people adopt, of how things are done, of social *practice*, and is scathing about those who seek to divorce the supposed objectivity of social science from the necessarily subjective attitudes which the social scientist brings to it. He argues:

> Social science must not only, as objectivism would have it, break with native experience and the native representation of that experience, but also, by a second break, call into question the presuppositions inherent in the position of the 'objective' observer who, seeking to interpret practices, tends to bring into the object the principles of his relation to the object. (Bourdieu, 1990a:27)

Elsewhere he suggests:

> The distinction between sociology and ethnography prevents the ethnologist from submitting his own experience to the analysis that he applies to his object. This would oblige him to discover that what he describes as mythical thought is, quite frequently, nothing other than the practical logic we apply in three out of four of our own actions. (Bourdieu, 1990b:66)

Bourdieu and Cohen are not always comfortable bedfellows, however, since it is exactly the argument that 'all the products of a given agent, by an essential overdetermination, speak inseparably and simultaneously of his class' (Bourdieu, 1977:87) against which Cohen is arguing when he speaks of social scientists too frequently conceiving individuals as 'replicates in miniature' of their society. I shall have cause to consider at more length the uneasy place of individual agency in Bourdieu's general theory in Chapter Three. For the present, while accepting that each one of us betrays through our actions something of our upbringing, class, enculturation, call it what you will, I have, as Cohen suggests, attempted to work inductively in this study. And it will be seen that the following chapters start at the level of the individual musical self and the way musicians conceptualize their sense of self, before moving onto considerations of how that self fits into the larger social whole.

Thus I seek to tread something of a methodological tightrope in this study, hoping to maintain my balance between, on the one hand, providing an ethnography which is full of experiential description but which has little theoretical framework through which it might gain a wider validity, and, on the other, presenting a study which infers rules, patterns or structures of great insight or complexity but which remain abstracted constructs which may lie contrary to the lived experience of individual selves in general, and myself in particular. Ultimately, of course, this balance must be struck in the writing of the ethnography itself, and I shall conclude this chapter with a brief consideration of some of the problems I have confronted, and the solutions I have adopted, with regard to this final hurdle.

The ethnographic text

In recent years a number of studies have examined the literary nature of anthropological texts and have argued that particular modes of writing are implicitly deficient.[15] Problematic issues have included, for example, the lack of consideration by male ethnographers of gender issues; the various methods of representing the ideas and voices of others in the text; the use of tense; the degree to which such texts can be considered 'fiction' or 'reality', and so on. While it is not appropriate here to review this material in detail, like all ethnographers I have had to make certain literary choices about how to present my material, and these require some justification.

Perhaps the most significant consideration is that I have chosen to write in the first person, in keeping with the role I have allocated myself within the text, while at the same time remaining wary of the danger of egocentricity this may imply; as a native anthropologist, however, it would be difficult, not to say contrived, to write otherwise and yet still include my own voice. Equally it will be clear from my discussion of self consciousness that I believe the notion of the quasi-detached participant-observer to be, not simply a fiction, but a misrepresentation likely to detract from the final ethnography. I would agree with Kirsten Hastrup that 'gender studies have taught us that the general pretence of neutrality must be abandoned. There is no way of eliminating our consciousness from our activities in the field; it is part of reality' (Hastrup, 1992:118).

Furthermore, to provide some counterbalance to my voice, I have incorporated verbatim transcripts of interviews and conversations with other musicians where possible, again in the hope that these provide a context for my claims which give to them a validity beyond my own subjective experience. Such practice, while desirable, is problematic because of the danger that it immediately establishes a hierarchical relationship between their voice and mine, with mine, given that there is much more of it, in the ascendancy. Where such quotations are included, therefore, they are separated from the text and italicized, to distinguish them from my voice, but not indented, a small gesture which I hope conveys that such voices are equal to mine and not in any way subordinate. I am still conscious, however, that *I* am the one doing the editing of these interviews and selecting the appropriate passages; it is through devices such as this that Hastrup rightly says: 'the ethnographer *authors* a truth about her people' (ibid.:126). But ethnographies are *constructions* of reality, they are not realities in themselves but synthetic concoctions inevitably permeated by this kind of editorializing creativity, a duty from which anthropologists cannot shy away even if they wished. The English language plays a cruel trick on anthropologists when it derives the word 'authority' from the same root as that of 'author'; for ethnographic purposes we must remain conscious that these two ideas can be very different. As Geertz puts it, 'the responsibility for ethnography, or the credit, can be placed at no other door than that of the romancers who have dreamt it up' (1988:140). As part of my own creativity, then, I have presented here the ideas, experience and opinions of other musicians as a framework within which to hang my own observations, showing at which points my experience resonates with theirs, and at other times demonstrating the tensions that must inevitably inhere between the different perspectives of individuals engaged within the same cultural field. Thus there is something of a symbiotic relationship between my voice and those of others in the text, with my informants providing depth and breadth to my own assertions while I provide the context within which their voices come to be heard (notwithstanding the unavoidable ethnographic editorializing I have already mentioned).

Throughout my research I made clear to all informants that absolute anonymity would prevail, particularly if any of my work was subsequently published, and I have been keen to retain such anonymity in my text. This relates not only to information taken specifically from interviews but also to that recorded in other contexts, and I have felt it necessary to change names, and on occasion gender, in order to prevent others attempting to match quotations or events I have related to known individuals or occasions. There will be those who feel such quotations *ought* to be identified, either for purposes of ethnographic integrity (to show that I am not simply making them up) or for the undoubted benefit of 'hearing' identifiable others within my text. But I have felt it more expedient to risk the ire of the academic community than that of the musical one upon whom this ethnography is centred. As I hope will be clear from what follows, the social and musical relations between musicians are both finely balanced and closely intertwined, and while such relationships do on occasion come under strain, it ill behoves the ethnographer to contribute to such difficulties in any way. The delicacy of these kinds of social relationships is, of course, a consideration for all ethnographers; but their significance is perhaps increased when, as in my own case, the ethnographer continues to live and work among the same people after the completion and publication of the research.

Positioning oneself clearly within the ethnographic landscape, however, is hardly an original textual device, and a number of other ethnomusicologists have also chosen to write in this way; thus a brief consideration of how such authors have approached this task may help to illuminate the position in which

I see myself, relative to those I have chosen to place around me. For example, Bernard Lortat-Jacob, in his largely narrative *Sardinian Chronicles* (1995), albeit a book unburdened by the need for extensive theorizing, also places the ethnographer distinctly within the literary frame. Yet the voices of others are seldom directly heard in Lortat-Jacob's essentially monologic text. Here he is the reteller of what occurred, relating events and occasionally providing explanations for or interpretations of them, but not attempting to balance his own voice with those around him; his 'I' is the overriding arbiter of experience. I have tried to balance my own experiences with those of others, allowing them, whenever possible, to be the channels through which data and observations become transmitted. Lortat-Jacob's work, although both revealing and absorbing, is not necessarily best described as ethnography: on my bookshelves it sits alongside the works of insightful travel writers such as Paul Theroux and, particularly, Patrick Leigh Fermor.

More reminiscent of my own approach is Timothy Rice's (1994) study of Bulgarian music, *May It Fill Your Soul*, in which the author has consciously sought 'to keep alive the sense of dialogue and discourse in which my knowledge of the tradition actually developed' (11). To achieve this Rice uses a mixture of textual devices, most frequently incorporating verbatim quotations directly within his own words and not separating them as I have done. Rice's justification of this is well made: although his own knowledge and learning of Bulgarian music began out of context in folk dancing clubs in the United States, his more intensive assimilation of it occurred largely in particular contexts during various periods of fieldwork in Bulgaria itself, in specific situations with identifiable others. Rice has been able to capture his experience of Bulgarian music within a specifically dialogic mode which reflects the context of his own learning process. I have not attempted to replicate his approach because, although the quotations I have presented were (largely) collected within specific dialogic situations (formal interviews), they did not form part of my own enculturation within this tradition in quite the same way; also my learning process covers a rather greater time span, and therefore, perhaps, a greater variety of contexts, than does Rice's. It would be difficult now to recall relevant conversations of the distant past with the necessary degree of exactitude, and it would be somewhat contrived of me to present my work in this way. As Rice himself points out, 'quotes often seem to exist merely to support the author's point' (11), and while I would object to his use of the word 'merely', I would agree with him that I have in part used my verbatim quotations for this purpose.

Anthony Seeger (1987) provides a third approach in his account of the 'Mouse Ceremony' of the Suyá people of Brazil. Seeger's work uses both first and third person narrative, with the 'I' of personal experience essentially providing bookends to the more avowedly 'they' of the middle chapters. Thus we are presented with the anthropologist in the foreground of the work in its early stages, yet who fades into the middle distance (but is never entirely absent) during the more detailed discussions of Suyá musical life. Personal experience, then, is clearly implied, but in Seeger's case it provides a frame of reference in which to present a more conventional ethnographic exploration of 'why Suyá sing', rather than a significant foundation on which to construct his theoretical argument: the exact inverse, in fact, of my own approach.

I have also chosen to write here largely in the present tense (or versions of it – see Davis, 1992) in spite of the various criticisms that have been made of this method, for example that it is an artificial construct which places a temporal distance between the anthropologist and the subject (Fabian, 1983). I am persuaded by Hastrup's argument that the ethnographic present is the proper place, indeed the only place, for anthropological texts because it is here that the anthropologist confronts the object of study and, literally, makes sense of that confrontation. She observes that 'although fieldwork took place some time in an autobiographical past, the confrontation continues. The past is not past in anthropology, it is ethnographic present' (Hastrup, 1992:125). Her point is twofold. First, although the fieldwork itself may have a particular chronology (albeit a more difficult assertion to make in a case such as mine), the ethnographic results of that fieldwork may surface many years later, with the anthropologist continuing to reflect on the nature of his or her experience, thus making sense of it *through* the writing of the ethnography. Second, the ethnographic present is not a present tense at all, but a 'world-out-of-time' (128), an artificially constructed chronology which has only an ambiguous connection with 'real' time, and which is presented in an ethnographic text which is itself allegorical (128). For Hastrup, the ethnographic present exists in the space *between* self and other, notwithstanding that the others become textually fixed and, therefore, hierarchically differentiated in ethnographic discourse in a way which they are not in fieldwork dialogue. She notes:

> At the level of dialogue, the individual interlocutors are equals. 'You' and 'I' are engaged in a joint creation. But we are both subjects engaged in a process of objectifying our reciprocal identities. There are selves and others, but no absolute and exclusive categories of *ego* and *alter*. Difference is continually transcended. However, at the level of discourse the 'others' are textually fixed; the absent people are recognised as embodying an alternative culture. (129)

I would take this analysis one stage further, however, and suggest that the ethnographic present exists in a space not only between the anthropologist and his or her subject(s), but within a triangle formed by adding the reader for whom the ethnography is intended. All writers produce their texts expecting that they will be read (it is a rather self-indulgent enterprise otherwise) and construct them according to their perceived target audience; but this is not to say that all readers infer the same from a given text. Interpretation is not the sole prerogative of the anthropologist and we cannot be sure that our texts will be received uniformly; in fact, we can usually be sure of quite the opposite, as the comparison of any two reviews of the same book will frequently reveal. And, just as the anthropologist may confront his or her fieldwork over a period of time, so too might the ethnography be interpreted by various readers in different ways over an extended time scale, as our changing perceptions of, say, Malinowski's work easily demonstrates. So, extending Hastrup's analysis, I would argue that the ethnographic present, while existing for the anthropologist in the act of writing the ethnography, is also created in the mind of the reader for whom that ethnography is intended; in short, it exists between those who must write, those who must know, and those who must suffer to be written of.

One final thread which I have attempted to weave throughout this work is a consideration of Merriam's paradigmatic assessment of musicians across different cultures as sharing three particular traits. I have already mentioned his seminal work *The Anthropology of Music* (1964), and his chapter on 'The Musician' (123–44) remains perhaps the most important overview of the working practices of musicians from a cross-cultural perspective. In it he suggests that the social positions and behaviour of musicians in a variety of different contexts are characterized by a general pattern of low status, high importance, and deviant behaviour subsequently capitalized upon (137). He writes:

> In nearly every case ... musicians behave socially in certain well-defined ways, because they are musicians, and their behavior is shaped both by their own self-image and by the expectations and stereotypes of the musicianly role as seen by society at large. (123)

Merriam draws on a number of examples from various non-Western societies to illustrate these points, as well as certain behaviour patterns noted among American jazz musicians. For the Basongye of Africa, for example, musicians were 'the butt of jokes in the society ... lazy, heavy drinkers, debtors, impotents ... hemp smokers, physical weaklings, adulterers, and poor marriage risks' (136). Yet the villagers were also unanimous in stating that 'musicians are extremely important people; without them, life would be intolerable' (136). Merriam also gives several examples of musicians being allowed to behave in ways which would not be tolerated in other members of the society, particularly with regard to sexual deviancy. He cites Gamble's (1957) observation that the griot musicians of west Africa 'had the right to mock anybody and could use insulting language without any action being taken against them ... In the past they had a reputation for drunkenness and licentiousness' (cited in Merriam, 1964:139). As a rather extreme example of sexual deviancy, Merriam relates Malinowski's account of a Trobriand singer engaged in an incestuous relationship with his sister. The subsequent discovery of this relationship leads to a scandal in the village, which, Malinowski suggests, would in olden days have ended in the suicide of the guilty pair. However, in this case, they were apparently able to brave out the situation, and lived in incest for several months until she married and left the village (cited in Merriam, 1964:135). From this admittedly slender evidence, Merriam puts forward the hypothesis that musicians, in view of the special licence allowed to them, are considered to be of such importance that they must be retained within their society, regardless of the often considerable social cost to the group involved (135).

Merriam's analysis remains a significant benchmark for studies of musicians, and as a musician myself I have been intrigued to consider to what extent classically trained musicians in urban Western society conform to this pattern, as distinct from the essentially rural societies from which Merriam draws the majority of his examples; and so I shall come back to 'Merriam's paradigm' at various points in my text. There is, however, a terminological inexactitude contained with Merriam's analysis in his use of the word 'status'. Like Neuman (1980:90) I prefer to reserve this term to indicate a more general class of social positions: married, uninitiated and so on.[16] So where Merriam might have used 'status' I have instead used a mixture of 'social rank', 'prestige' and 'stature', according to context, to express ideas based on some form of social or cultural hierarchy.

Ultimately, then, this is a study of musical specialists, and it therefore seeks to take its place among, not only studies such as those mentioned above, but also others such as Howard Becker's (1951) study of New York dance band musicians or Martin Stokes's (1992) investigation of Turkish arabesk musicians, among others. What follows is drawn, at least in part, from the accumulated experience of one musician among a community of professional musicians whose beliefs, ideas and expertise he has pillaged at will; for better *and* for worse, this *is* a native's point of view.

Notes

1   I was later both gratified and disappointed to find that, as in so many other things, Frank Harrison got there first, when he wrote: 'The material of the musicologist remains, as always, music ... but his aim becomes the study of men in society insofar as they express themselves through the medium of music' (Harrison, 1963:78–9).

2   See, for example, Stobart (1994).

3   I am aware that John Cage, for example, strove to incorporate natural sounds within the context of his 'chance' performances; yet even performances of such aleatoric music exist within a socially defined time frame – something of which Cage himself was acutely conscious.

4   See, for example, Tomlinson (1984).

5   As exemplified, for example, by the online journal *Critical Musicology Forum:* http://www.leeds.ac.uk/music/Info/CMJ/cmj.html

6   Schwarz *et al.* (1997), for example, provides a good cross-section of these
       various perspectives; Cook and Everist (1999) provides another overview of
       recent developments.
7   For example, Shepherd (1991) or Chanan (1994).
8   See, for example, Sloboda (1985) or Kemp (1996).
9   For example, Hargreaves and North (1997).
10   Institut de Recherche et de Coordination Acoustique-Musique.
11   Sociological examples would include Westby (1959), and Faulkner (1973a,
       1973b); psychological studies would include Davies (1976, 1978) and Lipton
       (1987).
12   It is inappropriate here to consider in detail the paths anthropologists have trod
       in their pursuit of a commonly acceptable definition of the word 'community'.
       Cohen (1985) gives an overview of many of these; Finnegan (1989:355–6, fn.3)
       also cites a number of different approaches from various disciplines.
13   See *Classical Music,* 18/07/98:8.
14   Like Cohen, I have retained the unhyphenated construction 'self conscious' to
       indicate 'being conscious of the self', in order to distinguish it from the more
       familiar and hyphenated 'self-conscious', with its possible implications of
       embarrassment or shyness.
15   The following represents a small sample of the many references that might have
       been cited in justification of this statement: Marcus and Fischer (1986), Clifford
       and Marcus (1986), Geertz (1988), Wolf (1992).
16   In fact Neuman goes further and uses the term 'social identity' to refer to 'any
       marker such as Hindu, Punjabi, disciple, woman, Brahman, *tabalchi*, which is
       socially significant' whereas 'status' refers to 'the rights and obligations
       associated with a given social identity' (Neuman, 1980:90). I have not felt it
       necessary to pursue this distinction myself.

CHAPTER TWO

Musicality and Individuality

Introduction

In this chapter I shall consider the nature of the individual musical self and certain issues related to the rather nebulous concept of musicality. I shall also look at the way musicians conceptualize sound, perhaps the most fundamental if least theorized component of their job, yet one which is also inextricably linked to notions of individuality.

I introduce a distinction here between musicality and musicianship which perhaps requires some explanation. Musicality I see as essentially an individual quality, the 'art' of being a musician; yet despite it being essentially individual I shall argue that it is not in fact entirely generated by the individual but, paradoxically, is a quality ascribed by others through complex patterns of social interaction and negotiation, which establish a sociomusical hierarchy whereby the musical production of different individuals is endowed with varying amounts of significance. Musicality is earned rather than learned, as will become clear below. Musicianship, on the other hand, is the 'craft' of music-making; it may well involve learned behaviour; it is how particular individual qualities are put to use, and comprises not only the way in which specific cognitive and motor skills – pitch and rhythm perception, digital facility and so on – are utilized, but also, and most significantly in the present context, the social skills which are both a necessary prerequisite for and an inevitable consequence of acts of collaborative musical production. These will be explored more fully in Chapter Four.

I also make a distinction here (and beyond) between self-conception and individual identity. Self-conception is essentially our view of ourselves, of how we see our own particular abilities, preferences and characteristics: a cognitive space where we decide who we really are and how we think we appear to others. Individual identity, however, is how we *do* appear to others, our individual attributes and our position in the larger social whole as it is conceived by those around us. Ultimately it is their views of us which ascribe to us our identity within a particular social or cultural group, an identity which may or may not be at variance with our own conception of our place within it, or our relationship to it; and, similarly, it is our views of others which in part determine their identity within the larger group. Self-conception and individual identity are rather separate ideas but they are not unrelated; indeed self-conception is to a significant degree derived from our engagement with our environment. As our self-image evolves we may seek to project ourselves differently to others, which might influence how they see us; similarly, assertions by others may cause us to reflect on our view of ourselves, particularly if made repeatedly or coming from sources whose opinions we value. These two interrelated ideas, and the way in which they are expressed and articulated by musicians (both verbally and non-verbally), constitute significant threads in the next three chapters.

Musicality and individuality

In the Western world the concept of being 'musical' or 'musically talented', or the stigma attached to being described as 'unmusical', is an issue of importance matched in degree only by the ambiguity of what is actually meant by such a description. Certain people, and this is particularly true I think among adults rather than children, do sometimes describe themselves as being unmusical, by which they generally mean they do not play an instrument or cannot sing well; yet in my experience these same people are frequently musical enough to judge between obviously good or bad performances, or are able to demonstrate preferences between different musical styles or pieces within them, all of which require what I would describe as musical skills. In colloquial usage, then, being musical is frequently associated with the idea of performance or possessing some degree of competence on a musical instrument or as a singer, rather than simply engaging with music in some other way – as a listener, perhaps.

This division of labour into those who are deemed to be musical and those who are not is particularly emphasized in Western societies, and our traditional systems of musical education and training often contribute to this rather artificial distinction. Certain individuals are particularly encouraged in music-making at home or school, and from this group a very small minority are then further developed through particular and intense channels of music education, producing a subgroup of musical specialists who are then at the service of the wider community. Those who do not see themselves as part of this group thus begin to think of themselves as unmusical, however inaccurate that description may be. All too often, then, 'musicians' are musical, others are not. However, while this thumbnail sketch may be broadly true, it also represents something of an oversimplification. As I have already observed in Chapter One and as Ruth Finnegan's (1989) work clearly shows, there is a broad range of amateur music-making in Britain, some of which overlaps with the professional world. And while the educational model I have set out will be familiar to those in the classical music world, it does not adequately describe learning practices in popular musics, which are often undertaken in less clearly defined environments, as Lucy Green's (2001) work demonstrates. But there remains a perception in the West that musicality is somehow invested mostly in those who are in some way trained for it, leading to curious descriptions of others as being 'quite' musical, or 'not very' musical.

Such distinctions, however, are by no means universally found elsewhere. Ethnomusicological work has shown that, while many societies have musical specialists, who may be recognized as particularly skilled musicians or simply allocated the role, this does not necessarily mean that others are deemed unmusical. John Blacking's work among the South African Venda people, for example, provides one well-documented example in which all members of the community were expected to contribute to musical activities, an attitude underpinned by the belief that 'all normal human beings are capable of musical performance' (Blacking, 1976:34). As Blacking himself observes, such beliefs are 'diametrically opposed' to those conventionally held in the West.

For professional musicians, of course, the concept of musicality, and the degree to which it may be said to be held, is necessarily more complex than the physical execution of musical tasks, since the act of playing or singing inevitably inheres in their job. They do describe particular performances or individuals as being less or more musical than others (or themselves) in ways which clearly imply that this difference has nothing to do with mere technical competence; that musicality is something completely separate from an ability to play an instrument. Indeed, technical virtuosity is sometimes taken as obscuring musical deficiencies.

If you play it technically well, with all the dots and dashes where they should be, but don't actually engage your audience then you haven't done anything very musical.

They can come and play a concerto and they might be superficially very efficient players, great facility. I think there's a great concentration on facility, on notes in other words, rather than the musical aspects.

I don't know anybody who doesn't know that record and not think it's just exceptionally good. It's got everything. It's musical, it's technically brilliant, but it's got that something. You can hear a lot of other players rattle stuff off, it seems these days more so than ever, and it doesn't do anything for you at all. It leaves you cold. But it's not that easy to get that something that's alive, that lifts, that brings a lump to the throat when you hear it.

These assertions on the musicality of others will be familiar to anybody who has attempted to describe or assess a particular performance; the distinction between technical facility and musicality as markers of musical competence is not confined to professional musicians. Like most people, however, musicians find it difficult to put into words exactly what it is about somebody's playing which makes it significant, sometimes relying instead on words borrowed from other contexts.

So often people can play everything perfectly but what they're actually doing with the music is not interesting. They don't have a sense of style, they don't have a sense of how to create different colours. And I keep coming back to these words colour and texture.

There's something about being able to express the unsayable in words, which I think gets to you.

Notwithstanding these difficulties of expression, however, these are essentially subjective observations which, taken together with other equally subjective observations, may over time establish a social hierarchy in which the musical interpretations and performances of particular individuals are invested with greater significance or importance than others. Thus what is described as musicality and considered colloquially to be an individual quality possessed in greater quantities by particularly 'gifted' performers is, in fact, the product of collective judgments and social ascription, reflecting as much about those who make such judgments as those upon whom they are made. This theme runs throughout Henry Kingsbury's book *Music, Talent, and Performance* (1988), where he examines the various ways in which musicality, otherwise described as 'talent' or 'potential', is construed within the confines of an American music conservatoire. He writes that 'an assessment of musicality or talent is not something that is ever proved or disproved. Rather, it is validated with reference to the same social process in which it first arose' (75). Furthermore, the notion of 'talent' can be seen 'more as the "property" of a cultural ideology than as a "property" or characteristic trait of the individual person ... musical talent is attributed to certain people in certain situations, rather than being an a priori physiological property of the person' (76–7). In other words musicality is not a characteristic with which individuals are born but a description with which they are endowed by others in society; over time this process, as I have said, imbues the musical production of certain individuals with enhanced significance. Such assertions are considered particularly meaningful if they emanate from those who themselves hold positions of high social rank; that is, significant performers, teachers, critics and so on, figures of authority whose specialist expertise determines that their judgments carry additional weight.

Musicality is also inextricably linked to individuality, and such judgments on the musicality of others are nearly always applied to individuals rather than groups. We do not generally describe 'people from Birmingham', for example, as being more musical than 'people from London'; nor do we consider violinists, perhaps, to be more musical than clarinettists, *per se*.[1] Part of Kingsbury's work concerns what he describes as 'the cult of the individual' (117 ff) and, given that he is primarily concerned with a music conservatoire, a type of institution which lays particular emphasis on the development of individual musical skills rather than collaborative ones,[2] his emphasis on the individual is to be expected. The presence or absence of musicality, then, and the degree to which it is considered to be held, becomes part of the individual identity we construct for others. And if such assertions are generally agreed upon or made frequently enough by people whose opinion in such matters is highly valued, this in turn becomes part of a musician's self-conception, of how they see their own particular musical qualities; validation from outside confirms (or in some cases disputes)[3] one's own convictions as to the quality or worth of one's own musical production.

Although Kingsbury's assertions are supported by evidence from the somewhat rarefied environment of a music conservatoire, I would suggest that those taking part in the rather more utilitarian world of professional music-making are equally engaged in a discourse which ascribes musicality to some more than others, thus creating a sociomusical hierarchy:

I don't know what it is but certain players, when they do things, you get that – all I can call it is a tingle factor. And there are certain people who've got that, and other people who are brilliant musicians, have a great sound, but, we could say, no soul. There's no tingle factor, there's no magic there. And they're doing everything right ...

I mean all the jokes about Nigel Kennedy and [adopts a slang accent] *'all that sort a stuff, 'n' his chat 'n' the way he talks', but I've been there when it's been hair-raising. Playing of a totally magical quality. You just can't argue with it. There isn't any story you can say, well, it was a good day or whatever; it was breathtaking. I wish somebody could account for that. That I think is going to remain a mystery for a long time.*

Such observations are typical of the way in which musicians retain a degree of awe, coupled with an apparent mystification of the forces involved, with respect to the ability of others to generate what they describe as very musical performances. These kinds of assertions not only occur in the context of formal interviews such as those above, but also, and perhaps more importantly, they are embedded within the social interaction which is a natural consequence of collaborative musical performance, as the following brief conversation, taken from a break in a performance, reveals:

A: You remember Barry?
B: No.
A: Barry. The drummer. He did Leicester.
B: Oh yeah. He was quite good, I thought.
A: Yeah, he had a great feel.
B: Yeah. We should use him again.

In this case we may interpret having 'a great feel' as a confirmation of being musical: producing musical performances which are then socially validated as acceptable or competent. Thus, although musicians, understandably, might not subscribe to the rather anthropological model I have borrowed from Kingsbury, they clearly appear to be taking part in social negotiations about musicality in much the same way as this model suggests.

Although musicians may not be clear in their own minds as to *why* one person seems able to produce performances they consider particularly musical and another does not, they are, in general, clearer about what does not give rise to this ability. In particular, it is not related to intelligence:

Sometimes some of the biggest thickies produce these extraordinary results and you think 'wow!' They're the sort of things that send shivers up and down your back. And I don't know how that happens.

Anybody, almost, can learn to have a facility on an instrument. It doesn't require special brains or anything. In fact if you've got limited intelligence that might be best, you won't find it boring to practise scales and stuff, studies. But it's the bit after that, the sort of intuitive bit ...

Furthermore, I think most musicians would agree with this statement from a string player who said: *I don't think you can be taught to be musical, you either are or you aren't.* But this raises an interesting paradox with regard to the role which teachers are seen to play in an individual's musical development. Many musicians, most of whom will have studied with a number of teachers during their apprenticeship, often regard one or two as being particularly significant or important in their musical development. They speak with some reverence, and of course affection, of the abilities of those teachers who can bring out these 'magical musical powers' in themselves. Being unable to verbalize accurately *how* they do what they do, they give particular import to those who they feel are able to tease these abilities out of them. This again resonates comfortably with Kingsbury's (1988:78) observation that 'musical competence grows – or withers – in the context of particular social relationships'; that is, favourable social environments, in which the musical production of the individual is legitimized by the teacher as being valuable or worthy, are essential for competent musical development to occur. It is those teachers who are most positive in fostering the development of a musician's musical personality and who encourage a self-conception which believes that one's musical output is significant, who are likely to be seen by the musician as most significant in the context of their own development. But there remains a paradox here between what is construed as innate musicality, the 'art' – you can't be taught to be musical – and musicianship, the 'craft', the idea that going to the right teacher can make you a better musician, a paradox which is symptomatic of the difficulties musicians have in dealing with these issues.

I think everyone's got the potential to be musical, but it can be drawn out by a teacher, or it can be drawn out by the experience that you're given. But if I take my own musicality, in a sense it's no different than it was as a child. It's either been tampered with or it's been encouraged. And it can disappear, with criticism, I think or with disappointment.

There seems little doubt that instrumental teachers do play a significant role in the early development of musical skills. Davidson *et al.* (1997:202) suggest that, whereas the personality of the teacher is important for younger children, performance skills and professional reputation become more significant later on, as the student's abilities and therefore aspirations increase. Many musicians gave me the impression that they developed significant relationships with a particular teacher during their late teens and early twenties; that is, at the time they sought to make the transition from amateur to professional:

I sort of hit it off with Dave. But then I've noticed that when he talks about other pupils he always refers to them with great respect, and is always very excited about what they do. He was so helpful really and positive. Whereas I think Bill was distant and slightly aloof and impenetrable. I never really knew who he was, what really made him tick.

I had a very good relationship with my teacher. He wasn't necessarily preparing me as a saxophone player, because the work that I've ended up doing hasn't been the sort of stuff I learnt with him. He would give you all the encouragement.

But the paradox lies in what musicians believe they gain from these teachers. Although, I suggest, most musicians believe musicality cannot be taught, they still seem to go to teachers for what they describe as musical rather than technical reasons. Consider the following extract from the same interview with the string player quoted on p.38.

I didn't feel that I really needed an awful lot of technique, it was more sort of musical things, and the fact that I hadn't really had a proper viola lesson, because all the lessons I'd had had been violinists teaching me the viola. So, the main reason was that he was a viola player, but a very fine viola player, and he was incredibly musical.

Having earlier suggested that musicality cannot be taught, he went on to assert that his choice of teacher was based on his assessment of the teacher's own musicality, which, presumably, he felt would be transmitted to him. So the paradox here is that musicians are frequently seeking from a teacher something that they themselves cannot define: a mixture of personal and musical skills which, to make a bad pun, strikes a chord with them and which they see as encouraging the development of their own abilities in what one described to me as a 'black art'. In fact, it is the endorsement of individual interpretations by this significant authority, the confirmation that 'what you're doing is very good, very musical', which validates a musician's production and contributes to both their self-conception and their individual identity as somebody of notable 'talent'.

Often the choice of teacher, which in retrospect can appear so important, is purely fortuitous. Many students starting at music college will simply be allocated a teacher on arrival, although they may swap at a later stage. In such cases an effective teacher–pupil relationship relies not only upon a good match between the social and musical traits of both teacher and pupil, but also upon the coincidence that brings them together. Reflecting on my own experience I can see that I exemplify many of these things. My early teachers were notable for their enthusiasm and their ability to generate enthusiasm in others, rather than for any great technical ability. But in my university and conservatoire years the technical and musical expertise, together with the stature of the teachers themselves, became more important. The technical ability of my first teacher left me so overwhelmed that I felt I either had to work very hard indeed or give up. The second placed more emphasis on matters of musical interpretation than technical wizardry, which again I felt was right for me at the time. For the third teacher I went to the Paris Conservatoire, to acquire something from contact with the long-established tradition of classical saxophone playing in France. Even now I cannot say exactly what it was that I thought I might gain from this, but it seems likely that it was both the added kudos arising from studying with a particularly eminent international teacher and the sense of authority inherent within this particular tradition.

The idea of establishing some connection with a perceived tradition seems often to be important for musicians. Kingsbury (1988:46) notes that in his first piano lesson with a new teacher he was advised that 'my teacher was Artur Schnabel, the famous pianist. Schnabel studied with Theodor Leschetitzky, Leschetitzky studied with Liszt, Liszt studied with Czerny, and of course Czerny was a student of Beethoven. So you see you come into a good pedigree here'. Kingsbury's point is that this lineage is taken to contribute to an enhanced understanding of particular artworks: if you are part of this tradition your interpretation of a given artwork is supposedly more meaningful than those who do not have this direct connection with the work's historical roots; yet this added authority must come from information imparted aurally (and orally) by the teacher, and not reside in the musical score which, of course, is available to all. One of my own pupils unwittingly touched on the same subject. In one of our lessons I caught myself half-way through relating an anecdote about something my teacher at the Paris Conservatoire had said to me, and I began to worry that this might be boring and irrelevant. I started to apologize for this when she stopped me by saying: *Don't be silly, that's why I'm here.* Her perception that she was part of a particular music lineage and that this might contribute to her musical development was important to her. Another musician made a similar point:

I see Dennis as a link with the great names of the past, and I don't mean that as being overwhelmed with nostalgia, I just think that, realistically, he knew people that don't exist anymore. He played for Beecham, he played for Pierre Monteux, big names like that. Yeah, he is a link with the past. It's like when he played for Adrian Boult. Well, here was a man who knew Elgar. Some people might say, 'So what? He's just an old man standing up in front of you.' But to me that was really important, that meant something.

At this point we are dealing with an area which has perhaps been unfairly neglected by scholars, and this is the oral/aural tradition of Western art music. Although such music arises from a highly rationalized system predicated on elaborate scientific principles governing temperament, functional harmony and so on, and underpinned by a sophisticated notation system, there is also a significant aural component in the way in which it is produced and reproduced. Traditional musicology's reliance on the overriding primacy of the musical text has perhaps obscured this point, but the discourse between teacher and pupil, and between musicians themselves, must inevitably affect the interpretation of individual works. This is reminiscent of the Indian *gharana,* wherein, as Neuman points out:

A musician's identity is always defined in part by the identity of his teacher who, in turn, is identified by the identity of *his* teacher back through the line. This taken as a whole comprises a given 'school', called a *gharana* (literally, 'of the house'), distinguished from other gharanas on the basis of its unique history, pedigree, and style of performance. (Neuman, 1980:31)

In the West this lineage is neither as explicit nor, usually, as accurately articulated as it was by Kingsbury's teacher, but it appears to remain an integral component of a musician's self-conception. This is evidenced not only by the quotations above but also by the fact that many musicians, particularly at the beginning of their professional careers, will automatically include the names of those teachers they consider most significant in their biography and CV, and this in turn becomes more widely disseminated through programme notes, CD liners, and so forth. Thus their affiliation with a particular teaching lineage becomes a significant component of both their self-conception and their individual identity within the world at large. The following extract from the biography of a recently graduated pianist, which I have extracted from a concert programme, exemplifies this point:

Last summer Andrew graduated with First Class Honours from the piano class of
Irinia Zaritskaya at the Royal College of Music, where he was a prize-winning
student. He has performed extensively as a chamber pianist and has been coached
by several eminent instrumentalists, including Dr. Felix Andrievsky, Itzhak
Rashkovsky, Christopher Bunting, Dr. Peter Katin, and the Chilingirian Quartet.
As a conductor, he was trained by the legendary professor Ilya Musin at the Saint
Petersburg State Conservatoire, Russia.

Of course, the whole ethos of Western art music, with its emphasis on the
production of specialist, professional musicians, encourages a belief in musical
individualism. As I observed above, it implies that certain people, by dint of
superior individual skills and extensive specialist training, are worthy of the
description 'musician', while others are not. For those musicians entrusted with
this responsibility, however, this has a further ramification in that they are
encouraged from the beginning to develop their own individual voice, to have
a strong sense of themselves as individual musicians. In particular, the whole
system of music education, especially in the post-school years, puts
considerable emphasis on producing soloists, or at least musicians who are both
predisposed towards and capable of playing in a soloistic manner.

This is demonstrated in a number of ways. Firstly, instrumental tuition
nearly always occurs on a one-to-one basis, a single pupil with one teacher;
only very seldom does group tuition take place and this is usually either for
reasons of financial expediency (that is, the local authority or school cannot
afford the teaching hours to pay for individual lessons for everybody) or in
occasional chamber music coaching, perhaps available once a student has
reached a certain standard. For many students the weekly lesson with their
instrumental teacher may be the only time they actually play with anybody
else present, and this is particularly true of instruments such as the piano. Of
course, many students do take part in school groups or orchestras, but this
tends to be more available to those who have already reached a particular level
of proficiency. Furthermore, the system of exams and competitions upon
which instrumental music education in this country is predicated (a hangover
from Victorian preoccupations with the need for paper qualifications)[4] also
encourages a soloistic attitude, as well as being a significant and obvious
mechanism through which assertions of musical talent are bestowed. As
students progress they are entered for an exam where they generally perform,
usually accompanied by a pianist if playing an orchestral instrument, in front
of a single examiner who then assesses the quality of the individual
performance against particular benchmarks (although my personal experience
of entering students for this suggests that these benchmarks, perhaps
inevitably, are widely variable). Competitions fulfil much the same purpose,
ascribing pre-eminence to certain individuals within particular instrumental or
vocal specialisms. Naturally the thumbnail sketch I have presented here does

not tell the whole story; there are competitions and exams for chamber music groups, choirs and orchestras, and approaches to teaching, such as the Suzuki method, which deviate from the norm I have suggested. But I believe that in general the most significant emphasis is on the development of a distinctive and individual musical personality, and I am not alone in this view:

I think, you know, sometimes as a classical musician you're always trained to be a soloist, and bit by bit you have the stuffing knocked out of you. You suddenly realise that you're not going to make it as a soloist, so maybe you'll be a chamber music player. A lot of people suddenly realise they're not going to be a chamber music player, so 'I'll go into an orchestra' and then some people don't even do that. So I think you're turned out to be a soloist and then you're left to do what you can with your life.

The accent [at music college] *was quite often on 'orchestral playing is bad for you, bad for your posture, bad for your playing' because ... I'm not quite sure why. But the ideal thing was to be a soloist if you were really on top, you know, but otherwise a chamber music player.*

Having been in the profession and at the sort of sharp end for quite a long time, and having auditioned virtually every fiddle player in the country, I know just how difficult it is. The way that specialist music schools and music colleges are actually geared, very, very misguidedly to turning out soloists. I was really quite against that. I still am. I mean the way they go about churning out potential soloists is absolutely ridiculous.

Indeed, when I pressed other musicians on what they considered to be the defining characteristics of a good musician, several included in their response the idea that their playing must be characterful, with a strong personality:

I think it is somebody who captures your attention, you have to listen to them, they grab you and they don't let go. You're sort of drawn in.

It doesn't have to be loud, but someone who really performs well, with great vitality and life in their playing.

Conversely, another musician bemoaned the fact that her particular experience at music college tried to take this individual character away from her:

Having been at university, that was when I felt that my voice was sort of there, and then the moment you go to music college they are trying to make you into this breed, and they are not developing your own natural voice, but they're trying to develop a way of flute playing. And I found that very damaging.

Anthony Kemp, in *The Musical Temperament* (1996), shows how this development of individuality, the deliberate cultivation of a conscious musical self, becomes a significant component of the personality of professional musicians. He notes that musicians have a tendency towards introversion – although this is not generally coupled with shyness, resulting in what he terms 'bold introversion' (46) – and independence. Indeed, it is a notable characteristic of professional musicians that they demonstrate a personality shift from dependency in their earlier educational years (while they need the teacher to develop their technical skills) to independence during their post-educational years (when such skills have become internalized and they concentrate on developing their inner aesthetic world (66)); this would appear to amplify Davidson's observations noted above on the role and importance of teachers in musical development.

In part, therefore, describing a professional musician as being musical implies that their playing has character, distinctiveness, that they draw attention to themselves. Yet, in most situations where professional musicians work, this quality must, through the necessity of having to combine their voice with others, be somehow subsumed; or, as another musician eloquently put it, *You have to not so much subsume it, but you have to submerge it, you have to craft it into different shapes.* In fact the vast majority of musicians very seldom perform as soloists as such, although some do have soloistic moments within orchestras and ensembles. There is, therefore, a tension to be resolved between the training most Western musicians undergo, which deliberately fosters a soloistic attitude, the development of a conscious musical self, and the performance situations in which they most frequently find themselves, where this tendency towards individualism must be restrained or modified for the purposes of collaboration with other equally self conscious musical individuals.

This tension between self and society is not, of course, unique to musicians, nor is the consideration of it peculiarly ethnomusicological; there are numerous academic works which have considered the issue from different perspectives and with regard to various subjects. But much of what follows in the rest of this chapter and in subsequent chapters is predicated upon the notion that musicians both deliberately cultivate and value highly a strongly developed sense of musical self, and that this is expressed and articulated in diverse ways both in their music making and in the organization of their professional lives. And perhaps the most significant and personal manifestation of this is revealed in their approach to and conception of their own instrumental sound.

Conceptualizing sound

Traditional musicology has frequently marginalized the study of musical timbre, largely because the notation system which underpins Western art music is all but incapable of conveying timbral information. Musical texts contain detailed instructions relating to pitch and rhythm, and less specific information about speed, volume and so on. Yet, beyond allocating particular musical lines to specific instruments, they reveal very little about the quality of sound expected from groups or individuals at any given time, except for rather inexplicit instructions implied by (often Italian) descriptors such as *cantabile* or *sotto voce*. Only in particular specialist areas such as orchestration textbooks, electronic music composition or the consideration of *Klangfarbenmelodie*,[5] does the actual quality of musical sound generate anything other than a footnote or cursory discussion, if that.

Scholars elsewhere, however, are more receptive to the idea that musical timbre can both represent and connote information which is significant, not only in itself, but also in terms of our perception of the music. John Shepherd (1991:164–73), for example, has suggested that different vocal timbres can be read as projecting different gender locations or images, with the rasping tones of overtly masculine 'cock rock' clearly distinguishable from the 'rich, resonating sound' of the 'woman-as-nurturer', or the more hard-edged female head tones of the 'woman as sex object' (167–8). Shepherd also characterizes the ideology underlying Western art music as insisting on 'standardised purity (which students are carefully taught to achieve) ... [and which] has in turn resulted in the unexamined assumption that timbre in "classical" music is a neutral and largely unimportant element, having little to do with the expressive quality of the music' (164). Neither Shepherd nor myself believes this to be the case, as will become clearer below.

Similarly, Theo van Leewen (1999) has attempted to set out a 'social semiotics of sound quality' (130), arguing that musical timbre can signify 'practical experience metaphorically' (140), as well as allowing us to understand similar metaphorical extensions represented by the sounds of others. In particular, van Leewen observes a relationship between the physiological states required to produce particular sounds, and the physical or emotional states that may be referenced by them. Sounds which may be described as timbrally tense (for example, voices which are higher than normal, or aggressive guitar or saxophone sounds) can relate to 'increased alertness, self-control, stress ... in short, to every situation in which it is not desirable or possible to relax or act without constraint' (140); nasality is similarly related to tension and may convey 'strong negative value judgments' (141); and so on. Equally significant is that sound quality is multidimensional, 'a combination of different features which all help define what the sound quality presents or represents' (140).

Both Shepherd and van Leewen are therefore suggesting that sound quality is capable of being decoded, that it can reveal underlying social or cultural constructs which may not be directly asserted in the musical patterns or texts of 'the music itself'. Perhaps the most ambitious attempt at this kind of decoding was Alan Lomax's Cantometrics project (see Lomax, 1968, 1976), which set out to relate the style and structure of folk song to types of social organization in general, and particularly to the degree of control exercised over women in a given society. It was Lomax's contention that 'song style seems to summarize … the ranges of behavior that are appropriate to one kind of cultural context' (1968:6), and his approach involved mapping the analyses of small samples of song onto a matrix derived from 37 ratings scales (22–3). In addition to considering ornamentation, rhythm, melody and other features of the songs, some of these scales dealt with timbral issues such as 'nasality' or 'rasp'. This in turn led Lomax to observations such as the rough male voice being more common where boys are trained to be assertive, a tendency found more often in hunting societies and less in agricultural societies (192). While the Cantometrics project has been extensively criticized on a variety of grounds,[6] it remains significant in the present context for the importance it attaches to the qualities of sound generated in particular circumstances, and for suggesting how such qualities may be related to underlying cultural constructs.

It is noticeable that all these scholars rely significantly on the qualities of the human voice as the basis for much of their work, although they do occasionally consider instrumental timbre also. Clearly the voice has a particular role to play here, in part because of the rich timbral flexibility which it affords, but also because of the range of inferences which may be drawn from, or the associations made with, the various musical contexts in which it is employed. Van Leewen, however, when not drawing on vocal qualities, often uses different saxophone players and their sounds as his exemplars. Like the voice, the saxophone is both flexible and capable of a variety of very distinct timbres, more so than many instruments. These range from the bright, aggressive tones of rock sax solos, through the smooth but breathy sounds of Ben Webster, perhaps, or the lighter, 'purer' sounds of Lester Young, to the more rounded classical sound of the orchestral saxophone, and many others besides. Although I see other instruments as having analogous variations in timbre, it is perhaps my own involvement as a performer on an instrument with such noticeable contrasts, and which can reference such a wide variety of musical styles, which provokes my own interest in and sensitivity to these issues. Such issues are not, however, restricted to saxophonists, nor even to wind players in general:

I believe the viola is more a lyrical, singing instrument than a virtuoso instrument – and I think I make a better viola sound.[7]

I think in timps the sound production is more important than on most other instruments. Most other percussion instruments it really is a matter of you hit it and it makes a noise. On the timps there is much more control over what kind of sound you get out.

Notwithstanding my own particular interests then, I suspect that all those who subscribe to a particular musical tradition develop an ability to make timbral judgments on the musical sounds of that tradition, however subconsciously such abilities may be exercised. Those parents who are subjected to the early musical efforts of their offspring as the latter attempt to master the intricacies of the violin or oboe in their bedroom, will often recognize that, not only has technical competence yet to be achieved, but also the instrument does not sound right, or at least the sound is not yet mature. And of course many people become skilled at identifying singers (the human voice again) from the quality of their vocal timbre, rather than because of the repertoire or any particular recording: Ella Fitzgerald as opposed to Billie Holiday, Frank Sinatra rather than Dean Martin, or whoever. Such issues become particularly transparent in the world of opera, where aficionados will vigorously debate the finer differences between one singer or another, notwithstanding that such distinctions may seem almost imperceptible to those who do not subscribe to these traditions. Inverting the argument for a moment, it is also clear that particular qualities of sound become identified with, indeed promoted by, certain institutions or traditions of one sort or another. The early music movement, for example, has engendered an approach to performance and recording in which a particular transparency, clarity or lightness has become *de rigueur*, to the extent that one can immediately identify so-called historically informed performances simply by the quality of the sound.[8] I also notice that one of Britain's few radio stations specializing in classical music transmits its signal with noticeably enhanced bass frequencies, no doubt in an attempt to produce a warm, rich sound, in keeping with the station's identity as a purveyor of 'smooth classics'. In both cases such timbral manipulations may be seen as supporting particular cultural ideologies.

Yet I suggest that, while these abilities to make timbral judgments are widespread, they are held most keenly by those in whom a musical tradition may be said to reside, by which I mean most obviously the musicians themselves, but also to a lesser degree others such as, in our own traditions, critics, record producers, composers and so on, who all have a vested interest in making such judgments. Professional musicians, however, have more interest than most in this issue, for a number of reasons. First, because musicians' perceptions of sound are closely allied to their judgments on musicality: 'she's very musical, she makes a lovely sound'. Because sound quality is the raw material in which musicians deal, and through which they interact with others, it forms a significant part of their assessment of the musical identities of those around them.

No-one's going to listen to you if you sound awful. The classic case on saxophone is they say you sound like a Kazoo. I mean, that's what you're trying to avoid, and it's something, with the teaching I do now, I say this is one of the most important things. You're playing an instrument and the reason you're playing an instrument, I presume, is that you're going to want to play for people. But it's got to be attractive. So for me, what makes a good musician, that's fundamental.

And it's the same with all musicians, for me, it's the sound. That's the first thing that attracts me.

Even more significantly, in the present context, the sound a musician produces or seeks to produce on their instrument is one of the most significant dimensions of their self-conception as musicians; the quality of sound which a musician conceives as being 'truly me' both symbolizes and is a constituent part of their conception of themselves as individuals, as well as being of fundamental importance in defining sociomusical relationships.

You hear an ideal sound within yourself. And that's the sound you want to reproduce. That's your aim. When you hear the sound isn't right, you keep on searching for that ideal. And when you find it, that's fantastic.

And to my ear, there's a certain string which I use which I think is best, and it makes the sound I want. There's an idea of the sound you want.

So [at music college] *everyone's almost sounding the same, they're trying to get the same sound from people, rather than trying to let their character shine. And I found that very damaging.*

This last musician's discomfort with part of her musical training underlines the significance of her own sound as a fundamental expression of her self-conception as a musician.

Such observations would appear to further reinforce Kemp's assertions on the importance musicians attach to internalizing musical information, and the imaging processes which accompany this. He writes that 'the ability to internalise sound and to develop a rich, imaginative, and comprehensive internal representation, not only of what has been previously experienced, but also for imaging new, innovative compositions and interpretations, would appear to be an essential feature of a musician's thinking' (1996:44). While Kemp appears to be emphasizing pitch and rhythmic information, I suggest that the timbral information essential to the conceptualization of a musician's sound is similarly internalized and, as I have said, comprises a significant component of their self-conception.

The notion of selfhood, of what constitutes the self, how it may be defined, or whether indeed it exists at all, has provided an important focus for scholarly work in a variety of academic disciplines, including philosophy, psychology, anthropology and others.[9] Here is not the place to review these various endeavours, but I suggest that, for musicians, this conception of their own individual sound forms a significant part of what psychologists would describe as their 'phenomenal' self, which may be defined as 'a person's awareness, arising out of interactions with his environment, of his own beliefs, values, attitudes, the links between them, and their implications for his behavior' (Jones and Gerard, 1967:716). Thus each of us has 'a potentially available overarching cognition of his or her interrelated dispositions' (Jones and Pittman, 1982:232) which we may consciously draw upon to determine our actions. Paraphrasing this for my own purposes, I am suggesting that a musician's conception of the sound he or she makes is one of the most significant components of those 'interrelated dispositions' which they feel characterize them as musicians, and which they call upon to determine their musical actions in a given context.

Furthermore, as is evident from the words of Jones and Gerard above, our conception of self is determined in part by our relationships with our environment, and is not something that can be established without reference to society at large. As Suls elsewhere observes, 'self-knowledge stems from the reciprocal relationship between ourselves and our social group. Conceptions of our traits, abilities, and opinions grow out of the reactions of others, and how we compare to them. In short, the self is made of social cloth' (Suls, 1982:vii). Such social cloth is woven particularly finely in musical co-productions, because of the need to manipulate one's sound for the purpose of blending, literally and figuratively, with others. Consider the example of the woodwind player who goes into an orchestral section for the first time. If he is, say, the second clarinet, he knows the other seven wind players who form the nucleus of the wind section will be listening closely to the type of sound he makes and the way he is able to manipulate it. He will need a sound which matches but does not overpower the first clarinet player, which allows him to blend with the particular musical characteristics of the woodwind section as a whole, but which is also confident and characterful enough to deal with occasional second clarinet solos. One clarinettist remarked to me that, while he thought he would fit well into the wind section of the London Symphony Orchestra, who he felt played with a certain individualistic style, he said he would not be so happy in the Philharmonia Orchestra, as he found everything just too smooth and 'over-blended'. Likewise, an essential part of the craft of playing in a large string section requires a similar ability to manipulate the quality of one's individual sound according to the occasion.

The difficulty of playing in a string section is that obviously the string section has to sound like one instrument. And you have to have the ability to make all these different sounds, everybody in that section has to be able to play the same way. And in a good string section if one person isn't doing it they stick out like a sore thumb. If you don't have that degree of control over your instrument you can't play in a string section.

*Probably the first thing to do is to be able to make a really beautiful sound,
and to realise that there are different characters of sound to be dealt with in
an orchestra. So that when you are asked to play in a subservient,
accompanying manner you can do that, and then when you are asked to play
in a rich, warm, soloistic manner you can do that. And these are important
things, you've got to know what sort of sound you've got to make.*

All of which would appear to demonstrate highly developed ideas about what
kind of sound is required for what sort of situation, as one might expect from
this very skilled group of musical practitioners. But it also demonstrates a
conceptualization of the individual in relation to the group, expressed as sonic
information. Although musicians have a strong sense of what constitutes their
own particular sound, they are also conscious of the necessity to manipulate
this sound in order to take their proper place in the particular sociomusical
world in which they find themselves.

However, notwithstanding the centrality of this subject in musical life, few
musicians show any degree of exactitude when verbalizing about sound, and
the various codes into which they lapse when attempting to communicate ideas
about sound to each other would form the basis of an interesting
sociolinguistic study. These seem often to be conveyed in terms of space or
architecture (fat, thin, wide, focused, tight, centred, toppy) or perhaps
instrument technology (reedy, edgy, stringy, brassy, metallic) or sometimes in
terms of musical style (straight, classical, jazzy, bluesy). All these and more
are employed in the attempt to communicate to others how one perceives a
particular instrumental sound. Van Leewen (1999:130) notes that such
adjectives often mix the purely descriptive with the evaluative. Thus it is
considered 'good' for a voice to be 'bright' or 'clear', but 'bad' for it to be
'piercing' or 'strident'. The ambiguity arising from the use of these terms
undoubtedly contributes in part to the ascription of musicality (or otherwise)
to which I referred previously; that such adjectives may be employed with
either positive or negative spin on them can be ascertained from a cursory
inspection of any page of recording reviews in a music magazine. So, although
I suggest that professional musicians have very sophisticated perceptions and
conceptions of sound, these are not supported by or expressed through a
rigorous, analytical verbal framework. Yet the various adjectives employed
must convey some kind of shared understanding or agreement, otherwise they
would be, literally, meaningless. One might reasonably argue, however, that it
is via the musical sounds themselves that musicians truly communicate their
intentions or understandings; mere words, in this case as in so many others,
are often woefully inadequate.

Concepts of sound production are frequently related to musical technology
and, like professionals in other fields, musicians are keen to discuss with
colleagues who share their instrumental specialism the merits or demerits of

one particular tool or another. One has only to look at interviews and reviews in the various journals directed at particular types of instrumentalists – *The Strad, Saxophone Journal, Modern Drummer* and so on – to see the many column inches devoted to this subject. I use the term 'concept of sound production' because, paradoxically, although musicians are keenly interested in the technology of their trade and its relationship to their own sound, most also agree that, ultimately, 'the sound is in your head'. In other words, once a musician has established what they take to be 'their' sound, they will reproduce it, or something close to it, regardless of the particular technology being used. This is not to say that the right reed, mouthpiece, string or head-joint makes no difference; it does, and the right apparatus certainly helps a musician *feel* more comfortable or confident about making their sound. But it is also true that changing mouthpieces or other technical paraphernalia does not necessarily radically change a musician's sound unless it is also accompanied by an intellectual and emotional desire to make a different sound. I have observed this in others and experienced it myself. For example, some time ago I swapped soprano saxophones from one brand to another. The feel of the new instrument was very different: different weight, different keywork, I felt it immediately needed a different mouthpiece and so on. Before purchasing it I asked a close colleague to hear me play on the new instrument so that he could assess my new sound against the one he was used to hearing, and so that I could weigh up his objective opinion of the sound against my subjective one. But when he heard me play, rather to my surprise considering what a completely different experience it felt to me, he simply said, 'It just sounds like you playing a soprano saxophone.'

That's always the thing, you know, somebody else plays your fiddle, and you think that sounds great. But they might not think it sounds great, when they're playing it.

You might go to a repairer or a maker who will make an adjustment, and you'll say, no I want it more like this, and they'll make another adjustment, and you're not happy and, I want it more like this. And they can't tell the difference.

Thus this concept of sound is an internal referent, an individual, internalized ideal which is not entirely dependent on physiology or instrumental technology, notwithstanding that the latter does have some role to play in generating it.

How might musicians arrive at these internalized sound concepts? This is a broad and difficult subject, but in part at least we return to the aural tradition of Western art music. In our early, impressionable years we are inevitably greatly influenced by those around us, including those teachers who provide our initial musical training. The oral/aural discourse between student and teacher not only provides technical details about the instrument, music notation and so on but is also the first step in moulding a basic sound which is aesthetically acceptable to both parties. The teacher naturally starts with an internalized conception of sound which is necessarily transmitted to the pupil.

He told me I had rubbish technique, but my sound was great. He said, you know, your tone and playing in tune, they're gifts really, now we just have to be able to get your fingers in the right direction.

Reflecting on my own work in this area I am conscious that I discuss with a pupil what I think is or is not good about their sound: whether it projects properly, whether it is too 'edgy' or 'woolly', too 'fat' or too 'thin'. Personally I try not to be too dictatorial with my students; as long as the sound they produce is at least basically acceptable to me I try and allow them to develop a sound with which they feel comfortable. Yet even this phrase, 'basically acceptable to me', reveals some measurement of their sound against my internalized concept of what constitutes a good sound; and I do demonstrate my sound and illustrate differences between theirs and mine which must inevitably influence their own conception of their sound, particularly among younger students who may not be advanced or mature enough to question ideas put forward by such an influential figure as their own teacher. Developing the ability to analyse musical sound, however, particularly one's own, is an essential part of the evolution of individual musical maturity.

This process then gets extended so that 'schools of sound' begin to emerge, in which particularly popular teachers influence numbers of students who consequently begin to sound like them, a sonic consequence of the *gharana* principle that I noted previously. I have observed, for example, that one of my saxophone teachers now encourages his pupils to play, as he does, with the saxophone at a much sharper angle relative to the jaw, which results in a greater proportion of upper partials or overtones in the sound, making it brighter and more penetrating. I find it interesting to see (because of this different posture) and hear a whole group of saxophone players so obviously imitating their teacher in this way. Moreover one can find analogous 'sound schools' in many other instruments. The thin, rather reedy orchestral oboe sound of the 1940s and 1950s has given way to a more mellow, rounded sound; the old-style, 'straight' English clarinet sound, associated in the minds of many clarinettists with instruments known as B&H 1010s, although still occasionally produced by certain players, has largely given way to a 'fatter', 'warmer' sound, and the French Buffet clarinets are now favoured for producing this. I have no doubt that people with more expertise than myself would be able to make similar observations in other fields. Taking this a stage further we can see that these schools of sound can be construed by musicians not only as representing associations with particular teachers but also as being emblematic of certain national identities: 'the German sound', 'the French sound'. And of course one can go on and suggest that east European brass and wind players sound different to their west European counterparts, as do the orchestras in which they play.

The sound of the Philharmonia is the most similar in London to that of the Vienna Philharmonic. It's a very rich, warm sound.

Because professional musicians are keenly attuned to these timbral variations they frequently attempt to decode certain pieces of information simply from analysing another musician's sound, in a similar fashion to the scholars whose work I outlined above, albeit that musicians perhaps do it more intuitively. Such appraisals of other musicians' characteristics and abilities are an integral part of professional musical life, and this is particularly the case among jazz players. Because jazz has even more of an aural tradition than Western art music its exponents are encouraged, indeed almost obliged, to listen extensively to other jazz musicians who are, after all, responsible for both creation and reproduction within the tradition. This leads to certain allegiances with particularly significant figures, which in turn often influences sound production. Among saxophone players I would argue that Jan Garbarek, Michael Brecker and, particularly, David Sanborn provide notable recent examples of this. It is worth noting that in these cases such widespread influence would be impossible without the advent of the recording industry, which provides another perspective on the issue of sound transmission, over and above direct teacher–pupil relationships or national performance styles. Even in Western art music the importance of aural tradition, as a conduit both for interpretive ideas and for providing models of sound types, should not be overlooked.

And he relied a lot on tradition, you know, learning from what's gone on before. It was very important to hear as many recordings as possible and to know how people used to perform things.

And Joe would just play me tapes, and I'd hear saxophone playing I'd never heard, but he would give you all the encouragement.

It should also be emphasized that for many professional musicians in London individual sound ideals are not only components of musical self-conception satisfying some inner psychoacoustic aesthetic. The manipulation of one's sound is also a necessary skill in a marketplace where a musician can be called upon to perform in many different musical styles. Again this may be a more significant consideration for wind and brass players than for certain other musicians, but I think the point is generally valid. The type of sound required for a big band or a West End musical is fundamentally different for an orchestral concert, and different again for a solo performance; yet many musicians find themselves working in all these areas and others I have not mentioned. The hypothetical clarinettist I introduced above might well find himself, the night after his orchestral engagement, playing among electric keyboards and guitars imitating a Jewish klezmer musician in a performance of *Fiddler on the Roof,* followed by a date with a small chamber ensemble performing an avant-garde piece requiring extended instrumental techniques. Such skills, albeit perhaps driven by economic expediency, are necessary extensions to the flexibility discussed above with regard to orchestras. Being sensitive enough to distinguish between these needs, conceptualizing the differences between them, and then being able to reproduce sounds accepted as aesthetically appropriate, as well, of course, as being conversant with the different musical styles themselves, greatly increases a musician's employability. Most saxophone players, and many trumpet and trombone players, and perhaps others besides, carry different mouthpieces with them in order to help produce these different sounds; however, as I have already noted, the technological paraphernalia is, I believe, of secondary importance to the cognitive skills employed.

So, by way of conclusion, I suggest that the particular quality of vocal or instrumental timbre a musician seeks to produce represents one of the most fundamental components of their self-conception as a musician. Yet, notwithstanding that this sound is conceived as the musician's own, it is both formed and informed in part through their engagement with the wider musical world and their interaction with other sound producers. While this sound is necessarily manipulated in different contexts, a sense of musical self prevails throughout, just as each of us manages to retain a sense of who we are in the many different social roles in which we may find ourselves in our everyday lives: as mother, wife, daughter, employee, churchgoer, neighbour and so on; each of these roles may require us to behave rather differently, but we still retain a sense of being 'me'. As Anthony Cohen (1994:9) writes, 'it [is] remarkable that, as individuals, we generally manage to cope with these many incompatible claims on our allegiance without cracking under the strain. It is little short of a triumph that we do so while also preserving a reasonable sense of loyalty to our own sense of self'. The loyalty musicians feel towards their own sound, and the manipulations to which it may be subjected for the purposes of collaboration with other individual musical sounds, provides both a metaphor for, and is itself an essential part of, the social relationships between musicians and the tension which inevitably inheres between the individual and the group in the essentially social act of professional musical production. Social interaction is timbrally formulated in musical contexts. Furthermore, for professional musicians this sense of self, symbolized here by the production and reproduction of their individual sound, must be retained throughout a variety of different musical genres and professional engagements, and one of the most significant ways in which this is demonstrated forms the basis of the next chapter.

Notes

1   We do occasionally refer to certain nationalities (for example 'the Welsh') as being particularly musical, but this, I think, has more to do with issues of stereotyping than empirical facts about collective musical abilities.

2   He writes that students feel that 'time spent in learning orchestral parts is time that might be spent developing one's own artistic skills on the instrument, and it is the latter that is quite generally perceived as the primary agenda for a conservatory student' (Kingsbury 1988:54). Many of my own conversations with orchestral musicians threw up similar perceptions of conservatoire attitudes.

3   See Kingsbury (1988:64–7), for example.

4   Ehrlich (1985:116–20) writes extensively on what he describes as 'the bizarre Victorian conception of a professional musician's career as a ceaseless quest for paper qualifications'. It should be noted, however, that, while this may very well have started as a peculiarly English tradition, it has been taken on with alacrity in all parts of the globe where Western art music has become established.

5   *Klangfarbenmelodie* was a term established by Schoenberg to express the idea that successive tone colours could be related to one another in a way analogous to the relationship between pitches in a melody.

6   See, for example, Henry's (1976) reassessment.

7   Cited in Danziger (1995:8).

8   Taruskin (1995:164–72) provides a typically pungent review of 'the modern sound of early music'.

9   There are many sources that might be cited as examples here. Suls (1982) and Suls and Greenwald (1983) provide a good overview of a variety of psychological approaches. Holstein and Gubrium (2000) provide both a review and a critique of various sociological and anthropological approaches. Goffman (1959) is an earlier but influential sociological approach, Giddens (1991) a later but similarly influential tome. Cohen (1994) will be already familiar to readers of the present work.

CHAPTER THREE

Self-Conception and Individual Identity: the Deputy System

Introduction

In this chapter I continue my consideration of the musical self, and particularly the way in which individuals engage with the wider musical community through the system of deputizing, a process which facilitates the substitution of one musician by another for a specific engagement. This process, which for most if not all musicians appears as a natural consequence of their professional responsibilities, in fact reveals a great deal about both self-conception and individual identity. Although my principal concern here as elsewhere is with classically trained musicians, I shall occasionally refer to those working in other fields such as jazz or musicals, some of whom might not describe themselves as 'classical' musicians as such. Economic expediency dictates that musicians must be competent in a number of different performance styles, leading to some overlap between musical genres, which frequently prevents the rigid categorization of a particular musician as being of one type or another, as I hope my analysis will show.

Variety as the spice of life

Two musicians were booked for an engagement in Thailand; one was a jazz musician and the other was a show musician, that is, a musician who specializes in playing musicals. In order to increase their rather poor fee for this gig they decided to try and smuggle some drugs back to England on their way out of the country. Naturally, they were caught and subsequently sentenced to death. When the day came for the sentence to be carried out they were both brought before a firing squad, and the captain of the firing squad went up to the show musician and asked him if he had one final request. 'Yes,' he replied, 'I would like to hear the entire works of Andrew Lloyd Webber once more before I die.' The captain was a little taken aback by this, but he agreed to it. He then went over to the jazz musician and asked him if he had a final request, and the jazz musician looked at him and said, 'Yes – can you please shoot me first?'

I have heard (and told) this joke in a number of situations among many different musicians, all of whom, it seemed to me, appreciated the joke. No doubt our collective appreciation was based largely on an implied judgment of the musical value (howsoever determined) of the works of Andrew Lloyd Webber. But in order for the joke to succeed another, more subtle, distinction is being made, between the image of a jazz musician and that of a show player. Or rather, for the joke to make sense it is accepted that such a distinction could be made, regardless of the potential inaccuracy of such stereotyping, as will become clearer below.

Playing jazz, of course, requires a very different set of cognitive skills and a different musical aesthetic to playing in a show, and these are only two of the various musical styles with which a freelance musician in London might need to be familiar. Other styles include, for example, classical and contemporary Western art music, commercial studio work and pop music. These different skills are fundamental to a musician's employability: the more styles in which you are convincing, the more work you are available for, and the busier and therefore wealthier you are likely to be.

I do not claim that it is only in London that musicians are required to cover such wide musical ground. I imagine that much the same occurs in other large cities, such as New York, where there are also a variety of musical styles available for popular consumption. Nor is this necessarily exclusive to Western culture: it is perhaps a feature of urban music-making generally. Neuman (1978) has shown how rural musicians in the Hindustani tradition evolved various adaptive strategies during the late nineteenth and early twentieth centuries as increasing numbers of them migrated to the urban areas of Delhi, an environment which encouraged them to become proficient in musical styles or instruments outside of their previous narrow specialisms; similar patterns of sociomusical change are evident among musicians in the Carnatic tradition in Madras (L'Armand and L'Armand, 1978:140).

In colloquial terms, however, London is frequently referred to as the musical capital of the world, and there are perhaps more professional musicians here than anywhere else. They are drawn by the numerous performing opportunities the city offers: five major orchestras and many smaller ones, together with a variety of ad hoc freelance groups and semi-permanent chamber ensembles; a constant turnover of West End shows, including some which seem to have established their own permanence and which attract a large tourist clientele; a thriving although badly remunerated jazz circuit; and, until recently, considerable commercial and studio work, although this has declined quite dramatically over the last decade or so because of increased competition from elsewhere.

In one sense this is a dynamic equilibrium, a constant but changing source of work supplied by a constant but changing pool of musicians; yet it is also rather unbalanced, since the number of musicians seeking work consistently outstrips the supply. The end result is that, in general, London musicians are more badly paid than their equivalents in other Western cities (competition keeps fees low) and frequently have to work harder by comparison. There is little empirical evidence to support this view,[1] but there is a great deal of anecdotal data. Consider the following statement from a South African orchestra player working with the London Philharmonic Orchestra:

> Musicians overseas think London is the centre of the universe, they all want to play here, and when they come they find people just killing themselves to play.[2]

This intense competition for work, while no doubt partially responsible for the continuing high musical standards in London, inevitably breeds a great deal of insecurity. The idea that 'you're only as good as your last gig' is an ever-present if seldom articulated worry. This insecurity is heightened by the fact that the majority of musicians are freelance, with little guarantee of future employment. A very brief description of the contractual situation in some of the different performing situations freelance musicians might encounter will illustrate this point.

In the classical world only those musicians working in the BBC orchestras can be considered employees proper, with permanent contracts. Players in the other major orchestras are technically freelance, although once appointed as members of the orchestra they are generally guaranteed first refusal of all work, subject to certain conditions. However the fragile economic positions of all these orchestras, the intense competition between them and their collective uncertainty about what the future holds still encourages a considerable sense of insecurity among the musicians involved. In smaller ensembles and ad hoc groups there is a general understanding that the fixer, the person responsible for booking the musicians, will usually call upon the same performers from one event to the next. But it remains a precarious situation, and if a musician is unavailable for certain events or falls out with the fixer, leader or conductor, then he or she risks being quietly passed over for future engagements, usurped by those more willing or able to give the commitment asked for.

Away from this classical world there is again very little security in other musical positions. Musicians booked for West End shows do have a contract of employment but this is only for the run of a particular show, akin to a musical lottery whereby the musician's employment is subject entirely to the often fickle demands of the marketplace; while some shows might achieve a degree of permanence, others close within days. For some musicians it is their dearest wish to land a long-running show, and while they may well laugh at the show-musician/jazz-musician joke related above they might think twice before telling it to the fixer for *The Phantom of the Opera*. For commercial sessions and studio work there are often signed agreements and contracts, generally regulated by the Musicians' Union, but these cover only the details of one particular session or group of sessions, giving some protection to any further exploitation of the musician's work but no guarantee of continuing or future employment. And the jazz world operates very largely on word of mouth, except for cruises or occasional residencies elsewhere, which again would generally be measured in weeks rather than months.

Although I have outlined only four particular areas of professional music-making in London, and not in any detail, it should be clear that, in terms of work guarantees and long-term employment, most professional musicians' lives are riddled with insecurity.

Deputizing

One direct result of this insecurity is that most freelance musicians, in order both to maximize their work opportunities and to retain the widest possible field of contacts, quite literally take on more work than they can do. All musicians eventually find themselves in a situation where, having accepted a particular engagement, they are subsequently offered different work covering the same period, and which, for reasons I shall come to, they would rather undertake. In order to manage this situation, musicians might adopt a number of strategies, which include the acceptance of both dates followed by a later withdrawal from one or the other; the provisional acceptance of both dates on the understanding that later withdrawal might follow; or perhaps the immediate rejection of the second date with a conversation along the lines of 'I'd really like to have done it but I'm already working that night. Thanks for asking and do call again.'

In situations where more than one date has been accepted, that is where a musician is committed to being in two places at once, the solution is to engage another musician as a deputy, commonly referred to as a 'dep', who is sent to play in the prior engagement, thereby releasing the first musician to undertake their preferred work. This process is properly known as deputizing, but more commonly described as 'depping' or 'sending a dep', and is long established, as Ehrlich's description of musicians' lives in the 1760s reveals:

> The need to piece together an income from diverse sources imposed a sense of vulnerability which tended to encourage mercenary behaviour, and the increasing influence of market forces required attitudes and skills more common among tradesmen than artists. If fees were tempting one might relax musical standards, take on more work than could adequately be performed, or send deputies to less remunerative functions. (Ehrlich, 1985:31)

Some two and a half centuries later deputising remains a necessary strategy for musicians in a highly competitive environment.

The other thing about freelancing is that it's one big juggling act. You've got to keep ten balls up in the air at the same time, you've got to keep lots of different people happy. Because if you are saying no to the same people all the time then they'll stop asking you. So you've got to occasionally say yes. If I was a freelancer who kept on saying 'I'm sorry' at the last minute, 'I can't do it', then eventually they would just stop ringing me. It's just a question of being intelligent and juggling things, and trying to keep all these balls up in the air.

For many of these musicians such ball-juggling is so familiar that it no doubt appears as a simple matter of logistics and expediency; however it is an operation permeated by questions of individual identity and both economic and musical value judgments, as the following explanation of the process will show.

There are two stages to the operation. First, and most obviously, the musician must decide whether or not to accept the second engagement offered. This is not always straightforward and cannot necessarily be resolved as a simple evaluation of financial gain. Second, the musician must find a suitable deputy for the job from which he or she is trying to extricate him or herself. Most musicians, by the very nature of the music business, know a considerable number of other musicians of similar type: 'it's not what you know, it's who you know'. The more musicians you know, the more potential deps are available to you and, crucially, the more people who know you, the more chance you have of receiving work opportunities from them. Thus any individual musician can be seen as one part of a web of sociomusical connections, often constructed over many years through school and conservatoire environments, playing with others, hearing others play, hearing *of* others play, personal recommendations, non-playing social events, and so on. This results in a list of players whom the individual is willing to consider as a suitable deputy for a particular engagement; I know a number of musicians who keep such a list at the back of their diaries for just this purpose. For others the list is more of a mental construct:

I have a sort of a mental list. It's not a written list and it's not a fixed list because if the date is different in some way, like it's contemporary or it's badly paid or it's well paid or it's orchestral or whatever, the list will change according to those categories. The same sort of order will appear, it'll still be roughly the same list that I'll hold, just a couple of people may swap places for different reasons.

Moreover, as is clear from the above quotation, each name on this list connotes an image of that person's musical and social abilities. For example, Jack is a great classical player but he doesn't swing very well, so he's inappropriate for jazzy shows; Sarah is a good straight player, and a good swinger, but her improvising is awful; Mark is a great improviser but his sight reading is very weak; Julie is an excellent classical player, but I know she hates the section principal in this particular orchestra; John would cover this show for me really well, but I know he's very established, and he'll want a lot of money to go to Manchester for one night; and so on.

Definitely in your own mind you know what you're happier on, and what you're not happier on. I think with other colleagues you draw on, you understand what they're happier on, and you build up a catalogue of what they prefer to do and what they couldn't do. From experience you best know what your colleagues can do.

To illustrate this process more clearly, as well as the various pitfalls that may be contained within it, I shall outline four incidents involving the use of deputies. Although I have presented these as hypothetical examples they are based on episodes in which I have been directly involved, or have involved musicians whom I know well; and I have discussed the issues arising from them at length with a number of other musicians, both in formal interviews and during the course of my performing activities. The whole process of deputizing is a constant source of discussion among musicians, and such discussions are, of course, one of the ways by which musicians construct their images of one another. I have no doubt that similar or analogous situations to those I describe are widely replicated on a daily basis, albeit for different musicians in a variety of contexts.

- Musician A has a temporary contract in the pit orchestra of a well-known musical, undertaking a long national tour, during which he is offered a few nights' work with a progressive modern dance company. After several months on the road he is bored with playing the same music every night and would appreciate the challenge of playing more difficult music. Although the dance company pays more than the show, he has to cover the dep's travel costs, and he is also bound by the convention of paying show deps extra money for out-of-town shows, to compensate for the frequently disproportionate travelling involved relative to the amount earned; so there will be little financial gain on his part. The show is at present in Newcastle, so, attempting to economize, he books a less familiar player from Manchester rather than using a musician he knows well from London. He sends the dep to do the show and works with the dance company, resulting in considerable extra travel and no financial reward, but he enjoys working with different musicians and likes the new music he has learned. He is subsequently offered further dates with the same company. On returning to the show he finds that his dep did not play to the satisfaction of the Musical Director and he is instructed not to use him again, but only to use musicians that the MD is familiar with from London. Therefore he will lose even more money in fulfilling the additional dance company engagements he has been offered.

- Musician B is working in a top West End musical. She has the relative security of knowing that the show is fully booked for the next six months, she is well paid, particularly in comparison to a touring show, and she is living at home. She is offered a date with a provincial orchestra playing a big nineteenth-century symphony. This involves several overnight stays and, being not as well paid as the London show, means she will lose money. Her normal dep on the show is not free for those days, so she must get another musician trained for her part and pay them to sit beside her for one or two shows to learn the music, meaning she will make even more of a loss. However, she takes the orchestra job because she really wants to be an orchestral player and needs to have this kind of experience on her CV for future auditions. While she is with the orchestra she plays well and is invited to undertake a trial for a position soon to become vacant. When she returns to the show she finds that her dep also played well, and she books the same dep to cover some of the time off she will need to do the orchestral trial.

- Musician C has agreed to a date with a quartet with whom he works regularly, performing difficult contemporary music which requires considerable rehearsal. The day before the concert he is offered some extremely lucrative sessions from a fixer for whom he occasionally works. He knows that the group, of which he is a regular member and who are also his close friends, cannot possibly find somebody else to learn such complicated music in the time available; he also shares with them an ideological commitment to the music the group is trying to promote. Regretfully, he turns the sessions down, resulting in a substantial loss of income.

- Musician D plays regularly with a small chamber orchestra, albeit on a freelance basis. She is offered some reasonably well-paid studio work at a time when she is already committed to a particularly prestigious Royal Festival Hall date with the orchestra. She agrees to do the studio work because this is through a fixer well known for his good contacts and for whom she has not previously worked. She books a dep who has played in the orchestra many times, but leaves it as late as possible before telling the fixer, presenting him with a *fait accompli* and making it appear that the other work has been offered to her at very short notice; this is because she has turned down the last two dates with this orchestra. Naturally, she is concerned about her future relations with the orchestra, particularly when she subsequently learns there is a short foreign tour for which she has not been booked. Two months later the session fixer rings again to offer her some more work.

In these examples we can see some of the factors that an individual musician must consider before deciding whether to substitute one musical engagement for another. For musician A the problems of finance and logistics (booking a deputy from London or Manchester) must be weighed against his desire to perform different and more challenging music; musician B also has slight logistical and financial problems, but her desire to become a full-time orchestral player is a stronger consideration; musician C would probably prefer to do the more lucrative commercial work, but he is bound by his musical and social obligations to the quartet; and musician D is most clearly the one who risks sacrificing an established contact for the uncharted waters of a potentially more lucrative one.

Sometimes I have been in a situation where if I was just doing tutti somewhere I've been so desperate I would just go to a diary service and say, 'For God's sake find me somebody. I've got to get out of this date.' It's going to cost me X amount of money. A lot of it again comes down to money. You might have quite a nice date when suddenly you're offered three days of film sessions, which you know are going to be mind-blowingly boring, but you're going to come away with quite a lot of money.

It is perhaps worth making clear that in most circumstances a musician will pay his or her deputy directly, rather than expecting the organization involved to take on this responsibility, although the latter does occur, particularly with larger orchestras and theatre companies. As with most other areas of social interaction, the exchange of money can lead to friction if the deputy feels that he or she has been underpaid in some way or, equally irritating, if payment is rather slow in forthcoming. Conversely, some musicians will make a point of paying their deputies even before they themselves have received payment for the original job, an attitude which, although laudable, can cause cash-flow difficulties.

Although freelance musicians are frequently called upon to resolve the kinds of conflicts I have outlined, it would be wrong to suggest that the deputizing process is always invoked when a musician wishes to withdraw from a work commitment. In certain situations, particularly with the major orchestras or significant commercial work, it is possible that a musician would simply phone the fixer or orchestral manager and request to be allowed off the date, leaving the fixer to book another player. Even in these cases, however, a musician will frequently provisionally arrange a deputy who they think the fixer/orchestral manager will accept, a sociomusical damage limitation exercise which attempts to lubricate the process of extricating the musician from their commitment while still maintaining sufficiently cordial relations for him or her to be considered for future work.

When you book a dep what you want is not somebody who's going to be brilliant, that's neither here nor there. What you want is somebody who's going to be competent, and almost invisible. If they're too brilliant then you don't get the job next time! The worst thing that can happen is for a fixer to say, that dep you sent in wasn't much cop. That's very bad news because you feel that you're under attack. So what you want is somebody who's going to go in, be no trouble, get on with everyone, get on with the job, and get out again.

Economic capital, musical capital, and self-conception

Clearly deputizing is essentially a two-stage process: first, deciding whether to substitute one musical engagement for another, by considering factors such as those I have outlined above; and second, if accepting an alternative engagement, assessing the musical and personal attributes of potential deputies who might be asked to undertake the first date. Although the system may seem superficially quite straightforward, and is used on a daily basis by musicians as a perfectly natural consequence of their professional situation, it is underpinned by a number of significant concepts which lend themselves to ethnomusicological examination. In particular, ideas relating to the accumulation of particular types of capital seem useful in considering the first stage of the process, while anthropological theories of reciprocity and gift relationships offer some insights into the second stage.

In invoking the concept of capital, one is inevitably drawn to the work of Pierre Bourdieu, where similar approaches play a substantial role. Bourdieu argues that culture can be examined in terms of a number of interrelated forms of power, the most obvious being derived directly from economic power: economic capital. But he also suggests that power can be achieved through the acquisition of other types of capital which may, under certain circumstances, be convertible into economic capital. He suggests that cultural capital, for example, is a measure of 'legitimate' knowledge of one kind or another, acquired through 'early, imperceptible learning, performed within the family from the earliest days of life and extended by a scholastic learning which presupposes and completes it' (Bourdieu, 1984:66); social capital indicates degrees of relationship with significant others; symbolic capital represents 'prestige, reputation, fame, etc.' (Bourdieu, 1991:230). I wish to suggest that the engagements which musicians trade between themselves through the deputy system I have outlined above can be analysed, not only in terms of the economic capital they imply, but also through the consideration of another quality, which I shall describe as musical capital.

Musical capital can be seen as a measure of the desirability, from the musician's point of view, of their participation in the event, as well as its value to them as they seek to establish a reputation and profile for undertaking particular types of work within their professional world. In this sense it has something in common with Bourdieu's notion of symbolic capital, in that it connotes differing levels of honour and prestige as being represented by different performance events; and it resonates with his ideas on cultural capital, in that the latter similarly and necessarily distinguishes between 'legitimate' and popular culture. It is also allied to Bourdieu's notion of 'taste', whereby consumers express preferences for cultural goods on the basis of social class and the educational opportunities afforded to them.[3] Yet none of Bourdieu's concepts comfortably encompasses the full complexities of the deputy system as I see them, and my notion of musical capital is distinguished from his various types in several important ways.

First, I see musical capital as something which can be accrued throughout a musician's career, and not as something that is completed once their education and training are finished. Unlike Bourdieu's cultural capital, it is not an experiential springboard which launches us on a trajectory in later life over which we have limited control, but an abstract formulation which allows musicians to conceive the significance to them of performing in a given event. In many cases their participation in notable events will be worked into their biographies or CVs, in an attempt to assert their professional profile and rank, or for the purpose of convincing others (fixers, orchestral managers, record companies) that they are capable of a particular job, or at least worthy of consideration. Such reifications of this otherwise abstract concept are important components of both self-conception and individual identity.

Second, I would argue that musicians are conscious of the different amounts of musical capital represented by these events, and are thus able *deliberately* to process them for their own ends. The musical capital they seek to accrue, and the conception of self which underlies the choices they make, is not primarily dependent on social class or educational background, although it may have some relationship with personality (see Kemp, 1996). It is only through such self conscious deliberation that we can see something of their self-conception and individual identity within the larger social group. This notion of agency, of the individual making conscious decisions about how to process various cultural goods or symbols, sits uncomfortably within Bourdieu's general theory. He does of course lay great emphasis on practice, wherein actors develop a practical logic of how to pursue their lives which they then use strategically to achieve particular ends. But for Bourdieu such practice seems not to be reflexively employed, but is presented rather as a consequence of the individual's familiarity with his or her social space; this is a 'practical mastery ... acquired by experience ... which works outside conscious control and discourse' (Bourdieu, 1990b:61), and the dispositions of actors 'are relatively autonomous with respect to their position' (Bourdieu, 1993:182). It is here that he and I take rather different views, and I am inclined to agree with Richard Jenkins's observation that 'actors must know more about their situation, and that knowledge must be more valid, than Bourdieu proposes' (Jenkins, 1992:97).[4]

Furthermore, because musicians in this context are not simply consumers, the economic capital inherent within each engagement necessarily confuses the issue. Bourdieu writes that 'art and cultural consumption are predisposed ... to fulfil a social function of legitimating social differences' (Bourdieu, 1984:7); in other words, we betray our social origins through the cultural goods we consume. But for musicians, the necessity of earning a living does not allow a completely free choice of engagements, nor the 'luxury' of one predicated solely on social class or personal taste. As I hope I have shown, musicians may choose to undertake an engagement they do not particularly wish to fulfil simply because of the financial rewards it offers. Their need to earn a living through their reproduction of culture does not allow them a choice in the way that Bourdieu's theory of cultural consumption suggests.

However, although my perspective may differ from that of Bourdieu, I nevertheless believe this to be a useful concept in the present context, and my argument here would be that London's musicians are, on a daily basis, actively engaged in juxtaposing varying amounts of both economic and musical capitals, according to their particular view of themselves as musicians; and furthermore, that this self-conception can be defined and objectified according to the balance they achieve, or attempt to achieve, between these different forms of capital, manifested through their manipulation of different performance events.

Figure 1 demonstrates how a relationship may be posited between these two forms of capital, and how the various work opportunities for London's musicians may be mapped against them.

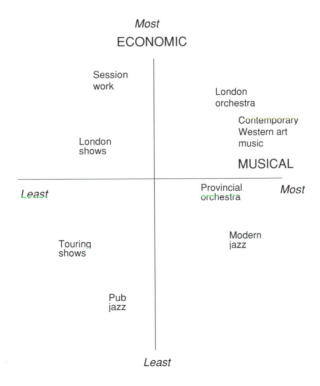

Figure 1: Economic and musical capitals

The vertical axis represents economic capital, the valorization of certain specific performance events, with the most lucrative engagements at the top and the least lucrative at the bottom. The horizontal axis shows the degree of musical capital associated with a particular event, expressed from the performer's perspective as the desirability of taking part, from the least on the left to the most on the right.

While economic capital can be assessed empirically, that is we can compare how much a musician is paid for one type of performance event as opposed to another, musical capital, in this case and elsewhere, is not only more subjective but also rather more nebulous. The desirability of certain types of work changes from one musician to another for many complex reasons: career aspirations, musical tastes, sociomusical connections and so on, and it is this which allows us to see how musicians conceive their sense of themselves as authorial individuals. Because I constructed this particular map it is very much a subjective expression of my own self-conception as a musician working in London. Others would certainly map different performance events in different places, more clearly reflecting their own perceptions of themselves. For example, because I am afflicted by an abiding interest in contemporary Western art music this is placed towards the extreme right of the musical axis; but I realize that my fellow musicians do not all see it in this light and many would place it much further to the left. Equally, others who aspire to a long-running West End show might well not regard this particular type of employment with the same mixed feelings as I do. So there is a necessary and in-built degree of flexibility within this map which not only allows for changing perceptions of musical employment but also for changes in the levels of remuneration of certain events. For example, although playing with a London orchestra remains a relatively prestigious occupation to which many classically trained musicians aspire, the competition between these orchestras for ever-decreasing funds has meant a corresponding reduction in the fees for individual concerts, so such events would be positioned at a lower point on the vertical axis than might previously have been the case. And of course the value ascribed to the event by the musician may also be influenced by who is conducting, or who they might be working with, or what the particular repertoire might be, and so on. Saxophonists, for example, are frequently called upon by orchestras for a small number of popular and therefore frequently performed pieces: Ravel's *Bolero* or Gershwin's *Rhapsody in Blue* spring readily to mind. The attraction to these musicians of once again having to perform these pieces may diminish over time, notwithstanding that such performances may take place with orchestras of international repute. Naturally this would influence their decisions on whether to undertake a particular engagement or not.

Seen in this way, the different musical engagements which individual musicians undertake in the course of their work become symbols of their involvement in this particular community. Each type of performance event, while superficially the same for each musician, is in fact both a flexible, abstract concept and an obvious economic reality, which musicians imbue with different meanings according to context, and which they process, as Cohen suggests, 'if not as wholly free agents then, at the very least, as interpreters' (1994:94).

Furthermore, while I am necessarily concentrating here on the professional musicians who are central to this study, I suggest that all those who are in some way paid for the provision of musical services, that is paid for playing, must also somehow resolve this conflict between musical and economic capitals, between art and mammon: the semi-professional violinist whose day job perhaps gives her financial security still has to make decisions about whether to accept a particular engagement or not, decisions that must assess both the remuneration on offer and her own desire to be involved with a particular event; the church organist no doubt regards the prospect of playing a Handel organ concerto with the local amateur orchestra, however badly paid, as being a pleasant change from yet another performance of Mendelssohn's wedding march. Harry Christianson's work among semi-professional jazz musicians in the north of England also seems to confirm this:

> Some [semi-pro jazz musicians] can earn bigger money playing with bands which play for ballroom dancing on Saturday evenings, but are only too glad to get the chance to play something more to their taste and with more freedom of expression even for very little money ... a bass player who gets regular well-paid work with a well-established folk group in the Black Country expressed his eagerness to be invited to play jazz at much lower pay: 'We play the same fifteen to twenty numbers over and over again that we have been playing for years. When we do a new number we rehearse it for weeks before we do it on a gig. It gets really boring. But when I play jazz we never play the same programme two gigs running. Even numbers we've done before we play differently each time.' (Christianson, 1987:224)

Individual identity and reciprocal obligation

I have deliberately used the term 'self-conception' to emphasize the subjective nature of this first stage of the deputizing process, and to contrast it with the concept of 'individual identity', which requires an essentially social view of the individual. But it is the question of individual identities, the way in which we see others and they see us, which provides the foundation for the second stage: choosing and booking a suitable deputy. This requires a musician to make a number of musical and social judgments about fellow musicians, and it is through such judgments that, in part, the identity of an individual is constructed within the larger social group. Such judgments rely on images of the abilities of others which may be built up over many years, in various ways and in many different contexts. I have overheard (and taken part in) hundreds of conversations in which somebody's abilities have been commented upon, either in praise or denigration, all of which feed back into the mental images I have of particular players' abilities and which sit alongside my own impression of their skills, if I know them personally. It is unusual, albeit not entirely unheard of, for musicians to book somebody they do not know, or who has not been recommended by someone whose judgment they trust.

I would always think about what it is that I'm doing, and whether that person would fit into that job. No, I wouldn't book just any old person to do any old job, unless I was absolutely desperate [laughs] *which I have done before now.*

Furthermore, the act of offering different types of work, each perceived as having varying amounts of economic and musical capital, is itself invested with all sorts of subtle messages. For example, if a musician has some relatively well-paid commercial work in his diary but is offered an even more lucrative date, he is in a strong position to offer the first work to other musicians that he perceives as being of high social rank; that is, those who are recognized as senior names in the business, either because of their playing ability or for reasons to do with the type of work they most commonly undertake. In offering work which is already well remunerated a musician obviously implies that he or she is able to give this work away because they are doing something that is even better paid. This in turn contributes to the image that the receiver has of the giver and, if such interactions take place often, will perhaps elevate the giver into a new social rank among his or her peers. Conversely a musician may be ill-advised to offer work to those for whom it is inappropriate, since this may prove counterproductive. It would be unwise to offer, say, one night playing second clarinet in a touring show to a musician whose regular work is with a top orchestra or who is a busy session player. They may feel slightly offended by the offer of what they would perceive as a relatively unprestigious engagement; and this in turn, if done in the wrong way, might result in a more negative image of the person offering the work.

Because the act of appointing a deputy is endowed with both musical and social significance it can be a source of tension between musicians if it does not go smoothly, and there are a number of ways in which it can go wrong. A few examples will illustrate this. In the first instance, an orchestral player was asked to advise on which musicians might be brought into the orchestra for a piece which required an unusual combination of particular instruments. Having been asked to recommend players, she passed over a number of people close to her, and with whom she had played for some time in a chamber ensemble, asking only one player from the group and not the others. The reasons she later cited ('A' is not really a classical player, 'B' isn't very reliable, and so on) are typical of the kinds of assessments musicians make of each other, although here I have stated them very baldly; the particular reasons behind a decision are often rather more complex. In this instance the musicians who had been passed over, but who considered themselves suitable for the job, learned of what had happened, which created considerable social tension and led in part to a schism within the chamber ensemble; there was clearly a significant disjunction in this case between the self-conception of the players passed over and their identities more widely perceived, leading to a Turneresque social drama requiring some kind of resolution. In another instance, a musician (I will call him 'Phil') booked a close friend and colleague ('John') as a deputy for a group with whom he (Phil) had played for several years, and which was a significant engagement for him in terms of its musical capital. A conflict arose when, after the original engagement, the fixer for the group then asked John to take on some additional (and unrelated) work with the group, which Phil would normally have expected to do. John was caught between his desire to undertake the work (for reasons of both economics and prestige) and his loyalty to Phil, with whom he had exchanged work on many occasions over the years and who he knew would be upset if he chose to undertake these additional concerts. John did undertake the work, Phil was indeed upset, vowing (in the heat of the moment) never to use John as a deputy again, and significant tension was generated between the two which took several months to resolve.

One final illustration of the difficulties that can arise in this process is known colloquially among musicians as 'being given the DCM'. 'Don't Come Monday' is the euphemistic description of the deputy who has been blacklisted by a fixer, musical director, conductor or other musicians, usually for reasons of musical unsuitability but occasionally because of personal behaviour (and sometimes, musicians will tell you, for no reason at all), thus preventing the musician who booked the deputy from using him again in this particular environment. This is often a difficult situation and musicians are not slow to castigate others, particularly those in some position of authority, if they feel a colleague has been rejected for no apparent reason, or for a reason with which they do not agree.

It's something you find very hard to say to your dep, presumably you've put in a friend, and you know that the next time you want to get work off with that particular fixer it's just going to be that little bit harder.

Such difficulties can again strain the relationships between musicians, even in those situations where a deputy realizes that the musician who booked him or her is not directly to blame.

Another issue which arises within the deputy system is that of reciprocal obligation. Offering work to another musician, particularly if done regularly to the same person, engenders some feeling of obligation, that is, that this favour should be returned. Musicians do have a sense of community and if one member of the community is seen to be helping you regularly then you feel obliged to give some help back if possible. One musician, who had recently been given a contract for a musical having previously depped frequently on another show, said that she felt very guilty because she had had few alternative engagements since her new show began, and therefore no opportunity to offer some deputy work to the person who had previously offered her so much. This sense of guilt was further compounded by the fact that the first show had now closed and the musician to whom she felt this obligation had no regular work.

Some people look at it as if I'm doing them a favour by giving them work, and they feel it has to be returned – if you give something then you're looking for something back. I mean I've been in a situation doing 'Oliver', for Julie, she asked me to come in on clarinet. Fine, I did it, and I was very happy to do it. But there's nothing that I do that I could give her back. Now I know she will never call me for anything again.

Ideally, the fulfilment of this obligation – the payment of the debt, so to speak – should be in kind. A prestigious orchestral engagement or lucrative session would, in an ideal world, be repaid by an offer of work of similar magnitude; and, likewise, an obligation incurred through the exchange of a less important date may be discharged with a similar offer of work. Naturally musicians do not live in such an ideal world; the exchange of work seldom proceeds in this equalitative fashion and there are numerous 'debts' which remain unpaid or are repaid with unequal offers of work. However, this principle of reciprocal obligation, of helping those who help you, although largely unspoken, remains a significant issue in the trading of musical engagements between musicians.

This web of reciprocal obligations which the deputy system engenders might be conceived of as a series of gift relationships. Mauss's pioneering study *The Gift* (1990; first published 1950) established gift exchange as an important component of economic anthropology, and the relationships produced through the exchange of musical performance events can be further illuminated by some consideration of subsequent work in this field. In particular, Sahlins, building on Mauss's work, has proposed a 'spectrum of reciprocities' (1974:193) defined by its extremes and a mid-point; these three positions he describes as generalized, balanced and negative forms of reciprocity. Generalized reciprocity characterizes transactions which are 'putatively altruistic' (ibid.), and which take place between those who are close, or related, or part of a restricted social group. There is only a weak obligation to reciprocate because the mutual dependence of the close-knit group provides a context in which 'the expectation of a direct material return is unseemly. At best it is implicit' (194). Negative reciprocity is the opposite end of the spectrum, and describes 'the attempt to get something for nothing with impunity' (195). This is the most impersonal form of exchange, in which individuals confront each other as opposed interests, each seeking to maximize their own gain at the other's expense. Balanced reciprocity occupies the mid-point between these two. Although the exchange is less 'personal' than generalized reciprocity, each party recognizes the other's distinct economic and social interests, with the material part of the transaction being at least as important as the social. In this last case, Sahlins suggests, the key indicator is the system's inability to tolerate one-way flows, since 'the relations between people are disrupted by a failure to reciprocate within limited time and equivalence leeways' (195).

It is this latter position which most closely describes the social interaction generated by the exchange of work opportunities among musicians, and the social relationships which are established or reinforced through such exchanges. As I have shown, musicians do have some sense of honour-bound reciprocal obligation, an expectation that a debt which has been established must, ideally, be repaid in some way. For the system to remain balanced the obligations implied by the offer of work from one musician to another must somehow be discharged and, as Sahlins so perceptively puts it, 'within limited time and equivalence leeways'. Such timescales would not be verbalized by musicians, although they would be measured in weeks or months rather than years. And the complexity of the urban musical situation often means that obligations may be discharged in unequal measure: musicians cannot freely determine what work is offered to them and this inevitably influences what they can themselves pass on. Indeed, as Sahlins himself notes, not all exchanges will necessarily fall directly into one of his three categories, but may lie elsewhere in the spectrum (196), suggesting sufficient flexibility in his model to allow for inequalitative transactions.

It is also possible to conceive of the relationships engendered through such exchanges as further evidence of a sense of community prevailing among London's musicians. Sahlins argues that his spectrum of reciprocities is often related to kinship distance; generalized reciprocity is more characteristic of close kinship, whereas negative reciprocity becomes increasingly common as kinship distance extends (196). He writes, 'it is not only that kinship organizes communities, but communities kinship, so that a spatial, coresidential term affects the measure of kinship distance and thus the mode of exchange' (197). As I have observed in Chapter One, the sense of community felt by London musicians is to some degree a mental construct, and subject to different inflections. Clearly it is not always characterized by obvious kinship relations, although close relationships may of course arise, especially among those working together frequently; yet neither do musicians confront each other 'entirely as opposed interests'. However, the balanced reciprocity they attempt to achieve through the mutual exchange of performance opportunities does imply some sense of loosely constructed community, one which is in part derived from the social relations both facilitated and underpinned by the 'gift of the gig'.

Music as capital and music as coin

I have suggested that performance events can be seen as symbols which musicians manipulate in various ways and through which they refract their sense of inclusion within this particular community. I would also argue that, at the second stage of the deputizing process, these exchanges of musical work might equally be read as the currency by which capital is acquired. Musical engagements can be considered as large, medium or small denomination, in terms of both the economic and/or musical capital with which they are endowed, and may be traded between musicians in a way that is analogous to monetary exchange: a large debt implies a large repayment, or a series of smaller payments, and so on. The system is not flawless and there are many variables within it. I have illustrated the deputizing process from my own perspective as a freelance wind player, and the nature of freelance work is perhaps a little different for wind and brass players than for string players, and certainly than for pianists, harpists, accordionists and so on. There is perhaps more variety of work open to brass/wind players than some of these other instrumentalists, who may find themselves less frequent visitors to West End musicals or Sunday lunchtime jazz gigs in the local pub. But I suggest that, even among these slightly different musical crafts, similar or analogous processes to those I have described also exist. A string player remarked to me:

I think the great thing about being a freelance player is the variety. One day you can be doing the quartet, the next day you can be doing a film session, the next day you can be doing Mozart players, the day after that I can be doing Ferneyhough with Music Projects, whatever. I mean that is the nice thing.

Thus the need to juggle different performance opportunities, and the inherent juxtaposition of economic and musical forms of capital this implies, would seem to be a feature of urban music-making generally, regardless of instrumental specialism.

The idea that musical performance events can be viewed as a form of currency is clearly resonant with Nettl's description of three types of 'coin' in *Heartland Excursions* (1995:53–5). Here Nettl discusses the exchange of what he calls standard coin (that is, real money), academic coin and musical coin between the three dominant factions in American schools of music: teachers, administrators and students. Standard coin is obviously a measure of the monies that are paid to or paid by the members of these three groups; academic coin is measured by, for example, academic titles (university professor, university scholar) or grades awarded to the students; musical coin is less clearly defined but, Nettl argues, arises from a conflict between, on the one hand, the musicians' desire to be paid for what they do, and on the other, the feeling that they should somehow be 'above the material world, and that the opportunity of making music, that gift from the supernatural, is somehow its own reward' (55). In other words, in the competitive world of the music school, being given the opportunity to perform is itself a kind of remuneration. In Nettl's analysis the highest form of musical coin, because of the dual role of the music school as a teaching institution and entertainment provider, is to be appointed to positions of leadership in musical organization; that is, to be made a conductor of ensembles.

While Nettl's analysis is necessarily different from mine, given that we are covering two rather different environments, there is an obvious similarity in our terminologies. Some of his assertions appear less appropriate in the context of my own work, particularly his statement that 'musical coin [is] translatable into academic and standard coin' (54). I can see that in an academic institution this may be the case: a good finals performance will lead to a good exam grade, or a more significant conducting position may lead to a pay rise. But in the wider world the relationship between these various issues is far more tenuous; as I hope my analysis has shown, musicians may choose to divest themselves of potential economic reward if they feel that the musical rewards compensate for this. Yet there are certain circumstances in which the acquisition of musical capital can lead, ultimately and perhaps by chance, to economic wealth. As an obvious example, those musicians performing the music of Michael Nyman or John Tavener 15 years ago would have found themselves very much on the musical and commercial periphery, and probably working for relatively little money. Tastes change, however, and this music is now commercially very successful. But this is not the same as suggesting that these various forms of capital can be exchanged at will. I might also argue that Nettl's tripartite division can ultimately be reduced to a bipartite one, since both musical and academic authority can be considered as different parameters of cultural legitimacy.

However, my analysis shares with Nettl a belief that the practice of music-making in Western society (and probably elsewhere) requires professional musicians somehow to resolve the conflict between, on the one hand, what they conceive as their art, and on the other, the financial vicissitudes of an insecure profession. In Nettl's paradigmatic Heartland School of Music the faculty, the administrators and the students trade different forms of coin to achieve certain clearly definable ends. For the musicians I have described these ends are less easily determined. The general accumulation of wealth or the desire for wider recognition are less tangible aims than the acquisition of a university degree or professorship. Having less concrete targets, the strategies these musicians adopt result, at least in part, from the antagonistic relationship between music as a cultural symbol and music as an economic process; and the manner in which they resolve this conflict creates and sustains both their self-conception and their individual identity in the wider social world.

Notes

1   Although one obvious indication of this is the much higher levels of state support given to orchestras in other European cities, and the reduced working hours of their members.
2   Cited in Tait (1996:15).
3   See Bourdieu (1984) for an extensive exegesis of this idea.
4   For a more extensive critique of Bourdieu's ideas on agency, see Bohman (1999).

CHAPTER FOUR

Musicianship, Small Ensembles, and the Social Self

Introduction

In this chapter I shall consider how the individual selves musicians are encouraged to develop are integrated within the context of musical ensembles, and I shall examine some of the inevitable tensions inherent within such collaborations. I shall also explore how smaller groups conceive and underpin identities for themselves, and the implications this has for the members of these groups.

In Chapter Two I outlined Kingsbury's argument that musicality should be seen more as a property of cultural ideology than as a specific characteristic of any given individual; in these terms it is essentially a social product, a component of individual identity which is socially ascribed through the judgment of others on the nature of individual musical performance, notwithstanding that, as a folk notion, it is often used in quite a different way and is intended as a description of characteristic qualities of a particular individual. Yet there are undoubtedly personal musical qualities and skills (intonation perception, finger technique and so on) which differ from one individual to another. Such qualities are also in some ways measurable, certainly noticeable, and all of them can be learned and improved with practice; although there will always be particular individuals who seem to remain especially adept in certain areas, for complex enculturative and/or neurobiological reasons.

I propose to subsume all these attributes, and others I have not mentioned, under the term 'musicianship', the craft of being a musician; that collection of individual skills which are beyond social ascription and not dependent upon social agreement for their validation, notwithstanding that the possession of them and the manner in which they are employed may indeed provoke significant amounts of social commentary. But I also intend to take this definition a stage further by including within it, and indeed concentrating upon, those social skills (by which I mean patterns of interaction between individuals in a social context) which are indispensable in the pursuit of a professional musical career, and which I at least see as being inextricably entwined with notions of collaborative musical production. Social skills are not themselves necessary for the act of playing a musical instrument, but they have a significant impact upon almost every context in which that act occurs.

Musicianship

The levels of technical and musical expertise expected of specialist musicians in the West, and the frequently stressful and demanding environments within which such expertise must be demonstrated, necessarily mean that the acquisition of those performance skills which are fundamental to a musician's craft occurs over an extensive timescale. Thus for the majority of musicians their musical training begins at a very early age, and is usually predicated from the outset on the development of individual motor skills through technical exercises (scales, studies and so on). Although such development is both significant and important, the means by which such skills are acquired and the relationship of this development to sociocultural backgrounds (to give just two possible areas of enquiry) are issues which lie outside the limits of this study.[1]

But it would clearly be inappropriate to suggest that, once a musician finishes their formal training, this is the end of either their musical development or their skill acquisition. Like all craftsmen, musicians continually seek to expand their skills and abilities: both musically, in the sense of increasing their competence in musical interpretation and thus enhancing their chances of employment, and technically, in developing their individual instrumental skills or acquiring similar expertise on related instruments. 'On-the-job' training is also inevitable. Musicians leaving college cannot prepare themselves for every musical eventuality, however hard they might try, and will sooner or later be presented with a technical or musical demand for which they are unprepared. Although in many cases a musician will just go and work at it until the problem is solved, the generally fraternal relations which exist among musicians, and the social network which is inherent within the professional musical world, mean that there is usually somebody that a musician can turn to for help, if necessary. Such help will normally be given ungrudgingly, since musicians (like most people, perhaps) are happy to have their own knowledge or abilities implicitly confirmed or recognized by others who require help or information from them.

Yet those individual cognitive and psychomotor skills which a musician does possess are important elements of both their self-conception and their individual identity. I am conscious that, for example, one musician I know has a weaker sense of rhythm than myself, but a more finely developed sense of intonation; another has faster finger technique than many; another is well known for her remarkable sight-reading abilities; and so on. Rightly or wrongly I conceive myself as having a good aural memory for overall musical structures but I am less proficient (or at least, unpractised) at playing music from memory; and so on. These various attributes are all necessary components of the musician's craft, but this does not mean that all musicians possess them equally, and the assessment by others of the proportions in which such skills are deemed to be held by particular musicians are significant parts of the process through which they decide who to work with or who to employ as a suitable deputy.

Furthermore, within the necessarily utilitarian world of professional music-making, such assessments of individual skill levels are often just as important as assertions of musicality, and sometimes more so. The importance attached to one or the other, or the balance that must be struck between the two, is, I think, explained by the degree to which a musician's work is exposed. Music conservatoires place considerable emphasis on individual performance and achievement; thus notions of musicality, that is, judgments on the quality of musical interpretation, are pre-eminent, particularly since benchmark levels of technical ability are to some extent taken for granted. Equally, musicians in the professional world who are performing in a particularly soloistic situation (concerto appearance, solo recital) are judged more by the manner of their interpretation than by their technical skills; working at this level one would simply be expected to have a significant amount of the latter, and it is their absence rather than their presence that would generally be remarked upon. In ensemble situations, however, the balance changes. Matters of musical interpretation remain significant but they are also mitigated by the need for technical competence of a slightly different kind: to have a good sense of rhythm, to play in tune with others and be able to modify intonation quickly, to be subservient to others where necessary, perhaps reacting to or following their musical decisions, and so on. Such qualities, while desirable and normally present in solo performers, are not as essential as in collaborative ventures.

It's much harder to play first violin in a string quartet than to stand up and play a concerto. Technically much more demanding, musically much more demanding. Partly because of the variety of things that you have to do. Whereas if you're playing a concerto you're just basically playing loud, and projecting.

In other situations, for example in orchestras and especially shows, a particular type of musical craftsmanship can be the dominant requirement, and musicians who come in and try to impose undesirable levels of their own musical opinion can be a serious liability, possibly resulting in musical or social disunity. Many of these points will resurface in the following pages, but at this stage I would simply observe that the degree to which musicians are called upon to display the various characteristics which I have subsumed under the headings of musicality or musicianship changes according to context: in certain situations the distinctive musical personality I concentrated on in Chapter Two is considered pre-eminent; in others a musician may need to achieve quite the opposite: sit down, play the music, fit in with everybody else and try to be as anonymous as possible.

For successful musical collaboration individual percepts and concepts must inevitably be combined with and perhaps moderated by those of other individuals, and the negotiations through which all of these things take place require various patterns of social interaction. Therefore, to be a musician, or at least to enjoy any level of success as a professional musician, requires a fundamentally social outlook, for several reasons. Perhaps the most obvious of these is that most musical performance requires musicians to work together somehow, to coordinate the individual musical self with other self conscious individuals for the purpose of producing an ensemble performance. There can be very few if any professional musicians in the Western tradition who do not play with others at some stage. Even those instrumentalists more likely to play alone, such as pianists or guitarists, will be involved in accompanying or perhaps in a chamber group at some point in their musical career; indeed making music with others is for most musicians usually more satisfying than making it alone. Furthermore, social skills of a more general kind are needed to interact competently with other musicians in the intricate web of relationships that constitutes the community of London musicians; that is, to retain one's place in the social fabric and negotiate with others within it. As I have already shown in Chapter Three, such skills are a significant component in the acquisition and undertaking of musical work.

The biggest reason why you need social skills in the first place is to get more work, it's not to be any better or worse a musician. You need social skills because otherwise you're not going to communicate, you're not going to get asked back, from a simple pragmatic point of view you need social skills. I don't think you need them to be a musician, just you'll be a very poor one.

Additionally, and apart from the rather self-serving necessity of interacting with others for the purposes of acquiring work, the frequently itinerant life of a professional musician can be one of enforced gregariousness, with musicians often thrown together for short periods, sometimes under difficult or arduous circumstances, and left to get on with each other as best they can.

Very often you're touring with these musicians, and you look down the room lists and you're told to share with whoever. You've got no idea who they are. Or a show where you're going to go into digs with all manner of people. And what I do like about music is that you have to mix with anyone. Anyone and everyone. It doesn't matter if you're posh, poor, it doesn't matter. Can you do the job? That's the bottom line.

While such transitory acquaintances inevitably make demands on the social behaviour of all parties, it is no less true that, in more permanent situations, those who have to work with a particular musician over a long period of time will need to be persuaded, not only that his or her playing is adequate, but also that they are the right person for the job. One orchestral player, who already had a job in a London orchestra, told me that he was thinking of undertaking a trial for a job in a smaller provincial orchestra, which would pay less well but give him more time off. He eventually decided against doing the trial for a number of reasons, including the fact that it would cost him too much. Not only would he lose better paid work with his own orchestra, but he was also budgeting a certain amount for drinks, meals and general socializing with the players in the other orchestra in order to establish the social relationships which would be necessary to be considered a serious contender for the job.

I am always struck by the fact that musicians who have just met will often have particular topics of conversation to hand, in order, as it were, to break the ice. Once the general niceties and personal facts (abode, marital status and so on) have been dispensed with they will often discuss other musicians who they know in common: 'Do you know so-and-so?', 'Oh yes, we played on this-or-that date together. Is he still doing such-and-such a show/orchestra?' 'Yeah, I think he's quite busy ... ', and so on. Apart from providing some necessary social lubrication such conversations also fulfil a number of important functions. Not only do they attempt to ascertain the other's position within the larger social whole, thus partially establishing an individual identity for them, but they are also a means of keeping abreast with personal and business developments within the community, potentially important information which can conceivably lead to further work opportunities: a bush telegraph *par excellence*. Moreover, musicians who have worked together in the past and who already know each other often recount, either for themselves or perhaps to a third party, anecdotes or incidents, especially if humorous, from their shared experience. This confirmation of a shared history strengthens the social bonds between individuals, reconfirms to each of them their joint membership of the larger community, and again lubricates the social interaction.

At other times, of course, the knack of keeping your mouth firmly shut is another skill worth cultivating:

I think a lot of this profession is about biting your lip and keeping stumm, not saying what you think, because if you did you wouldn't work. The number of times I've gone into an orchestra and been sitting at the back and a viola solo comes up and I just think 'Jesus Christ, what are you doing?' But if I said that out loud that's the last time I'd go in there so you just keep quiet and, you know, you go up in the interval and say 'great solo, really nice'. I mean, I probably wouldn't do that, but people do do that.

It would be wrong to suggest that the hypocrisy suggested by this last sentence is widespread among professional musicians, but it certainly exists, perhaps in greater quantities than people wish to admit. In a business where musical abilities, employment prospects and social relations are so closely intertwined, people do not always say what they mean or mean what they say.

It is also clear that the social qualities needed to engage with other musicians can change quite noticeably according to musical context, as the following string player made clear:

There are lots of social skills about being in an orchestra which you're not really trained to do, you just pick them up bit by bit. Like don't practise your concertos in the bandroom. And there's a lot of etiquette within an orchestral section. If you're on the back desk of the violins never ask the conductor what he thinks about something, ask the principal violin. There's a lot of etiquette which you're not really taught and I think it's very important. I know lots of people who have been rubbed from dates because their etiquette wasn't correct. People standing up and talking to other sections from within a section. They should always go through the principal of a section, that's why they're there.

Obviously, such behaviour would not be considered necessary and indeed would often be seen as undesirable in smaller groups and chamber ensembles, where the musical contributions of each individual are perhaps more transparent and thus the interaction between musicians more immediate and less hierarchically organized. Such fine distinctions in the appropriate pattern of behaviour for particular contexts are seldom taught, they are only learned.

Musical issues must also be negotiated within the social context in which musical performance occurs. The perception and conception of basic musical parameters such as rhythm, timbre and intonation, and of course matters of musical interpretation, about all of which musicians inevitably develop strong personal opinions, can form the basis of misunderstandings and disagreements which may require considerable social interaction to resolve.

It's no good if they're totally inflexible: 'this instrument was tuned in the factory therefore you're out of tune', is a sort of attitude that I think we've all come across, when someone thinks they're right.

Musical ability and social competence are again revealed as being closely intertwined, and the social skills necessary to resolve these sorts of conflicts are prerequisite for a successful career; inevitably those who are inflexible in this respect soon find themselves unpopular and less frequently employed. But if such issues are important in any situation where musicians must work together they are perhaps most keenly felt in those contexts where the same musicians must regularly collaborate, in permanent ensembles and orchestras where particular blends of individual musical and social characteristics are regularly melded and subsequently tested in the furnace of musical performance. It is these more regular combinations of musicians, and the tensions and bonds which arise between them, which form the focus of the rest of this chapter.

Ensembles and individuals

In a quartet you can talk about the way a particular phrase is going to be played, or whatever. There's a lot more time to put what you feel into the music.

The whole point of being in the quartet is obviously that you have a voice.

Playing in small groups seems to provide for many people the perfect balance, musically speaking, between self and society; between, on the one hand, the cultivation of an individual musical voice and, on the other, the integration of this voice with other similar voices for the purposes of musical production. As one musician remarked to me in passing: *I think making music with a small group of people who you get on well with is just the best thing*. Such sentiments would appear to be underlined by the numerous groups within the professional music world which offer these kinds of performance opportunities. The exact number of groups working at any one time is difficult to determine, and this is an area of professional music-making which is in a constant state of flux as groups are regularly established or disbanded for a variety of reasons, some of which will be outlined below. But a general indication of the popularity of these ensembles can be inferred from the *British Music Yearbook*, a trade directory for the music business in Britain. The 1999 edition has some 16 pages of such groups, numbering in the region of 900 and ranging from duos to flexible ensembles which may have up to 20 or more players. These bald statistics obscure as much as they reveal, however, since many of these groups may work extremely irregularly (perhaps less than once a year) and others may be semi-professional groups possibly giving performances for rather smaller fees than professionals would expect (or hope) to receive.

Even among the professionals, however, very few of these groups constitute a full-time commitment for the players involved: perhaps only a handful of string quartets, a combination for which there is a small but continuing market (festivals, music societies and so on). Thus only a small number of musicians are able to regard such a group as their main source of employment. All the other groups lead a rather more transitory existence, coming together for brief periods of time to rehearse and perform perhaps just one concert, before the musicians involved separate to continue their freelance lives elsewhere. Indeed some of them may meet again quite soon, under the auspices of another group vehicle, particularly in London where many different groups are constituted from the same pool of available players. In this sense such groups can be seen as nodal points within the larger social matrix; they are among the most significant places at which social and musical interaction takes place, ideas exchanged, gossip and news disseminated, work discussed, and so on. It is through the navigation of this matrix, via the internalization of specific musical values or monetary potential perceived as being attached to such groups, that musicians in part construct their self-conception, in much the same way as I demonstrated in the previous chapter for the performance events in which these groups participate.

There are two significant types of group, essentially differentiated by size, with each type constituted on slightly different grounds, and this in turn generally affects the degree of commitment from individual members towards the group itself (although, as one might expect in such a fluid situation, there are exceptions to this kind of broad categorization). In the first type, smaller units of from two (although duos are not generally considered 'groups' as such) to perhaps six or seven players combine in such a way that each member is considered integral to the group. Only in exceptional circumstances would members be allowed to use deputies, often to the annoyance of the other musicians since this may well involve them in additional rehearsals, given the intricacies of much of this type of music. Usually musicians would be paid simply for the concert, and this fee would be expected to cover rehearsal time as well; in real terms rehearsals would effectively be unpaid, and thus having to undertake more of them dilutes the overall remuneration on offer. This type of group often requires considerable commitment from the individual members (as shown in my example of Musician C in the previous chapter; see p.63) and I shall consider some of the reasons why this commitment is forthcoming below. It is this model which is numerically most prevalent, particularly quartets and quintets, and on which I shall concentrate in this section.

In the second model, larger ensembles may be put together either by individuals or by a small core of sufficiently motivated musicians sharing a common outlook, to form a group which will frequently specialize in a particular repertory (contemporary music, baroque music and so on). Given that these involve larger numbers of musicians, with the attendant problems of musical coordination this inevitably implies, such groups frequently require a conductor; indeed many of them come about at the instigation of and to provide a vehicle for a particular conductor, who seeks to gain conducting experience and demonstrate his or her particular skills to the wider world. Once these credentials have been established, and particularly if the conductor achieves success elsewhere, the group vehicle may fall into disuse, or at least less regular use. Examples from the London scene over the last decade or so might include Jan Latham Koenig (*The Koenig Ensemble*), Richard Bernas (*Music Projects/London*) and Odaline de la Martinez (*Lontano*). In this model the group usually draws regularly on the same core of players, adding extras where needed, who will endeavour to make themselves available if they possibly can, so as to retain their position as the first point of call when a concert is being undertaken. But the relations between the individual musicians and the group are less binding, deputies are more frequent and can be accommodated more easily, and rehearsals will usually be paid, albeit sometimes rather poorly. One notable variation on this latter model occurs when a particular composer puts together a group largely to perform their own music, possibly as a result of a degree of commercial success. *The Michael Nyman Band* is perhaps the most well known example of this, but *The Steve Martland Band* and *The Graham Fitkin Group* provide further demonstrations of this trend.

Significantly, these kinds of ensembles continue to exist in the minds of those who contribute to them, notwithstanding that the group itself may come together quite infrequently and perhaps have no confirmed forthcoming engagements. This is particularly the case in the first model, where individual commitments towards the group are most keenly felt. In such cases the association with the group remains an important part of a musician's self-conception, especially so when the group is aligned with a musical style or repertory towards which the musician feels particularly drawn. Such mental constructs, where the group represents a reification of an otherwise abstracted system of cultural values, provide the rationale for musicians occasionally to make financial sacrifices in order to work with the group, although such sacrifices have to be carefully balanced since everybody, ultimately, must earn a living.

And it's the loyalty thing as well. Two years ago I was over-loyal to the quintet, I think, almost to the detriment of my own career. And it's only in the last few months that I've started to think, do I want to do this forever? Do I want an orchestral job? If I want an orchestral job I've got to start thinking about it now.

The processes by which groups come together are inevitably varied, although I have given some indication of possible mechanisms for the second, more loose-knit model. The first model might occur for a number of reasons. Many groups are established, at least embryonically, while their members are students or young professionals beginning a career. Forming a group offers them additional performance experience and a vehicle which they can market in order to get more paid work, an important aspect of conceiving oneself as a professional. More established musicians may form a group because of a preference for playing a particular repertory, which they are perhaps unable to perform as often as they would like, or because they see a gap in the marketplace for a particular ensemble. Orchestral musicians often enjoy playing chamber music because it gives them more opportunity for self-expression, something which they may feel is denied to them in their orchestral job; collaborating in a chamber group enables them to have more immediate control over their musical output, notwithstanding that such collaborations continue to necessitate degrees of musical compromise.

I think if I was offered a chamber music concert to do that would be something I would jump at. I don't do much chamber music. I don't think I'm all that good at it, not as compared with those who are doing it all the time, but I do like to do that sort of music. It's nice blending in with others as a member of a quartet, that's a nice thing to do.

Other groups might evolve as a consequence of being brought together for a particular musical engagement, with the musicians having enjoyed the experience sufficiently to want to recreate it. In another case a group had been formed in order to facilitate its members' attending a music course, and had been encouraged to stay together by their tutors. So, while the actual mechanisms through which groups become established may vary, it is clear that small-scale musical collaborations attract musicians across a wide range of musical styles.

The reasons for choosing which particular individuals to put into a group are inevitably complex and require a detailed and particular appraisal of another musician's personal and musical characteristics. Because of the pressures of the performance situation, the very high demands made upon musicians in chamber groups in terms of rhythmic coordination, intonation and so on, and the prolonged contact between individuals that inevitably occurs within successful ensembles, it is obvious that the individuals concerned must blend both musically and (ideally) socially; and while musicians may find it difficult (or simply be reticent) to verbalize exactly why one particular musician does or does not fit the bill, they are not slow to feel that something is not working.

You get certain people and they're really soloistic and that doesn't work, and you get certain people who are timid and that doesn't work. But somehow when you get someone who's so in touch with the whole thing, they just slot in.

We tried three or four different people. First of all you make sure that their playing is of a sufficient level, and then you try and find out how you're going to work with them, and what their response is to criticism, to being asked to do something totally different to what they want to do or what their nature is. And then finally you get into a performance, what they actually do in a performance, what their attitude is in the performance. Some people are after their own glory, and other people are doing what you've rehearsed and a bit more. And how they work under pressure, because that's when you find out the truth.

It took us a year to find a new person. We played with every single oboist in town you can imagine, and in a sense that was quite interesting, because we realized it had to be a woman. We're five women, so it had to be. Just by the nature of getting one man in, it changed. It altered the group hugely.

Given the problems of finding someone to 'slot in' it can be difficult to foresee how successful or otherwise, both musically and socially, a group may be, although Murnighan and Conlon (1991) have undertaken a detailed study on professional British string quartets which provides some interesting insights in this area. They suggest that shared backgrounds in terms of school and learning environment, similar ages and same sex groups (as noted by my own informant above) all encourage stability and success; that the more successful quartets managed conflicts within the group without necessarily resolving them directly: they would ultimately be resolved over time and perhaps unconsciously; and that the most successful groups had a form of what I call directed democracy,[2] in that one person, the first violin, would lead and take certain musical and pragmatic (rehearsal) decisions, but not in such a way that the others felt excluded or that their views were not taken into account; in the less successful quartets either the leader was too authoritarian, not allowing the others sufficient input, or did not provide enough leadership for the group to function effectively. This study concentrated on professional string quartets only, and I imagine – although this is not made explicit – that a number of these quartets, particularly the more successful ones, were full-time occupations for the musicians involved, unlike most ensembles (I have already noted that the description 'professional' is by no means unproblematic). But my own experience and my knowledge and observation of other groups, perhaps less rigorous than Murnighan and Conlon's statistically led approach but over a much longer timescale, lead me to feel that their observations for string quartets are more generally true for other ensembles.

At this point I should perhaps reiterate my own involvement in this world, having led a small chamber group (a saxophone quartet) for some 18 years, which undoubtedly explains my interest in this area and which also necessarily serves as a frame of reference for my observations. As I indicated in Chapter One, I feel it is important to explicate the nature of my (the ethnographer's) relationship with the object of study, and so a few explanatory remarks are in order here.

'My' quartet[3] was formed while we were students at music college; three of the four players are original members, while in the fourth position we have used four other musicians, although one of these was for twelve years. It is thus a very stable group, with little turnover of personnel, and exhibits many of the characteristics outlined by Murnighan and Conlon, including similar ages, sex and educational backgrounds of the individuals involved. The group specializes in performing contemporary music, and the musical demands made on us are perhaps a little different from ensembles performing standard repertoire, although this is not to privilege one type over the other. Much of the music we play is rhythmically extremely complex, and issues of interpretation – how to inflect a particular phrase or articulate the musical structure of the piece – can only be dealt with once we have devised solutions to the sometimes severe ensemble difficulties a piece presents. Like all chamber groups, however, we spend time arriving at 'our' interpretation of a particular piece, an internalized image of the way the music works, how all the parts fit in with one another, what needs to be brought out where, and which corners we need to be particularly wary of. Each of us must have a conception of our own part and our responsibilities, and how this fits into the piece as a whole. This evolves into a relatively stable group conception of the music, which we can then repeat during performances, suitably enhanced by the touches of adrenalin such performances bring.

The internal dynamics of a saxophone quartet are slightly different from a string quartet. One of Murnighan and Conlon's investigations was into what they termed 'The Paradox of the Second Fiddle':

> Second violinists have unique task and role problems. They must have consummate ability that rarely finds complete expression; they must always play the role of supporter during a performance, even if the first violin seems wrong ... Second violinists are critical to their group's success ... but they are rarely recognised. (Murnighan and Conlon, 1991:169)

To be second violin is a very difficult role, because you don't get the glory of the first violin but you have many moments when you've got to be fantastic, and you've got to leap out and play as well as the first violin, and then get back into the role of being second violin, supporting. And it's got to be something that is a natural thing for a person.

In my group, partly because we use the French formation of soprano, alto, tenor and baritone saxophones,[4] each musician has a timbrally differentiated musical voice, and although I undoubtedly get more of the musical limelight there are many occasions when the other players get a chance to shine. Furthermore, because of the nature of our repertoire, the musical structures are frequently not along the traditional lines of melody, bass line and inner parts, a format which has an in-built musical hierarchy; and we also play numerous pieces which require us to change to different instruments, including on occasions all four of us playing sopranos. So this is perhaps a slightly more egalitarian situation, musically speaking, than a traditional string quartet texture, although it is still the case that such a group needs the 'directed democracy' approach which I mentioned above.

In another common ensemble, the wind quintet, the situation is further complicated by the fact that there are three instruments (flute, oboe and clarinet) which share the musical lead, with the other two (bassoon and horn) often, but not always, designated as accompanying instruments:

And this is a huge problem within the group, because it means that there's no leader. In a sense the flute leads it for everybody, but then you're passing round the leadership, and that's a problem with us running the group and playing in the group, passing round the leadership. Anything works, a business works, when one person is running it, and everyone's working towards it. Democracy doesn't always work in that situation.

As another example, in a successful London-based percussion quartet (a slightly unusual musical ensemble with no obvious hierarchical characteristics) there is again a rather more egalitarian distribution of the musical responsibilities, with each member where possible allocated to instruments which they consider their strengths; but there is still a lead (both musically and administratively) given by two members of the group, again satisfying notions of directed democracy.

Naturally, the high levels of interdependence which develop in small chamber groups can lead to very close sociomusical relationships between the individuals involved; indeed, given the intricate nature of most chamber music, such a level of musical interdependency may be said to be fundamental. Understandably, when the social relationships go wrong, it can be difficult in both emotional and musical terms for the parties involved; emotionally because one is having to break ties with a colleague with whom one has worked closely for a long time and establish new relationships with somebody who may be relatively unknown; and musically because replacing one musician in such a small group inevitably requires new working practices, musical adjustments, additional rehearsals, and the need for the incoming musician to learn a significant amount of new repertoire, or learn that group's particular interpretation of works he or she may already know.

I mentioned above that in my quartet we have had to change one 'chair' (musical position) on three occasions; in each case there was no single event which led to this change, rather it was the culmination of a number of different factors – musical aspirations, availability for rehearsals, personality, a feeling that the group was not working cohesively – in different proportions according to the particular circumstance. On each occasion the decision was taken reluctantly, almost unwillingly; but having acknowledged that there was a problem of some kind it became necessary to deal with it. If the working environment of the group becomes sufficiently difficult that individuals are reluctant to make the necessary sacrifices, or cease to enjoy the work, then the strains this imposes on the group may threaten its survival. And of course, when musicians have worked closely with each other over many years, there can be some bitterness over splits which are less than amicable. When three members of the Audubon Quartet (based in the USA) decided to sack their first violinist, he responded by suing them for damages, and was subsequently awarded over $600 000; he then began bankruptcy proceedings against his former colleagues, forcing two of them to sell their house.[5]

Crisis management is certainly an integral part of chamber music-making. As Murnighan and Conlon point out, a successful group learns how to manage problems so that they do not impede its function. One of my favourite but probably apocryphal stories about the Amadeus String Quartet describes how another musician overheard a particularly angry conversation in a rehearsal, with one of the quartet saying: 'But I've played it this way for 20 years', to which another replied: 'Yes, you've played it that way for 20 years, and for 20 years I've hated it!' Yet such conflicts did not prevent this quartet from being one of the most successful in the world. In my quartet we have also had our fair share of disagreements, shouting matches, and what I might describe as musical stand-offs. A musician in another group offered a similar view:

We managed to survive for most of those 20 years with a good amount of humour, and occasional shouting matches, letting the steam out.

In the case of my own group I see these as inevitable consequences of the difficulty of what we set out to do, and the pressures of professional musical performance. It is noticeable that such arguments have become fewer over the years, as our working practices have evolved and we learn more about each other's personal and musical foibles. Like any longstanding set of relationships we have learned to try and avoid actions or expressions which we know may provoke others, and we have instituted a few simple rules, such as not discussing any negative aspects of a performance immediately in the dressing room afterwards. Other groups adopt different practices; indeed the New Zealand String Quartet apparently uses an outside mediator and engages in quarterly meetings to air grievances.[6] One of my own informants offered the following eloquent and perceptive comment on the role of musical performance itself in conflict management:

Usually, I have to say, things were repaired in the concerts, when the music took over and we realized what we were all about and why we were doing it. And when you sit down and play a great late Beethoven string quartet, the humanity of the stuff you're playing makes you think what idiots you are to be so petty, really. So the grandeur of the music was usually our way out.

Since many of these disagreements between musicians result from different interpretations or understandings of the musical text, we have once again returned to those considerations of the oral tradition of Western art music to which I drew attention in Chapter Two. It is often presupposed that a musical score is simply a list of instructions to be executed by musicians and that everything they might need to know is contained within the text. But this is not the case; indeed the text is frequently so inexplicit that considerable negotiation is required to agree on how it might in fact be reconstituted. Details relating to timbre, dynamics, tempo and character are only given approximate values in conventional Western notation, if notated at all, and are often grounds for considerable debate among those performing. Ruth Finnegan makes a similar observation in her study of amateur musicians in Milton Keynes:

> For performers a whole series of small decisions had to be made about (for example) the detailed exposition of the text, the numbers and blend of performers, whether words should be sung in the original or in translation, whether repetitions, even whole movements, should be omitted. This process, recognised or not, could have a large cumulative effect on the shape and impact of the work as actually performed. (Finnegan, 1989:174–5)

I would argue, therefore, that the musical notation which underpins performance events in the Western art tradition is as much (and perhaps more) a text in the Geertzian sense, as something ethnomusicologists might pore over *in situ* to discover local meanings, as it is in the traditional musicological sense. Musical texts become sites through which social relationships are negotiated. The intensity of these negotiations in the context of chamber music groups who work together regularly requires the establishment of a particularly finely-tuned set of personal relationships; hence the importance of the preceding observations about getting this blend just right.

It is because of these complex social interactions, and the musical consequences of them, that I would disagree with Christianson in his article on British semi-professional jazz musicians, in which he examines the motivational factors for putting together small groups among jazz musicians in the north of England. Comparing such groups with the formation of classical music groups, he writes:

> Where the composer is the ultimate arbiter and the reproduction of his intentions is the primary aim, what is required is the assembly of suitably competent performers who can be assumed to be more or less interchangeable. Their personal styles of performance are not the primary consideration. A formal procedure of advertising for performers and then organising a musical combination from the competent ones that respond is appropriate. (Christianson, 1987:236)

I believe most classical musicians would dispute this. Basic musical competence is only a small part of what is required to play in a successful chamber music group, and 'personal styles of performance' most definitely are a primary consideration. It is simply not accurate to suggest that, because the music is notated, all musicians play it the same; in fact musicians become highly skilled at noticing minute variations in the execution of particular phrases, variations which, in a chamber ensemble, might necessitate modifications in their own performance. Most musicians find it uncomfortable, to say the least, to have to work closely over a long period of time with another musician whose style they dislike; in a chamber group this would be counterproductive to the reasons for being involved in the first place. This is also the case in orchestras, where it can take many months, sometimes years, to fill a particularly important vacancy, with a number of musicians being given long trials before a decision is taken; again such decisions have both a social and a musical basis. It is true that the method Christianson advocates for putting together a classical chamber group is one that is occasionally employed, albeit rather rarely. In general, because of the close network of relationships which already exists within the community, musicians will often know who they want to work with and devise their groups accordingly, although some advertising may take place to fill individual positions, particularly in the case of musicians leaving well established groups.

Assuming, however, that the necessary checks and balances, both social and musical, between a small collection of individual but compatible musicians can be achieved, the group vehicle can become a powerful symbol of shared musical aspirations, leading to internalized conceptions of what the group represents which become reified through choices of repertoire, publicity material, CD covers and so on. A glance through a trade directory or a comparison of brochures quickly reveals the various visual images which groups feel best epitomize their own particular conception of themselves. Many choose a rather serious, conventional approach, often wearing the formal attire in which they would give concerts, as if to emphasise the gravitas they attach to their involvement in the Western art music tradition. Others, especially younger groups, will try and present a fresher, more relaxed image, perhaps underlining their youthfulness and vitality. Others again will align themselves with perceived images of particular repertoires; groups specializing in modern music, for example, will often present far bolder brochures and pictures, sometimes borrowing ideas from the pop music world, as if to say 'innovative, new, exciting'.

Less obvious, but just as significant, is the way certain ensembles collate pieces to create a repertoire which they feel both represents their musical aspirations and gives a distinctive musical identity to the group. Looking back on the practice of my own group, I can see that over nearly two decades we have been through a variety of phases, in which we have sought to align the group with different contemporary styles (although it should be kept in mind that the repertoire for saxophone quartet is in any case considerably smaller than for, say, a string quartet). Initially we had a broad repertoire, with a number of pieces written for us by jazz musicians. Later we sought to redefine the group as a more 'heavyweight' ensemble, constructing our programmes to some extent from what many would describe as the rather more difficult side of modern music, with composers like Xenakis, Globokar and Finnissy featuring significantly. After this we moved on to the rather more popular style of minimal music, performing music by Philip Glass, Steve Reich, Terry Riley and related composers. These different phases represent our changing aspirations for the group, as both the ensemble itself and the individuals within it evolved in particular ways. But through all of this we have attempted to establish and be identified with a repertoire which we can conceive as 'ours': a thread of collective self-conception woven throughout the fabric of our professional activities. In particular, we have always been keen to perform works which we have commissioned or which have seldom been performed by other similar groups, if at all. Such works also become part of our perception of what the group represents, and I see this reflected in the work of similar groups working in this field. Indeed one group has quite explicit instructions to composers on the style of music it would like them to write for the group.

This identification with particular pieces is perhaps less significant among those groups constructing programmes entirely from standard repertoire (traditional string quartets, for example) where there may be some overlap between the repertoires of similar groups, although even here some ensembles may become known for their interpretation of the works of one particular composer or musical genre.

We particularly liked the Czech music and Janacek was not much played in those days. And then we did a lot of Dvorak and Smetana. I think our hearts were very much in that Czech tradition. And then we also wanted to do the English music tradition. So we did Benjamin Britten, and gradually we got into younger English composers: Gordon Crosse, Michael Berkeley, William Mathias, a whole lot of English people [sic] *because we felt we had a duty to put these things out as well.*[7]

Such groups may also become known for their style of playing ('lyrical', 'forthright' and so on) or for the sound of the group, something I shall return to below. Even groups performing largely mainstream material may commission a new repertoire for themselves, and this again encourages a group to associate itself more closely with particular works.

We've recorded one piece that we commissioned ourselves, because it was ours, and that's nice. It's personal to us.

In the contemporary music world, where I have more personal experience, constructing a repertoire for a group becomes increasingly significant. Because Western musical performance is to some extent reproductive rather than creative (by which I mean creative in the sense of creating new material),[8] generating a large number of pieces which are unique to a particular ensemble can establish a distinctive profile for the group, something which undoubtedly informed the direction of my own quartet. The following extract, taken from the programme notes of a London concert given by a young saxophone quartet called *Saxploitation*, a concert in which they had invested significant amounts of time and money, clearly illustrates both their desire to be identified with a particular repertoire they can consider their own and their intention to exploit the theatrical parameters of concert presentation in an idiosyncratic fashion:

> With these two concerts Saxploitation aim to redress what we see as a lamentably stagnant state of affairs ... We will not sit down. We will not wear puffball evening dresses or dinner jackets. We will not perform a programme of music that any other saxophone quartet has performed before us. Indeed we will not perform a single work from the established repertoire. We will engage a 'cellist and a DJ and we will introduce our audiences only to music that has been either arranged, commissioned or composed by ourselves or by musicians or composers we respect. In addition we will engage dancers and a specialist in lighting and visual projections whom [*sic*] will interpret the music as it is presented.[9]

This is something of an extreme example, but it underlines the point that such ideologies are surface manifestations of a collective identity otherwise internalized by the members of the group.

Of course, not all members will necessarily support a group's activities to the same degree. I know from my own experience that there have been times when one or the other of my own group – including myself – has been unhappy about playing a particular work, or performing in a certain manner, either because the piece itself was felt to be of limited value or because individuals were being asked to perform in ways they considered inappropriate; again these tensions must be somehow managed within the group if a schism is to be avoided. But it does illustrate that while a group may indeed represent an amalgamation of shared musical aspirations, individual musicians within it refract components of their self-conception from the group vehicle on their own terms; we cannot tar them all with the same brush.

Recordings

Another significant reification of this group identity is through the production of recordings, particularly commercial recordings. Again I must declare my own involvement here in that my quartet was heavily involved in producing a (for us) significant disc for part of the period I was undertaking this research; naturally the issue has been at the forefront of my mind. CDs provide a very tangible expression of group identity; they generally, subject to the whim of the record company, allow performers the chance to select a part of their repertoire to which they feel particularly drawn (for whatever reason: because they think the pieces are musically strong, or show off the group's abilities well, and so on) and they provide a physical representation of what the group does which may not only be sold commercially but can also be passed around the sociomusical network surrounding the group – other musicians, agents, friends, or perhaps potential employers: 'this is us', 'this is what we do'.

I think it raises the profile of the group. I think it's a real challenge to be pushed as a group, just by the actual few days of the recording, and I think it's quite good to have something that's solid, not so transient. Something that you can actually hold on to and say that we have got something to show for all this work that we put in.

This is perhaps more true of less established groups or those working in specialist musical genres, where there is unlikely to be a great commercial demand for the disc. In these cases – and there would be many equivalents in the pop and jazz fields, perhaps more so than in classical genres – the distribution network may be limited, confined to a small number of interested parties; digital technology these days makes relatively small print runs much more economically viable than was previously the case. More established and successful groups would not regard recording another disc in the same way; indeed very successful and internationally recognized groups would certainly not see it in this light now, although doubtless they did in the initial stages of their career.

It was very important. If you didn't have records people were not interested in you, really. And when you went abroad your records would always be advertised, and that was very much your calling card. And then we got a contract with DECCA, and that was very important because that was obviously a worldwide institution.

These issues provide an interesting counterpoint to conventional musicological approaches to the role of recordings. Whereas such recordings have been used to obtain information about performance practice, either with reference to developments in musical style[10] or as a way of comparing variations in performance practice among different artists,[11] their iconic or symbolic significance has often been overlooked. One exception is Nicholas Cook's (1998a) paper on the reception of record sleeves, where he examines the degree to which the sleeve images contribute to the construction of musical meaning, and to a lesser extent vice versa. As Cook himself observes, 'record sleeves transcend their origins ... and become part of the product, or at any rate part of the discursive framework within which the music inside them is consumed. Seen in this way, they function as agents in the cultural process, sites where meaning is negotiated through the act of consumption' (106). By extension then, I would argue that a similar relationship to the one Cook asserts between LP covers and the music they contain exists between CDs (today's equivalent of the LP) and the groups which produce them. These recordings come to be seen as embodying principles underlying the group itself, through their choice of repertoire, cover imagery, liner notes and so on. This is a symbiotic relationship. The group gives meaning to the disc through its choice of repertoire, the production and packaging (to the extent these are within their control) and their performance style. And, similarly, such characteristics are endowed in the group by those who encounter the disc, and who subsequently invest the qualities it represents into the identity they construct for the group. Such relationships have been well articulated in the case of popular musicians,[12] but they have been glossed over with regard to classical music groups. And the most important dimension of these CDs, the one which most clearly epitomizes the group from the perspective of the musicians involved, is the musical performance itself. Such performances now exist in perpetuity, providing an essential resource through which the musicians can re-internalize the performance aesthetic of the group, discuss their performance among themselves and with others, and listen to themselves repeatedly and with an objectivity not otherwise achievable in live performance. Their perception of the performance will not necessarily be how an audience hears the group. In my experience musicians listen differently to recordings in which they are involved than would a truly objective audience; but it is as close as any musician can get.

Thus recordings are concrete products which come to represent the group and its aspirations, and which have a permanence and immutability in contrast to the essentially ephemeral act of live performance. And of course they have a functionality beyond their iconic status. They can be passed around the support circles of friends, family and other musicians who take an interest in the group's work. Most importantly they can be distributed amongst promoters and critics, thus holding out the prospect that, even if the recording itself does not sell in large quantities (and very few of them do), it may result in additional bookings or other work elsewhere, as well as contributing to raising the profile of the group. Kay Kaufman Shelemay (2001:17–18) notes similar *modi operandi* among early music groups in Boston, observing that recordings play a particularly crucial role among such groups since they provide 'detailed documentation of repertory, texts and translations, performance practices, and the group's statement of purpose'; furthermore, recordings could make a substantial difference to 'a group's ability to obtain engagements and maintain an active relationship with their audience between live concerts'.

The importance of CDs in the working lives of such groups has, I think, increased as the digital revolution of the last two decades has proceeded. This has meant that the recording, editing and production of high-quality CDs has become much easier and somewhat cheaper; and the distribution of such CDs by myriad smaller, specialist companies has led to a fragmentation of the recording industry, with the power and control of the major labels diminishing somewhat over this timescale, a trend which appears to have accelerated in the last few years (the same is of course true in popular and world musics). It is in large part because, at grass roots level at least, musicians can have greater input into what they can record and how it might be produced and marketed, that CDs increasingly function as both icons of and symbols for internalized ideas of group identity. And the rise of the Internet as a distribution tool means that groups can now sell into markets well beyond their immediate geographical area, which in turn can lead to increased conceptions of the group as an international entity, not simply a domestic one.

I see these developments as in some way parallel to the importance of cassette cultures in certain other traditions. As Shelemay has observed elsewhere (1991:285), the cassette revolution of the 1960s and 1970s returned recording technology back to the individual, and this led to 'the essential democratisation of the relationship between recording technology and music-makers cross culturally'. The affordability of the equipment for both recording and mass reproduction of recordings meant that the musicians themselves gained more control over the way their music was presented (control wrested not only from the record companies but also from ethnomusicologists and their field recordings) and the resulting cassettes could be easily distributed among diasporic communities (285–6). Among London's ensembles similar trends prevail. It is the groups themselves who frequently determine what they will record, and under what circumstances; and although negotiations are inevitably needed if the disc is to be distributed by a record company, many discs are produced and retained only by the groups themselves, to sell into shops where they can, to sell at concerts (often more successful and profitable) and for use as marketing tools.

Thus the equilibrium existing between the record companies, the artists and the consumers is rather more complex than used to be the case. Traditionally the record company, who would be financing the whole arrangement, would determine to a considerable degree what would be recorded and how it would be marketed. Groups aspired to be taken on by such companies because their patronage gave kudos (or symbolic capital) to those whom they deemed worthy of such support. Now, however, artists can circumvent these arrangements. By associating themselves with smaller, often specialist, record companies, or by taking on the role of the record companies for themselves, they can readily produce recordings more or less regardless of the commercial viability of the project. It is fair to observe, however, that those groups who do obtain recordings with the major record labels continue sometimes to regard such relationships as being qualitatively different (and often more important) from those with smaller labels.

That the CDs themselves do represent a reification of internalized ideas, a manifestation of group identity which is intrinsically meaningful to the group members, would appear further demonstrated by the fact that, in many cases, and particularly among less established groups, the musicians are often not paid for the recordings; indeed on numerous occasions musicians fund at least part of the costs of the project themselves, hoping for rather than expecting some later financial return, although this is frequently not the primary motivation. That such musicians, who in general are not some of society's most highly paid artisans, will use their own money to pay for recordings which they feel are representative of the aspirations of the group (in addition to their obvious marketing potential) would appear to demonstrate another permutation of the juxtaposition of musical and economic capitals which I outlined in Chapter Three, and further underlines the significance musicians attach to those performance opportunities which they feel most closely reflect their own internalized musical aspirations.

I think you've got to invest. If you're investing all this time and energy over years into a group, then in a sense to invest a thousand pounds, or whatever, isn't a huge amount; you've done that over the years anyway.

And although I have suggested that making such recordings is cheaper today than previously, the costs are still significant. At 2003 prices, a group would expect to pay from £2–3000 for recording and editing costs, possibly more if a recording space needs to be hired. Printing, production and pressing costs could amount to another £1–2000, for perhaps 1000 CDs. One well established production company currently advertises on its website an inclusive package of £4000 for 1500 finished discs.[13] Record companies may pay all or part of these costs, depending on what particular deal is negotiated. Even so, these remain significant amounts to be generated for less established groups, some of whose turnover may not amount to these kinds of figures in a whole year. Again Shelemay notes similar obstacles among early music groups in Boston, suggesting that 'the investment of time and resources necessary to produce a commercial recording is mentioned as a barrier for all but the largest and most well established groups' (2001:18).

But if these barriers can be surmounted, what CDs and other recordings do provide, rather obviously perhaps, is the opportunity for groups to hear themselves, and this is significant because good ensembles who play together over a period of time consciously foster a group sound, which not only functions as an aural reference point for their own work but can serve to differentiate the group from others of a similar type. I have already considered individual musicians' conceptions of sound but there are further points to be made here about the collective sounds to which ensembles aspire.

A certain amount of time is always spent at the beginning of a recording session trying to capture the kind of sound which a group feels it makes, yet which is also satisfactory for the producer and engineers who are responsible for the technical aspects of the recording. There are a number of issues involved in this which are not particularly relevant here, to do with room acoustics, distribution and type of microphones, positioning of players, and so on. But the end result is always a product of negotiations which arise largely because of an internalized sound ideal that the group has of itself: 'that sounds more like us'. The following anecdote illustrates this point. Some years ago I was discussing the work of a particular group, already defunct by then, with the (ex) leader of the group. The demise of the ensemble had been a rather fractious affair, brought about in part by the somewhat dictatorial style of the leader himself. Although the group, which was once quite successful, no longer gave concerts, they would still occasionally get together for commercial recording work. The leader remarked to me: *It would take us about ten minutes to get our sound back together, at which point I would start to feel physically sick.* As this graphically illustrates, the collective sound produced by musicians in a group situation is itself capable of significant symbolic representation for the individuals concerned, over and above the actual repertoire being performed.

I have observed similar issues when undertaking recordings with my own group, which have illustrated to me over the years the generalized conception we have of our own sound. In one of our early recordings the quartet sounded a little distant, a well-rounded and balanced sound certainly, but without the 'grit' or 'edge' which we felt characterized our playing. With a later recording we placed the microphones nearer the instruments, resulting in a much closer, more distinct sound; a bit more 'in yer face', as somebody remarked. For us, such a sound more accurately represented our internalized idea of how the group should sound. Whether the audience or listener perceives it that way is a different matter entirely, but it was important to us that we heard ourselves coming off disc as we imagined the group to sound in performance. Musicians in other groups made similar observations:

I think we had a very well matched, blended sound. Obviously at certain times we could vary that. But our basic sound quality was one that was very resonant, quite a big sound, full, and very rounded.

With our new cellist, who's Russian, we've got a totally different mixture of sounds now. Yet we've found our own sound very quickly, I think.

One musician, a member of a particularly long established ensemble, even speculated that the sound of the group had evolved as the members of the group had themselves matured:

Our first 20 years were obviously our best times in many ways, because it was very exciting. Everything was very new and building up. What we have now is somewhat more relaxed, I should say. We don't feel we're in such a desperate hurry to get everywhere and to be everywhere. And so the sound quality is not so youthful and vibrant, but is more mellow. Maybe that's the term for it.

Thus the perception of a group's sound, although no doubt varying slightly between individual members of the group, becomes a significant component both of the identity the group seeks to project and of the relationship between the individuals and the group itself. As with individual instrumental sound, timbre becomes a potential source of symbolic interpretation for musicians, who are themselves highly skilled at detecting and producing minute timbral variations, a skill they employ to underpin ideas of collective identity.

Another potent representation of group identity can be the name which a group uses to describe itself. This works at several levels, because of course this name not only iconically references that particular collection of musicians for society at large, it also symbolically represents a shared identity through which the individuals involved in part conceive their relationship with the group. For these reasons choosing a name can be a particularly difficult operation, notwithstanding that a proportion of ensemble names simply follow certain well established formulas. Two of these seem particularly prevalent. First, a number of groups choose to associate themselves with a particular geographical location, of which 'London' is by far the most popular, and not only, I think, because of the numerical superiority of musicians in the capital city. The word 'London' often has a significance (because of the capital's reputation as the centre of professional music work in Britain) beyond its strictly geographical reference. In such cases the descriptor 'London' is effectively being used as a synonym for 'national', and thus implicitly as a metaphor for national artistic excellence. The 1999 *British Music Yearbook* has no fewer than 30 ensembles (not including orchestras) who use this in their name. Secondly, among string quartets particularly, the surname of the leader may be invoked as a suitable moniker for the description of the group, and this doubtless relates to the issues of directed democracy which I outlined above.

It is perhaps difficult to convey the problems musicians can experience when naming ensembles (or CDs, for that matter).[14] For society at large the seemingly innocuous iconic function of a name no doubt appears unproblematic, but its symbolic nature for the musicians involved may increase considerably the importance attached to it. The name must say something about the group, whether by allying it with the conventional patterns I have mentioned or by seeking deliberately to differentiate it from these and thus imply that the group also seeks to differentiate itself in some way from what is perceived as a traditional approach to performance. In the case of my own quartet, after several false starts, we reverted to the area of classical language and mythology, another common source of inspiration for such things. Although the name did not, initially, say anything in particular about the group, it has come to represent, in the verbal constructions we use between ourselves, a convenient shorthand way of representing our musical aspirations: what we play, how we sound, how we approach performances, and so forth, although I doubt that it has this function for others, or at least not to the same degree. In moving away from these formulas, however, certain groups betray some indication of how they view themselves, particularly those who are prepared to incorporate puns and other word-play into their titles. Descriptions such as *Ensemble Bash* (a percussion group), *Brass Belles* (an all-female brass quintet) or *Saxploitation* seem to imply not only a good marketing strategy – having a name which is both distinctive and memorable – but also a desire to set themselves apart, to differentiate themselves from the traditional while at the same time clearly remaining part of the tradition.

Ultimately, all of these shared concerns – chosen repertoire, approaches to performance, conceptions of group sounds, financial sacrifices, recordings made, names discussed, and so forth – contribute to a mutual understanding of what it means to be a part of the group, and this sense of belonging is well captured by Gary Fine's notion of 'idioculture'. Fine suggests that every small group or team has a unique culture of its own, 'a set of customs, rituals, behaviors, and meaningful images that constitute the way a team views itself' (Fine, 1987b:111) and, moreover, that this group idioculture comprises a system of knowledge and beliefs 'to which members can refer and employ as the basis of further interaction' (Fine, 1979:734). In the case of musical ensembles I suggest that this idioculture comprises not only those patterns of behaviour which can be elucidated from observation or which arise from agreed conventions or a shared past, but also, and more significantly, 'meaningful images' of how the group itself plays and sounds, of what it means to be a musician contributing to the group's performances, and of how such knowledge can be employed either in the reconstitution of works already rehearsed and collectively internalized, or, indeed, when approaching and making sense of a work which is new to the ensemble. Furthermore, while such idiocultures are constructed, augmented or reaffirmed by each contributor to the group, they also generate significant components of a musician's self-conception, underlining the symbiotic relationship between the individual and the group in this most democratic of musical activities.

Notes

1   Such issues have, of course, been the subject of much work by other writers, particularly those who have approached them from the direction of developmental or cognitive psychology, such as John Sloboda (1985) or David Hargreaves (1986).
2   Murnighan and Conlon refer to this as the 'Leader versus Democracy paradox' (1991:169).
3   I refer to this group as 'my quartet' for convenience, but I am acutely conscious that, while I am nominally the leader, it is very much the product of and dependent upon all four individuals.
4   Rather than the American permutation of alto, alto, tenor, baritone.
5   The details of this rather messy divorce are available at various sites on the Internet (for example *http://www.bolzcenter.org/portal/print.php?sid=118*). Unsurprisingly, perhaps, they are not listed on the website of the Audubon Quartet itself.

6   According to *BBC Music Magazine*, April 2003, p.35.
7   I have transcribed this interview quotation verbatim, although it should be pointed out that William Mathias is very much a Welsh composer.
8   A more extensive discussion on the issue of creativity in Western performance will be found in Chapter Five.
9   *Saxploitation* concert programme notes, The Place Theatre, London, 29 November 1997.
10   See, for example, Philip (1992).
11   See, for example, Bowen (1999).
12   See, for example, David Buxton's (1990) paper on the role played by record sleeve imagery in creating pop music stars.
13   *http://www.classicalrecording.co.uk*
14   Composers often have similar problems finding titles for their works.

CHAPTER FIVE

Orchestras, the Self, and Creativity in Musical Performance

Introduction

In this chapter I examine musicians' work in those ensembles which are often taken to be the flagships of professional music-making, symphony orchestras, and I shall endeavour to outline something of the very particular mindset which often accompanies performance in this most demanding of musical arenas. As I made clear in Chapter One, my own experience of orchestral music-making is less extensive than in some other genres, and so I am more reliant on the words and ideas of others at this point. I have attempted, at least in the first half of the chapter, to take my place in the background rather than the foreground of the picture. I have not detailed the history and development of any particular orchestra, or indeed the London orchestras collectively. Such information can be discovered in greater detail elsewhere than I would be able to provide here,[1] and I am in any case more preoccupied with individual lived experience than with attempting to outline the social history of London's orchestral landscape. While I would suggest that a good ethnographic study of London's orchestral scene (or that of Berlin or New York for that matter) is long overdue, this is not what I have attempted here. Indeed it is one of the subtexts of this book as a whole to demonstrate the variety and extent of professional musical life in a city such as London, which goes far beyond the major orchestras which are so frequently taken as representing it.

I am also concerned here with notions of individual creativity and the degree to which musicians regard what they do as being genuinely creative. This does perhaps more closely reflect my own concerns, since, as will become clearer below, although I was initially drawn to a professional musical career because I saw it as being a creative occupation, I am now considerably more ambivalent as to where the boundaries of such creativity might lie. And I see such uncertainty reflected in the minds of other musicians, all of which provides interesting perspectives on the notion of individuality among professional musicians.

Orchestras and the self

In Chapter Four I observed that, for many people, the small group situation provides an ideal platform for expressing their sense of musical self within a social context. This is not to suggest, however, that all musicians would like to be performing chamber music all the time. Some might (and do), but as a number of the quotations throughout this book demonstrate, many freelance musicians derive great pleasure from the variety of work their rather precarious situation offers them, enjoying opportunities to craft their musical abilities in different ways and in situations which may be less or more rewarding according to circumstance. This necessarily implies, rather obviously perhaps, that in these different contexts the degree to which a musician's individual contribution is heard or recognized can vary quite considerably. But this can be seen in a positive light, a musical equivalent of moderation in all things:

In a sense the idea would be to do both. A chamber group gives you that security of a small group almost like a family, and you can come out and be a soloist and retreat back into it. But you don't always get the huge expanse of an orchestra, so I think the two together, that would be my ideal.

But these two performing situations – the ensemble and the large orchestra – make rather different practical and emotional demands on musicians, thus encouraging different relationships between the individual and the group, and it is both fruitful and relevant to consider the experience of the individual musician in the largest groups in which one generally gets to play: symphony orchestras.

It may be something of a truism to observe that musicians find it frustrating to contribute to situations where they feel their sense of self, the particular individual qualities they possess as musicians, is either inadequately utilized or subsumed to such a degree within the larger musical whole that they feel inconsequential. For example, the endless repetition of a long-running show, where one regurgitates the same music every night (and twice on Wednesdays and Saturdays!), would for me at least be a good instance of this. But perhaps more surprising is that similar tensions build up within orchestras. I describe this as surprising for a number of reasons. First, because, unlike a show, orchestras do have a regular turnover of music, particularly in London where the intense competition among the orchestras and the relatively fragile state of their finances means that each of them needs to take on more work than they would wish, simply to stay in business. (It is still the case, however, that much of their repertoire is confined to a disconcertingly small number of pieces largely derived from the late-eighteenth and nineteenth-century classics, with a variable degree of twentieth-century music added to the mix; one orchestra player told me that within a year of joining the orchestra he had played the majority of pieces he was ever likely to play with them.) Second, orchestras are regarded as among the most significant organizations – along with opera houses – within the Western art music firmament. These are the institutions which are most usually seen, rightly or wrongly, as being at the apex of the professional musical pyramid. When in 1997 the *Times Educational Supplement* ran a front page feature on cutbacks in instrumental tuition in schools, it was the knock-on effect on orchestras which was taken as being the greatest cause for concern:

> The future of Britain's orchestras is being jeopardised by a dramatic slump in the number of children learning to play an instrument at school ... The threat to traditional orchestras is made more acute by the fact that less popular instruments such as the bassoon and the French horn are in the greatest decline.[2]

Although such cutbacks have a serious detrimental effect across a wide range of music-making, it was the orchestral flagships (who employ only a fraction of the country's musicians) for which the paper was concerned. Significantly, such orchestras are also seen by many musicians themselves, particularly during their college years, as the ultimate achievement, the highest goal for which they can aim:

When I was a student I never imagined I would be in the Philharmonia. It was like one of the orchestras in heaven that you just aspired to in your dreams. Sometimes I remember that with a shock. I think, God, I'm playing in the Philharmonia.

That many musicians who achieve this goal develop a rather ambiguous attitude towards its merits does not seem to percolate down into the lower reaches of the profession to any meaningful extent.

The roots of any frustrations are not difficult to fathom. In London, particularly, the insecurity of freelance orchestral playing,[3] the severe work schedules the orchestras must undertake to survive, the continual under funding and so on may all contribute to a general feeling of dissatisfaction. But there are other problems inherent within the working practices of such large groups which can also generate discontent, and these seem to divide into two main areas. The first arises from a feeling that one is making a contribution to the end product which appears to be undervalued or unnoticed. Unsurprisingly, perhaps, such sentiments appear more common among the massed ranks of the string players than among the wind or brass:

Sitting in the middle of any string section there are obvious frustrations, you feel your chance to blossom is pretty limited sometimes. I have to bend what I'm doing to make it work with the principal viola and when you want to do it your way it can become a bit frustrating.[4]

I've heard from a lot of my colleagues that when they're at the back they just feel 'what if I just went up in a puff of smoke now – nobody would notice. It wouldn't make the blindest bit of difference because I'm sort of tickling away at the back, not really doing anything'.

An orchestral clarinettist observed:

I think that's the nature of violin playing, I think it's an awful job. They have the most expensive instruments, they are the least well-paid, they never get a number off, or very rarely. They don't get any of the thing about being complimented on good solos, they just get a lot of flak thrown at them if the section's not together. And sometimes sitting at the back it's impossible to play.

However, those who find themselves in this position, who must retain their sense of musical individuality even though they are playing exactly the same as 11 or perhaps 20 or more other players every time they play, necessarily devise strategies to deal with this, to preserve their self-conception as individual musicians.

There's always something that the individual can give, without sticking out like a sore thumb, without interfering. I think there is. There should be. Even if it's just somebody thinking 'right this is a nice tune, I'm glad we've got to play it, I'm going to make a really beautiful sound and I'm going to feel that it's all fitting'. You can get that sort of feeling, although you wouldn't ever put it into words particularly. It would just be a thought – 'Right here we go' – and you'd do it. There is individuality, and there is room for each individual to have a feeling that he's creating something.

Such strategies are widespread throughout the various orchestral sections, demonstrating the understandable necessity for all performers in an orchestra to assert the importance of their own contribution, even those such as the second violins or double basses who would not ordinarily attract the eye or the ear as much as other sections.

[A bass player]: *It's like putting colour onto a painting. We are the primary colours, and the others thin them down. That's why I love this instrument.*

Second fiddles need to be pretty hot players. We're the real motor of the orchestra: while the firsts are running around the place, having a great time playing the tunes, we keep the music going.[5]

This need to actively conceive of one's contribution as both distinct and significant is perhaps slightly less pressing for wind and brass players, who do get opportunities to display their individual musical qualities in a more obvious way, and this is particularly true of principal players;[6] indeed those players who can both submit to the rigours of orchestral discipline and produce outstanding solo playing when required are highly valued:

Alex used to say Dave Brown, for example, on the first horn, could lift an entire performance.

And he could do this, he could turn out, say Giselle, on a Saturday matinee, and it would sort of bring a lump to your throat. And that's quite something, that's really special.

So while there may superficially appear to be a great deal of uniformity about orchestral playing, particularly within the large string sections, it is clear that individual musicians, who have been encouraged to develop their own musical personality from an early age, do develop cognitive strategies which allow them to manage the inherent tensions between their individual aspirations and the necessary conformity their collaborative venture demands.

Another source of tension arises from the necessity to tailor one's own personal musical aesthetic to that of the conductor. The approach and musical agenda of this controlling figure may differ radically both from that of individual musicians (in their interpretation of a particular phrase or part) or from the collective approaches to music-making which inevitably develop among a highly-skilled group of people working together regularly, and who may have played a particular piece many times before.

The whole nature of being an orchestra musician is that you basically subjugate your whole person, all your ideas, your own personal ideas, you have to just completely throw them away. Just say, right, I don't matter. The guy on the box, on the podium, he's the guy that matters, and you have to give them what they want.

As a musician, even when you're young, you have a musical opinion. Then you join an orchestra and you have a musical director who imposes his own point of view, more or less skilfully according to how professional he is. Little by little you change your ideas, and you reach a compromise with the conductor. You end up saying, 'Well, I always saw it that way.'

When I'm in an orchestra I'm just a robot.

Thus there can be a considerable degree of tension existing between the interpretive agenda of the players and that of the conductor, and there is often relatively little scope for individual musicians to influence the musical decisions of the group, either within the context of a particular piece or in terms of the overall choice of repertoire the orchestra performs.

It's a little bit like being in a communist state really, being in an orchestra, in that you've got this Chairman Mao in front of you saying 'This goes like that.'

If you're lucky you might be able to discuss it with him, but usually there's no time. I mean, you know what it's like in this country, it's usually a three hour rehearsal and that's it, a concert, and there's no time to discuss anything.

Nor, these days, given the overwhelming influence and authority that conductors have and the enormous fees some of them command (see Lebrecht, 1991), is there any particular need for the conductors to cooperate with the musicians, and musicians can be particularly scathing about those who they perceive as being overly dictatorial.

The real martinet conductors, well there are fewer of them now, I think. Probably the last few are people like S— and D—, people who are probably fundamentally shits really – some of the others were also shits but they actually had a bit more charm.

The whole job of a conductor is to play an instrument, and he's the most privileged musician of all, because he's got 100 musicians, good ones, in front of him, and he has the chance to do what he wants. What he should really be is an enabler. He should allow all those musicians to give of their best. There are very few who can do that, there are some, but there are very few.

Like all those who have played in orchestras, I have my own recollections of being glowered at over the tips of angry batons, having played something which was evidently not to the conductor's liking. Learning to deal with this kind of behaviour, and particularly the abuse that can be given out during rehearsals, is an essential survival strategy for musicians.

I suppose the only preparation I got from music college was being absolutely torn apart, which you might be by a conductor, and having that experience, being able to pick yourself up and cope. If I hadn't been to music college I might have fallen apart at that, in the profession. Whereas I think I probably got destroyed enough at music college.

Inevitably, conductors who allow musicians to feel that they are really putting something of themselves into the performance are generally more highly regarded than those who seek only to dictate what should be done.

It's a two-way thing. They stamp their mark, but they allow you a certain amount of leeway too. And that's something that a lot of conductors find very difficult, to trust the orchestra.

I think you have to let your own voice shine. I think a good conductor does allow that.

Of course, given that symphony orchestras may have upwards of 80 players, a group discussion over every decision would be impractical. But because musicians perceive conductors as the figures responsible for curbing their own creative instincts, subduing their own musical personality, they are most frequently the objects onto which the musicians' frustrations become projected. This situation is imbued with even greater piquancy when, as is sometimes the case with the London orchestras, the 'guy on the box' is being paid more for his night's work than the rest of the orchestra put together. It is noticeable that one of the opening scenes of Channel 4's documentary on the Philharmonia Orchestra, *The Phil*,[7] shows the leader of the orchestra chopping wood on his farm. As he begins he says: 'After a hard day's work with the orchestra, you pretend this [log] is the conductor's head, and you do *that!*' – at which point he smashes down the axe and splits the log in two. With such sentiments common among musicians it is unsurprising that a whole genre of musicians' jokes and stories has built up around the conductor figure, and these will be considered in more detail in Chapter Six.

It is not only the conductor, however, who makes performance decisions which directly influence the contribution of other musicians. Whereas in a small chamber group the rather more egalitarian structure allows each individual to influence the musical product, the necessarily hierarchical relationships within the orchestra create particular channels of authority which again impact upon the individual musician's work. The leader of each string section will make certain decisions – about when the bow changes direction, thus influencing musical phrasing, for example – which the others must follow. In most of the other sections, particularly among wind and brass, the principal on each instrument will make interpretive decisions which other players in that instrumental group must be aware of, and which they will use as the basis for their own performance, and so on.

In some ways it's much easier being a principal because people have to follow you, they actually have to match you, play with you. In the old days, certainly, principals were fairly autocratic and they expected people to play with them.

But again there's always this hierarchy that the front of a string section, you're playing with them. You're always under the person who's in front of you. And I think that's difficult, because if you're at the back you daren't put a foot wrong. I mean, by far the easiest place to play in a symphony orchestra is on the front desk, because everybody else is mirroring what you do. It doesn't matter if you get something wrong, because what you're doing is right.

So while the large-scale nature of the symphony orchestra necessarily requires such hierarchies in order to function effectively, they are also a potential source of frustration for self conscious individuals who find their ideas in conflict with others. Inevitably, those who do not conform to these agreed behavioural norms, both musical and social, may become seen as a liability to the group as a whole, regardless of their musical expertise:

You have to feel able to fit in, and people who can't do that, you always seem to hear them playing a bit louder, or a bit more aggressively than others. They can be annoying, and also people who move about a tremendous amount when they play. They can be upsetting in a string section.

I think the personality is in some ways the most important thing, because some of the most awkward and difficult people, really however wonderfully they played, have been a complete menace in orchestras.

This last reference to personality resonates with Anthony Kemp's observation that within the orchestral environment different personality types are drawn towards particular instruments. He suggests, for example, that string instruments attract more introverted types who demonstrate aloofness and heightened levels of self-sufficiency. Woodwind players also show introverted traits but these are allied with a degree of imagination and radicalism not shared by string players. Brass players (to nobody's particular surprise, perhaps) show considerable extrovert traits allied to lower levels of personal discipline (see Kemp, 1996:139–65). Such observations again underscore the fact that collaborative musical ventures are executed by groups of individual musicians who possess highly developed conceptions of self which must be necessarily compromised, moderated or adapted for the purposes of musical production. The manner in which such compromises are negotiated inevitably requires sophisticated and delicate forms of social interaction, and it is for this reason that, as I observed in the previous chapter, I see social skills as being fundamentally intertwined with notions of musicianship, the craft of being a professional musician.

John Blacking's observations on the essentially social experience of human music-making provide an intriguing dimension to the frustrations which can be experienced in orchestral performance. Blacking's work with the Venda people of South Africa (fieldwork which formed the bedrock of many of his ideas about music and culture) led him to believe that human music-making is highly significant for constructing and maintaining social relations, and that music is most affective when experienced communally; thus the larger the group in which the individual participates, the more significant the cultural experience. However, in Blacking's view, this remained true only inasmuch as such participation allowed individuals to preserve their sense of individuality within the larger social whole, and the value of the experience was diminished when that sense of individuality was reduced. For example, in writing of the effectiveness of *tshikona*, the national dance of the Venda and a ceremony which had the largest number of participants in Venda society, he asserts that 'it is not a case of MORE = BETTER: it is an example of the production of the maximum of available human energy in a situation that generates the highest degree of individuality in the largest possible community of individuals' (Blacking, 1976:51). In other words, simply making music with increasing numbers of participants does not in itself represent a more significant human musical experience. What made this ceremony particularly notable, both in terms of its overall importance for Venda society and for the individuals who took part, was that their sense of belonging to the community was reinforced precisely because they were able to retain their sense of individuality in their communal music-making; thus their self-conception was enhanced through their participation in the communal event because it contributed to their sense of understanding of 'who I am'. Furthermore, participation in *tshikona* was particularly potent, since this large-scale ceremony symbolized the largest society known to the Venda in the past; the system of *apartheid* (racial segregation) prevailing at that time restricted their wider participation in South African society, preventing them from identifying with the modern political nation state, which sought to limit and control their individual freedom. Thus for the Venda *tshikona* epitomized the principle of individuality in community (101–2) reinforcing their self-conception *as* Venda.

It is not, I think, too whimsical to observe certain parallels with ensemble music-making in the West. In the orchestral context a musician's sense of individuality is also circumscribed, not through an overriding political ideology, but through the hierarchical structure prevailing within the group and, most significantly, because of the paramount authority of the conductor. Indeed some musicians clearly argue this can on occasion appear as a type of dictatorship, providing further resonances with the Venda's position. In terms of intrinsic personal satisfaction, therefore, it is again not simply a case of 'more = better'. The fact that many orchestral musicians appear to place a premium on their participation in unconducted chamber ensembles demonstrates their need also to 'generate the highest degree of individuality' within the range of communal music-making opportunities open to them. Such aspirations are more readily achieved through the social and musical egalitarianism inhering within chamber music ensembles than they are within the rather more rigid and hierarchical structures found within orchestras.

Creativity

My interest in musicians' perceptions of their contributions to group collaborations is in part driven by my desire to establish whether musicians feel that what they do is actually creative. In my teenage years I decided to embark on a music degree rather than a more vocational alternative because, as I remember explaining to my father, I wanted to do something more creative. At the time I saw professional musicians as obviously being creative people; now I am more ambivalent as to where the boundaries of this creativity lie. Given the centrality of the musical score in Western musical performance, and the near extinction of improvisation in all but a few genres, much of what Western musicians are required to do might reasonably be described as re-creative, since they are usually reconstructing musical ideas outlined on a page by some absent Other. My own interest in contemporary music no doubt stems from my desire to exploit the creative parameters of professional musical performance, since I personally find it more creative to be working with composers generating new material than simply regurgitating the masterworks of the past; thus the management side of my work – running an ensemble, organizing commissions, arranging concerts – I see, paradoxically, as being as creative as the actual playing, and others in my position share this view:

I think there are two sorts of musician. There's the passive musician who just goes into an orchestra and sits down and does a job, and there are the other ones who make things happen, and I'll definitely say that I'm the second one, because the whole Quartet, I mean this is not being big-headed, but it just wouldn't have happened if it wasn't for me. I've started it, I've made that happen. I commission works, so I'm creating music which wouldn't have been there otherwise.

Naturally the actual commissioning of new work is not undertaken by the majority of London musicians, and my particular perspective comes from my perhaps slightly unusual position within this community.

Kay Kaufman Shelemay (2001:9–10) similarly observes that, among Boston's early music groups, 'creativity … operates actively in all domains of program planning and performance practice'. And she goes on to note that 'musicians in all of the ensembles with which we worked testified to the centrality of creative activity in their conceptualization and performance of musical repertory' (10). But I would argue that this represents something of an oversimplification of this issue, since musicians do conceptualize different degrees of creativity, and they all have views as to what they do and do not regard as being creative; or at least, they construe particular activities as being more or less creative than others. Such views are frequently allied to their perceptions of their own contribution to a particular musical whole:

But the creative things, mainly, don't earn the money in music, so the bread and butter things I don't find creative. I go into them with a slightly different approach. I have to. I know it's not going to be creative doing a show every night.

We've worked with composers in a workshop situation where we really did have a hands-on approach. So I felt very much part of that creative team. The end result was all our work.

I think when I go and do orchestral dates I find that very, very uncreative. I know I should feel proud to be part of this great organism that produces such a majestic sound, but frankly I'm just bored and waiting for the cheque to turn up.

Unsurprisingly, perhaps, the last of these musicians does not in fact undertake a great deal of orchestral work. Those musicians who do, however, adopt cognitive strategies whereby they also conceive what they do as creative:

It's creative because I think there is always scope to go a little bit beyond the simple rows of dots that are in front of you, and the expression marks and the conductor who's giving his interpretation.

If you're in an orchestra there are boundaries which you never cross, because if you did you'd be chucked out. You can't suddenly decide to play a bar totally differently to everybody else, because you're part of a section or part of an orchestra and there's never time to discuss with a hundred other people how that bar should go, and you're under one person who's telling you what to do. It's not that I don't think orchestral musicians are creative because of course they are, but they do have boundaries which they are not allowed to go beyond.

For most musicians, then, being creative is essentially synonymous with having the opportunity to express musical individuality, with feeling that you are putting something of yourself into the performance; and those situations which allow musicians more scope to do this are inevitably conceived of as being more creative than those where the musicians' actions are more rigidly governed by external factors, where they have less scope for expressing what they might conceive of as their particular interpretation of a phrase or piece.

Equally, although the ability to be creative and to have strong interpretive ideas is often seen as essential or at least desirable, there are many situations in which the ability to produce repeatedly competent if unspectacular performances becomes a significant and necessary quality. This is particularly true in situations such as, for example, a touring ballet, where the ability to reproduce the music night after night, without letting the standards slip, is what is required:

We need people who can produce a very good standard every time. And if people say to me, well it's just a Saturday matinee, I say, yeah, but the people who have paid their money, they're just as entitled to a good performance as the people who came to the first gala night. For them it's the first time. It sounds quite corny, but you've got to make it good, and treat it like it's got to be a special night for them, otherwise why are they going to want to come back? They're not interested that you've sat there seven times this week, that you're tired, that you're on tour, that your wife's left you. You've still got to do it, or go somewhere else.

West End shows make similar demands for much the same reasons:

You can't be like a jazz player and try and phrase it differently every night, that's not what's required. I suppose it's a bit like a pistol shooter – you've got to hit the bulls-eye every night. There's no wavering, you can't negotiate that.

Again, the soloistic tendencies cultivated in one's training, which in such cases might be manifested through taking the opportunity to try different interpretations on different evenings, must to some extent be reined in.

A different perspective on the same issue is provided by the deputy system. Here a musician must literally step into another musician's shoes, creating as little disturbance to the overall musical production as possible:

I always think deputizing for someone is a nil–nil draw – you go in and try not to be noticed. Obviously you've got to play the notes but it's great when other people say, 'Oh, I didn't realize you were in tonight.' That's a compliment, which in most other things would be an insult. You say, 'Great, so it must have sounded the same.' So you don't rock the boat.

In such cases the craft of being a musician lies not so much in imposing your own musical ideas upon the performance, but in being sensitive and capable enough to modify them to suit the occasion; this may in turn simply mean attempting to replicate somebody else's performance or to produce unspectacular but efficient performances night after night.

This ambivalence about the degree to which musical performance can be seen as creative is reflected in the scant literature on creativity among musicians, much of which, unsurprisingly perhaps, concentrates on composer figures rather than performers, with the latter being more often deemed interpreters. Indeed, if one were to take the perspective offered by Stravinsky and others, performers should in fact be regarded as nothing at all, merely vessels through which the music should flow, uninterrupted by any encumbrance arising from the performer's aspirations or opinions.[8] Schoenberg held a similar view, arguing that performers were totally unnecessary other than that they 'make the music understandable to an audience unfortunate enough not to be able to read it in print' (Newlin, 1980:164, cited in Cook, 2003:204). From such perspectives the composer as a heroic, god-like figure is writ large; his genius – and it is all too frequently 'his' – is laid out explicitly in the score, and woe betide any performer who seeks to think it might be in any way improved.

Leaving aside the debate as to the extent to which any score genuinely represents the composer's intentions, the evolution of the artist as hero is a peculiarly Romantic notion, developed largely over the course of the nineteenth century, yet one which has remained a powerful image throughout the twentieth century also. And not only in music, of course, but also in the visual arts, literature, drama and so on. In all cases these supreme individuals are seen as providing the fundamental objects, works, ideas or benchmarks upon which any particular tradition is predicated; such beliefs, inasmuch as they relate to musical creators, will be more closely examined in Chapter Six. Yet in our later, postmodern times several writers have taken a more flexible approach to notions of creativity, arguing that those qualities which mark a given artwork or event as innovative and significant cannot be determined solely through any particular characteristics ascribed to its creator, or, necessarily, only to the details of the work itself. Thus the traditional approach has been augmented in two particular ways. First, several writers have suggested that any artwork must be seen as a product of numerous inputs, not just that of the artist/originator to whom it is nominally assigned. Howard Becker, for example, in his examination of *Art Worlds* (1982) asserts that 'all artistic work, like all human activity, involves the joint activity of a number, often a large number, of people' (1), and that in examining the worlds which surround the creation of such works he was himself 'more concerned with patterns of cooperation among the people who make the works than with the works themselves or with those conventionally defined as their creators' (ix). Carl Rogers (1970:139) takes a similar view when, in advancing his own theory of creativity, he observes that 'the creative process is ... the emergence in action of a novel relational product, growing out of the uniqueness of the individual on the one hand, and the materials, events, people, or circumstances of his life on the other'. Thus, in both cases, the creator as hero becomes subsumed within a matrix of cultural dispositions and social influences, all of which indelibly leave their mark in some way on the finished work.

Furthermore, and notwithstanding the disparate forces which may lead to the creation of a particular work, the work itself makes its impact only at the point of reception, not during the process of production. In Roland Barthes's view, this privileges the latter event over the former, as he suggests in his influential essay on 'The Death of the Author' (1977:142–8). Although his emphasis here is on literary works, his ideas can be extended to artistic production of all kinds. Barthes's semiotic perspective leads him to conclude that any text can be understood only in terms of those other texts (broadly construed) which surround it; to examine it in its own terms or to seek its meaning simply as a product of its creator is not in fact to examine it at all. He writes that 'a text is not a line of words releasing a single "theological" meaning (the "message" of the Author–God) but a multi-dimensional space in which a variety of writings, none of them original, blend and clash. The text is a tissue of quotations drawn from the innumerable centres of culture' (146). Thus it is the reader who creates and gives meaning to the written work, and it is for that reason that 'the birth of the reader must be at the cost of the death of the Author' (148). I have already noted a similar idea in Chapter One, in relation to the construction of the ethnographic present, which, I argued, exists in a space between the author, the writer and the subject (see p.28). By extension, then, the meaning attributed to a non-literary cultural text, such as an act of musical performance, is not contained within any script on which such act may be predicated, nor indeed is it entirely evinced through any interpretation offered by the performer who enacts it; instead it may be seen as being construed to a considerable degree by those who receive the performance and whose discourse gives meaning to it, notwithstanding that such reception may indeed be influenced by the performer's work. Therefore, in seeking to determine the nature and significance of the creative act, we should pay more attention to its reception than to its production. Creativity is bestowed through retrospective appraisal. The assertion that a particular event is in some way creative or innovative becomes a socially validated response construed by others after the event. As Jason Toynbee (2003:103) puts it, 'creativity is manifested precisely through post hoc evaluation, a process of diffusion and reception that is cultural in the widest possible sense'. And this is as true of ephemeral events such as musical performances as it is of material works such as paintings, novels or scores.

Ultimately such observations have distinct parallels with the social ascription of musicality which I advocated at the beginning of Chapter Two. There I argued that to describe a particular performance as being 'very musical' or to declare that a given performer has 'innate musicality' in fact represents a social evaluation of the performance output of that individual: musicality is earned rather than learned. Thus, in the case of both creativity and musicality, what are commonly taken as inherent qualities of certain individuals and their work can in fact be read as socially mediated expressions of cultural preferences. Yet I suggest that it is the confluence of these two ideas, and by extension the implicit (and often explicit) proposition that to perform music, to be musical, is also by definition to be creative, which attracts many individuals – including myself – towards specializing in musical performance.

As a musician you're always creative because of what you are doing.

Furthermore, it is the degree to which such creative aspirations are (or are not) felt to be realized in the context of a given performance event which leads musicians to express their preferences for certain types of music-making over others, in order that they may conceive of themselves as a creative musician.

Yet, as I have already made clear, musicians do not regard everything they do as creative, and Elliott Jaques (1990) provides some insight into the potential frustrations musicians sometimes face when he characterizes the creative process as a type of work, albeit one which is clearly distinguishable from employment work. In marking the distinction between the two, he observes that 'creativity emerges from individuals finding or being given opportunities to work at their full level of capability', but that 'work becomes uncreative when people are underemployed; this is to say, when the level of work they are doing is beneath that which they could do' (vii); many musicians would, I think, identify with such assertions. From his particular psychoanalytical viewpoint Jaques lays considerable emphasis on the nature of the individual's internal world, suggesting that 'creativity ... is work whose direction and goals arise almost exclusively from the inner world of the individual rather than from external injunction or for external purposes' (viii), although this is not to suggest any contradiction with my earlier observations on post hoc external appraisal. Indeed Jaques makes clear that, whereas employment work is defined by 'an instruction from an employer, who inspects the final product and who must be satisfied if the employment is to continue' (171), creative work, although 'not at all externally prescribed' does evoke a response in the minds of others, and thus 'the creative artist requires that his external audience should also work' (171).

The distinction between these two types of work lies at the heart of the difficulties articulated by certain musicians in the orchestral context. Musicians want to feel as though they are being creative. More than this, as I have already shown, they are intensively trained to develop their inner world and to have strong conceptions of themselves as self conscious individuals, with particular creative agendas which they are able to call upon according to context. Frustrations arise, however, when in certain situations the final shape of the objects of their creation – their musical performances – are not entirely in their own hands, either because the musical production is so routine that there is little scope for alteration, or because it must be scrutinized and validated by others who may superimpose their own potentially conflicting agendas. Although smaller chamber ensembles can negotiate and manage conflicts within the group, in larger directed ensembles such as orchestras or theatre pit bands, the musician's work is frequently more subject to scrutiny from a conductor figure who may be said to represent symbolically (and on occasion literally) 'the employer', and whose aspirations prevail over those of the performer.

This is not to suggest that good conductors and orchestras are not aware of these issues. Many of them are, and as Jane Davidson has pointed out (with reference to Allmendinger *et al.*, 1994):

Contented orchestral members tend to be those who feel that they are valued, and more importantly, have sufficient time to prepare their repertoire, as well as to sustain and develop their playing technique ... The possibility for every individual to be heard seems vital for empowerment and motivational reasons ... Indeed ... there needs to be some acceptance of the role an individual has within a group. (Davidson, *et al.* 1997:218)

Continuing with these psychological perspectives, we must also return to Kemp's (1996) work on musicians' personalities. In his discussion of the Myers–Briggs inventory of personality traits, Kemp notes that musicians resemble 'judging types' rather more than they do 'perceptive types' (62),[9] yet it is the latter which are more directly linked with levels of creativity (61). This may appear paradoxical in the light of my assertions on the creative roles which musicians seek to ascribe for themselves. But it further demonstrates the degree of ambiguity one encounters in attempting to determine to what extent musical performance can be designated as a creative act. As Kemp himself observes:

> The question that, of course, arises in this context is whether the rank and file musician can be viewed as a creative type. Certainly, the disciplined and repetitious nature of much of the musician's working life, particularly as a professional performer, would seem to suggest an orientation towards judgment. However, when we come to study the more creative musician – the composer – we might expect to find a distinct move toward perception. (62)

Clearly there are degrees of creativity implicit in Kemp's observations, just as there are among the less rigorously argued evaluations made by musicians.

It is also worth noting in passing the slightly different approach to personality studies put forward by Michael Kirton in his book, *Adaptors and Innovators* (1989). Kirton's theory has a rather narrower focus than the traits inventory outlined by Myers and Kemp, and is designed to account for the different ways in which problem solving is achieved in organizational settings. In seeking solutions to problematic tasks, individuals can be described as either adaptors or innovators, according to the particular stratagems they employ. Kirton emphasizes that his theory is a measure of cognitive style, not cognitive level (26); that is, it is not that adaptors are *ipso facto* better or worse in any respect than innovators, it is simply that they achieve the required ends in rather different ways. Kirton believes this allows for more subtle distinctions within large groups which might otherwise be generalized as being by definition creative, or not. He writes:

> Many articles and manuals ... imply or state that artists and possibly architects are creative and engineers and possibly scientists are not. Examination of only a small range of ideas and artefacts from each field must show that such crude division is nonsense. People can be found who paint within the current paradigm with originality, taste and competence or with dull repetition or lack of skill. Those who paint in a style that breaks the current conventions may either (eventually) become famous or may be unable to persuade their neighbours to take their creations as a gift, much less hang them in their garages. Much the same goes for the other fields. (26)

It is noticeable that the list of qualities which Kirton ascribes to adaptors contains a number of traits identified by Kemp as being possessed by musicians. For example, Kirton suggests (31) that habitual adaptors are more introverted than innovators, and in this respect one might recall Kemp's observation that musicians can be described as 'bold introverts', as I noted previously; adaptors tend to have higher anxiety levels, and likewise Kemp (1996:106) notes relatively high levels of anxiety as a personality characteristic of musicians; Kemp (100–102) also observes that low self-esteem is often coupled with anxiety among musicians, and Kirton again notes this as characteristic of his adaptor type. Adaptors also demonstrate a reduced capacity for discharging positions of high status, and here we may recall Merriam's observation on the low status (or social rank) of musicians cross-culturally. This is, however, something which appears to be thrust upon them, rather than a position of their choosing, and thus may be less relevant here.

In other respects there are traits of the adaptor type which do not seem to be particularly applicable to musicians. According to Kemp (63–4), at least, musicians are not particularly conscientious, and would often be seen as 'undisciplined' and challenging rules and customs, all characteristics which Kirton (1989:8–9) sees more as representing the innovator type. Thus, while this typology does not neatly categorize musicians as being completely one or the other (which would in any case have been quite contrary to Kirton's intentions), it does provide a useful alternative perspective on the creative nature of musicians' activities; and I, at least, feel comfortable with the idea that classically trained musicians might frequently be recognized as adaptors (sometimes literally, in the sense of adapting somebody else's score for performance) rather than being described as true innovators; that is, they often demonstrate a preference for 'doing things better' rather than 'doing things differently' (see Kirton, 1989:7). That this does not represent a value judgment or an attempt to demean or reduce the importance of what they do, but is simply a different way of expressing the nature of their creative output, would, I think satisfy many musicians also.

We're artisans rather than artists. What an orchestral musician is doing is taking somebody else's creative idea which they put down as dots on paper and actually turning it into sound. So we're more like bricklayers – the architect would do the plan and then they actually put the bricks into place.

Although Kemp and Kirton tackle this issue from rather different angles, they both offer insights into the somewhat ambiguous issue of whether performing musicians may be described as creative, or to what extent they might describe themselves in this way. And from these different perspectives we can begin to understand the different types of creativity musicians must employ as part of their work, and the various roles they have to fulfil in different contexts. In the case of original works – new compositions or arrangements – they may well be part of the art world which creates the work, their skills and predispositions influencing the ultimate shape of the final artwork itself. With regard to the reconstitution of extant works, the degree to which they exercise control over the details of the performance obviously determines the nature of their creative involvement with that performance; this in turn affects the way in which that performance is perceived both symbolically, that is, the place allocated to it within a tradition of similar performance events, and aesthetically, that is, the way in which the audience responds to the music itself at the moment of production. And, by extension, musicians also play significant roles in determining the reception of the work: not only through generating aesthetic responses which lead individuals to evaluate how 'nice' or 'good' they feel the piece to be (or not), but also through the decisions the musicians make about whether and when to programme the work, in what contexts to perform it and with what other pieces, whether to record the piece, and so on, all of which affect the way the work is perceived by society at large. Thus the notion of creativity is something of a moveable feast. On the one hand, most musicians like to believe that what they do is creative, and that their performances are in some way emblematic of their individual musical qualities. On the other hand, many are quick to acknowledge that certain aspects of what they do are not, in fact, very creative, and simply require them to reproduce musical information in as straightforward a manner as possible, unfiltered, to a large extent, by their own interpretive ideas.

In the performing situations I have examined in these last two chapters, the small ensemble and the larger orchestra, I have tried to illuminate something of the nature of musical collaboration, the tensions inherent within such collaborations, the way in which individuals retain a sense of musical self within these environments, and how they conceive their position within and relationship to the larger social group. Implicit within this analysis is the idea that musical collaborations can be considered part of a continuum according to the degree of self-expression, otherwise construed as creativity, that musicians perceive themselves as having within specific performance situations. At one end of this hypothetical continuum are those events where the musician does not feel he or she is making a contribution which really reflects something of their own musical personality. For many, this would certainly include West End shows and particular types of commercial work, the essentially reproductive elements of professional music-making: turn up, play the dots, go home. At the other end would be those environments where musicians feel they are being called upon, not only to execute their purely technical skills, but also to have control over musical decisions and interpretive parameters which make available at a surface level internalized individual musical preferences. Like myself, I think for many musicians this would be certain types of solo work and chamber music in small groups; orchestral playing would come somewhere between these two poles.

Ultimately, perhaps, this model has some resonance with the musical axis of the model I advocated in Chapter Three (see Figure 1), since those events which a musician considers particularly important are likely to be those in which they also feel they make a significant contribution. But there are some differences; for example, I would still place my involvement in a contemporary music event somewhere to the right of this axis, as being for me particularly desirable or meaningful, even though my individual contribution to it may be relatively insignificant or moderated by a conductor, so that I may not in fact have a great deal of control over the ultimate musical output. But I would argue that, although these are models designed for the purpose of ethnographic analysis, the principles underlying them are significant considerations for musicians, and influence not only their choice of which engagements to undertake but also their assessments of their own contributions to those engagements. Yet through all of this assessment, negotiation and juxtaposition a sense of musical self prevails, a conception of their own individual qualities as musicians, in much the way that Anthony Cohen (1994:29) – following Ralph Turner – suggests that 'people are not just miniature reproductions of their societies … a person's experience of his or her engagement with the social structure gives rise to a "self-conception", a symbolisation of self which runs consistently through all of the person's activities'.

Notes

1   See, for example, Nettel (1948), Russell (1953), Ehrlich (1985), Stewart (1994), or Lawson (2003), among many others.
2   *Times Educational Supplement* 31 October 1997, p.1.
3   As I noted in Chapter Three, musicians remain freelance even when they are allied to one of the main symphony orchestras, although this is something of a technicality, given the fairly binding nature of the relationship between musician and orchestra. Only musicians working for the BBC orchestras and the opera houses have employed status.
4   Cited in Danziger (1995:7).
5   Cited in Danziger (1995:48).
6   The player with the highest social and musical rank within each instrumental group: first clarinet, first trumpet and so on.
7   Documentary broadcast, Channel 4 television, 24 January 1999.
8   Stravinsky's opinions on such issues can be found in numerous writings. For example, in his *Poetics of Music in the form of Six Lessons,* he observes that 'the sin against the spirit of the work always begins with a sin against its letter' (Stravinsky, 1947:124).
9   Kemp (1996:62) lists the various traits associated with these different types. Judging types are noted as being 'more decisive than curious', 'dislike unexpected happenings', 'are self regimented, purposeful, and exacting' among other things, whereas perceptive types tend towards the opposite characteristics, being 'masterful in handling unexpected happenings', 'flexible, adaptable, and tolerant', and so on. The full list is adapted from Myers (1993:75).

CHAPTER SIX

Myth and Humour

Introduction

In this chapter I shall consider the significant and related issues of myth and humour within the context of musicians' lives. I begin with a broad consideration of the role of myth in sustaining the whole edifice of Western art music, before looking at the impact of certain types of mythologies within the professional music world. I am not concerned here with the use of mythological tales as the basis for particular artworks (Wagner's 'Ring' Cycle; Tippett's *King Priam* and so on), but with a more anthropological perspective on the way in which particular composers and performers themselves become seen as quasi-mythological beings by those who 'believe' in the tradition of Western art music. I then examine musical stereotypes, the notions of which embody both myth and humour, before considering the various uses to which humour is put, and the ways in which it sustains the community of professional musicians who are the object of this study. Finally, I consider one particular category of musicians' humour – jokes about violas and their players – the abundance of which would seem to demand particular attention.

Myth

Michael Chanan's book, *Musica Practica,* opens with a whimsical sketch inspired by a nineteenth-century silhouette drawing which shows the great composers of the Western art music canon lining up in heaven to pay homage to their acknowledged master, Beethoven. Chanan fills out this picture with his suggestions of what the various composers might be discussing:

> Beethoven has accepted the honour with a mixture of satisfied self-esteem and humility, for he protests that 'Handel is the greatest of us all.' Handel, of course, won't hear of it; in any case he's too busy arguing with Verdi about Italian opera and nationalist politics which, cosmopolitan that he is, he barely understands ... Mendelssohn is somewhere in the middle of the queue, heatedly discussing the metaphysics of musical expression with Stravinsky ... Meanwhile, Wagner is sulking in a corner, peeved that the only person who nominated him for the seat of honour was Bruckner, yet even now Bruckner has wandered off somewhere, looking for Bach, to continue their yesterday's conversation about the monumental architecture of proper church music. Brahms is contentedly chatting in another corner with Charles Ives about polyphony, eager to learn as ever but completely bewildered. (Chanan, 1994:3–4)

As Chanan himself enquires: 'What is it about music that lends itself to such fantasies?' From this starting point he embarks on a wide-ranging sociohistorical review of Western musical practice, which takes in not only particular musical rudiments (notation, musical grammar, instrument technology and so on) but also how musical works are integrated into the social fabric: in short, the production and consumption of Western art music. Given his avowedly sociological perspective it is perhaps unsurprising that not only does he confine himself to Western music, but also he finds it necessary to ask the question, 'why does it seem so difficult to talk about music in social and historical terms?' (4); to which an ethnomusicologist might reasonably respond that this is not necessarily the case, it is simply that most musicological work on Western art music has chosen to leave the social and cultural aspects of the music conveniently undisturbed. This is not to denigrate Chanan's work, however, since he is himself in part concerned with addressing just these sorts of issues. But my purpose in introducing this part of it is not so much to give it the reasoned consideration it no doubt deserves, but, rather more superficially, because it conveniently links the two issues I wish to discuss in this chapter, that is, myth and humour. I have put them together because in certain important ways, and particularly in the contexts in which I wish to deal with them, I believe them to be related.

That I find Chanan's sketch humorous reveals certain things about my relationship with the Western art music canon and my perceptions of its more significant creators. The fact that I even recognize the names, that they are somehow meaningful to me, implies a connection between myself and this particular cultural tradition. In order to appreciate his joke I must share with Chanan the images presented to us of these composers; in some senses, therefore, we can both be considered 'believers' in this tradition. Bruno Nettl has written on this analogy between the 'Great Masters' and a pantheon of deities, suggesting that, in the Music Building of his paradigmatic Heartland School of Music, 'musical life is built on a group of widely articulated beliefs, mainly about composers, and these have something (but not necessarily much) to do with historical reality' (Nettl, 1995:19). Furthermore these beliefs lead to certain perceptions about both the musical and the personal nature of these 'demi-gods'. In particular, Nettl suggests that 'Mozart is the concept of genius who accomplishes without effort; Beethoven ... symbolizes great human achievement requiring enormous effort ... Other composers also have unique personalities, much like gods' (20). Such perceptions of these composers and others are necessary to enjoy Chanan's joke. The idea that Handel, the solid, baroque, eighteenth-century cosmopolitan, and Verdi, the romantic nineteenth-century Italian, might discuss Italian nationalism is faintly absurd, as is the idea of Brahms, the conservative, traditional German, debating the subject of polyphony with Ives, the mould-breaking American experimentalist. But in order to appreciate the humour one needs to believe in the images of these composers as both shared and propagated by other believers, including Chanan himself.

Such myths are perpetuated despite frequently being contradicted by musicological fact. We construe Mozart's music as being 'supremely beautiful', 'effortless', 'heavenly', despite knowing that the composer himself was a childish adulterer, given to scatological humour, and for whom composition was at times difficult and painful. Some perceive Delius as being one of the quintessential figures of English 'pastoral' music, notwithstanding that he was born among the dark, satanic mills of Bradford and spent most of his life in France. So in order to sustain these myths we employ a similar suspension of disbelief to that required when Jerry flattens Tom with a large brick, only for Tom to bounce up and start chasing him all over again; because we find Mozart's music beautiful we are encouraged to develop an image of him which fits this perception of his music, and we sustain this image despite its contradiction by objective reality.

In some senses these are large-scale or 'fundamental' myths shared by all those who believe in the tradition of Western art music; these are the creators upon whose apparently 'God-given' talents the whole tradition is predicated. But this is not to suggest that all composers are everywhere perceived similarly, nor that their relative hierarchies are always agreed upon. One only has to look at the broadcasting or concert schedules between different countries in which Western art music is performed to realize there is little unanimity about exactly who is important and who not; in particular, countries tend to give extra significance to those composers they feel most accurately reflect their own sense of national identity. Here the 'pantheon of deities' is amended for regional or national purposes, in much the same way as Frith argues that rock and pop music are globally shared but locally adapted.[1] It is still the case, for example, that works by Vaughan Williams and Elgar are much less frequently performed outside the British Isles than they are within.

On another tack, Nettl (1995:27) points out that for Americans it is Beethoven who is regarded as 'the quintessential great master of music. This is, after all, the culture in which hard work was once prized above all and labor rewarded; you weren't born to greatness, but were supposed to struggle to achieve it'. He goes on to suggest that, by contrast, it is Mozart, supposedly the genius who composed beautiful music entirely without effort, who is more highly esteemed in Europe, perhaps reflecting cherished European notions about monarchies, privileged elites and being born to be great (26). Nettl's distinction is rather too clear-cut for my liking, and he offers little empirical evidence to support it; but I enjoy the idea that he may be right, and I am prepared, literally, to 'believe' in his assertions.

Myth creation of this sort is, and I suspect always has been, allied to marketing and image-making. For example, I am on the mailing list of several in-house magazines from music publishers, all of which have a section giving information on forthcoming anniversaries of significant dates (births or deaths) for composers for whom they control copyright material; these are intended to persuade those responsible for concert programming to make a feature of one or another composer on the basis that 'we must celebrate his (or her) work in this significant anniversary year'. Like Hollywood film stars, a composer really needs to be dead before myth creation can begin in earnest.

This perception of the demi-god nature of composers is further reinforced by the reverence given to the places they lived, the artefacts they used, and of course to the original musical manuscripts they left behind. There are numerous buildings all over Europe which, having at some stage been inhabited by one composer or another, have been turned into shrine-like museums, often displaying the said composer's original desk, or quill, or better still piano, so that those devotees who have made the necessary pilgrimage can admire them with suitably awed expressions. Nor is such reverence confined to the great masters of the distant past: the Arnold Schoenberg Centre in Vienna currently maintains a reconstruction of the great man's office, with all the necessary articles imported from California (to which he had emigrated in the 1930s) some time after his relatively recent death in 1951.

Manuscripts are given particular significance as hallowed objects, because of their symbolic as well as their practical importance. A recent example culled from a national British newspaper explicitly demonstrates this parallel with a supernatural belief system. Having chanced upon a score containing Mahler's own handwritten revisions to his First Symphony, the musicologist who discovered it in an Israeli academy was quoted as saying, 'I got shivers down my spine … I was really shaking. I realised that I had given a lecture on Mahler's First Symphony, holding his own score. This was something sacred.'[2] And the potential sanctity of the manuscript was further underlined by the newspaper's headline suggesting that the score might be 'worth millions'; clearly the desirability of owning such an item can be conceived in monetary terms, notwithstanding – or perhaps because of – its quasi-religious importance. That the annotated manuscript of a dead Austrian composer should make headline news in Britain, after being discovered in Israel and validated with reference to scholars in Paris and America, reveals a great deal about the widespread diffusion of this quasi-belief system.

While these images of composers are necessarily shared in some way by all Western art music aficionados, they are perhaps more keenly felt by those professionals whose job it is to recreate the texts left by the Great Masters and present them to the other followers: the musicians, conductors and administrators who, through the presentation of their regular concerts, simultaneously acknowledge and reinforce these myths. To some degree this is a by-product of planning and programming, since it is for these musicians to produce coherent programmes in which the competing claims of particular Masters are presented sympathetically. This leads to beliefs that certain composers complement each other better than others, beliefs which are only partly founded on distinctions in musical style, and which further reinforce notions of what these composer's works might 'mean' or represent.

Furthermore, and perhaps more significantly in the present context, it is also through these musical performances that certain performers themselves become elevated into quasi-mythical figures, and again this is as much a historical phenomenon as a present-day one. Liszt and Paganini provide ready examples of performers who, in their day, were so revered they were credited with having god-like (or, in Paganini's case, devil-like) powers. Today conductors have joined this trend, with certain individuals promoted, largely by record companies, into superstars whose interpretations of 'The Great Composers' are deemed to be particularly meaningful. Norman Lebrecht's exposé of the shadowy world of the international conductor superstar clearly reveals this in its title: *The Maestro Myth* (1991). Modern performers are very aware of the power of image and marketing, and it is worth noting that one British violinist recently emerging from his 'retirement' (aged 41) has made it known that he now wishes to be known only by his surname, Kennedy, without the use of any first name. The Kafka-esque overtones[3] have already been noted by certain music journalists, but they have missed, I think, the similarity with another recent musical demi-god, the conductor known universally (although not officially) as Karajan.

Performers, however, do not seem to have the same longevity as mythical beings as composers. I suspect that the general listening public no longer recalls the great virtuosi of the eighteenth and nineteenth centuries (with the obvious exceptions of those like Liszt and Paganini who are also remembered as composers) because their performances can only be relayed to us through the writings of others, and therefore have considerably less meaning than those we are able to experience for ourselves. But even in this century, when performances may be preserved as recorded sound, it would appear that a performer's importance diminishes after his or her death. Of course, we do sometimes hear their work again, occasionally resurfacing as recordings of historical interest or on specialist radio programmes, but such recordings seem insignificant compared to the marketing hype put behind the most recent version of Brahms's violin concerto, perhaps, by the latest young star. So there appears to be a contrast between, on the one hand, those who provide the primary texts of the tradition – composers – who may remain in relative obscurity during their lifetimes and only achieve notable significance after their deaths, and, on the other hand, those who interpret these texts – performers – who may achieve considerable importance during their lifetime, but which gradually diminishes after their death. It is only fair to say, however, that this is rather a subjective impression for which I offer no empirical evidence.

Yet it would appear that even within Western society there remains an implication that musicians have some kind of secret or mythical powers. Lévi-Strauss, in *The Raw and the Cooked* (a book which relies on musical structures and metaphors a great deal in its exploration of mythology), writes:

We do not understand the difference between the very few minds that secrete music and the vast numbers in which the phenomenon does not take place, although they are usually sensitive to music. However, the difference is so obvious, that we cannot but suspect that it implies the existence of very special and deep-seated properties ... [and] since [music] is the only language with the contradictory attribute of being at once intelligible and untranslatable, the musical creator is a being comparable to the gods, and music itself the supreme mystery of the science of man. (Lévi-Strauss, 1986:18)

Similarly, Susan McClary suggests that our musical world is frequently perceived as being divided between 'a priesthood of professionals who learn principles of musical order' and 'a laity of listeners who respond strongly to music but have little conscious critical control over it'. This laity, being unable to account explicitly for the way in which music affects them, behave as though the process was indeed mystical, and thus refuse 'to attribute to mere mortals the power to move them so' (McClary, 1987:16–17).

Both Lévi-Strauss and McClary, I suspect, are more concerned here with composers – the creators – than performers, who are more frequently cast in the role of re-creators. But these assertions that musicians are in some way 'other worldly' would appear to have a direct relationship with the psychological profiles which performers cultivate. Kemp has shown that musicians develop personalities which are taken by the rest of society as making them qualitatively different from 'ordinary' people. He suggests that pathemia[4] is a significant component of their personality, one which is revealed by high levels of sensitivity and imagination. Yet these traits are, paradoxically, internalized and obscured from others, so that musicians 'conceal the very thing that motivates them most highly, thus obscuring their *raison d'être* and rendering them somewhat enigmatic to others' (Kemp, 1996:84). Such behaviour not only marginalizes them within society (because those around them cannot see what it is that drives them) but also contributes to the assessment of them as having apparently magical powers. Thus there would appear to be a clear link, even within our own largely urban Western society, between the powerful and mysterious emotions that music can evoke in us (a process which, despite all our technological advances, we still have trouble explaining) and our perception that those who produce the musical sounds which give rise to these affects are themselves mysterious, enigmatic, social 'others'.

But equally of interest here are those myths and stories that evolve among musicians themselves in the course of their work, and which frequently involve extreme situations or heroic (used in a very broad sense) deeds of one of their own, even if the names of the individuals involved are long forgotten. Such stories, while not woven together sufficiently to be considered a belief system proper, provide a shared history which supplies musicians themselves with images of the more colourful or deviant behaviour patterns which they feel in part characterize them as a group; equips aspiring professionals with images of the way they think professional musicians behave; and furnishes non-musicians, such as journalists or authors, with stereotypical images of musicians' behaviour which can be subsequently regurgitated to a wider public, thus reinforcing such stereotypes. The following quotations exemplify this kind of myth-making. They are taken from a short, quasi-autobiographical book by Basil Howitt, an experienced freelance cellist who worked for more than 20 years with a small Manchester ensemble called the Manchester Camarata:

> I must resist all temptation to spread scandal by including here the wilder, more colourful drink-related cameos from my touring collection ... all night parties with unmentionable consequences in one of Europe's poshest hotels; a ravishing but far-gone and fickle hornist banging on a violist's door in the middle of the night and screaming for his services; the first ever infidelity of a quattrogenarian fiddler ... One might be pleading for a sub on his pay after blueing in [*sic*] all his subsistence money in Lisbon or Hong Kong on the first night of a tour (ask no more); another might have roughed up a hotel room during a party which got out of hand in Frankfurt. (Howitt, 1993:32–3)

I have no doubt that such descriptions are based on real events, and any musician, including myself, would be able to recall a number of similar episodes in which musicians are seen as deviating from behavioural norms. My own favourites include a trombonist 'flying' an inflatable (and inflated) sex doll through the skylight of a coach as it travelled down a German autobahn, and the musician who fell into a drunken sleep in the greenhouse of the country residence where he was working, thus missing most of the performance for which he had been employed. Indeed it is noticeable that such anecdotes frequently involve sex or alcohol, twin attributes of 'deviant' behaviour which musicians often attribute to themselves, and which will resurface below. Stories of this kind become detached from these real events and evolve into part of a shared mythology of the musician's craft. This in turn creates stereotypes which aspiring musicians use as role models:

> One violinist said to me: 'There's a lot of folklore attached to music, and people who play brass instruments are seemingly expected to behave in a certain way, therefore when they're trying to get on in the profession they do behave in that way, and then spend the rest of their lives trying to live it down, to some extent.' A trumpet player said, similarly: 'I think these impressions are made on you when you're at college; I think there's a certain pressure on you to live up to a brass player's reputation.' (Brearley, 1991:12)

I suggested above that myth and humour are in some ways connected and this seems clearly demonstrated in this mythologizing of certain specific events. Anecdotes which begin: 'Guess what happened to so-and-so the other night?' or 'I remember when ... ' become embellished in their retelling, so that over time the original event becomes not only magnified or exaggerated for the purposes of greater impact, giving these events and the participants in them a quasi-mythical status, but also part of a large stock of jokes and stories, the sharing of which among musicians fosters a sense of common heritage and group identity. This in turn leads to the creation of stereotypes both about musicians generally and about particular categories of musician. Consider the following descriptions of three brass players from Jilly Cooper's novel, *Appassionata*:

> Victor (Viking) O'Neill – First Horn and hero of the orchestra because of his great glamour, glorious sound and rebellious attitude. The godfather of the Celtic Mafia; Blue Donovan – Second Horn of the RSO – blue-eyed Irishman of great charm, who covers for Viking O'Neill both on the platform and in real life; Dixie Douglas – A Glaswegian hunk, whose light duties as an RSO trombone player leave him rather too much time to hell-raise and troublemake. Another member of the Celtic Mafia. (Cooper, 1996:xx–xxiv)

And it is perhaps in this concept of stereotyping, and of course in the nature of the stereotypes themselves, that myth and humour become most closely entwined.

Stereotypes

Stereotypes constitute a significant base for humour yet, like myth, they belong within the category of beliefs. Gould and Kolb suggest that the word 'stereotype':

> Denotes beliefs about classes of individuals, groups, or objects which are 'pre-conceived', i.e. resulting not from fresh appraisals of each phenomenon but from routinized habits of judgement and expectation ... A stereotype is a belief which is not held as an hypothesis buttressed by evidence but is rather mistaken in whole or in part for an established fact. (Gould and Kolb, 1964:694)

Thus stereotypes, like the perceptions of composers to which I referred above, require a certain suspension of disbelief; we persist in stereotyping even when confronted with evidence which defies or contradicts the stereotypical image created. Stereotypes require exaggeration, a distortion of traits which may be founded in objective reality and thus recognized as being 'real', yet exaggerated so that these traits become caricatured. For this reason, however, humour derived from stereotypical images impinges on many of the areas covered elsewhere in this study, since musicians' humour naturally draws extensively on qualities and characteristics of musicians' lives, on their concepts of 'musician-ness'.

Most of the work concerning stereotyping of musicians has come from psychologists, and particularly from those interested in the study of personality. Some, such as Davies (1976) and Lipton (1987), have concentrated on perceptions of orchestral groupings (brass, wind, strings, percussion), while others, such as Abeles and Porter (1978) and Bell and Cresswell (1984), have examined instrumental stereotyping among younger people; Kemp (1981a, 1981b, 1996) has been particularly interested in the relationship between personality and instrumental choice. Given this large body of work done by others, from which I have cited only a few sources, I will not go into detail on the correlation of stereotypical images and observed behaviour, but there are a few points worth making.

First, most studies attempt to establish the authenticity of stereotypical models, that is, how closely the traits attributed to one particular musical group actually reflect the personalities of that group. For my purposes, however, what is more significant is that musicians *believe* these models or images to be true, regardless of empirical fact. As I mentioned above, suspension of disbelief is an important element in sustaining these stereotypes. I know a number of trumpet players who do not in any way fit the stereotypical image of yobbish, drunken brass players, but that does not prevent me from cracking jokes at their expense, based on our shared understanding of the stereotype. Viola players are frequently the butt of jokes in which they are portrayed as incompetent idiots, even by those who work alongside them every day and know this is not the case.

It does get on my nerves sometimes, especially if we're working with somebody we don't know, and I might say something which is a bit silly, and then somebody will say 'Oh, he's a viola player, just, you know ...' It suddenly colours, I feel, the way somebody might respond or think of me. And I think that is then quite dangerous because ... well it's untrue and it's not fair in a way. Why should I have to suffer because of some historical joke? But I mean in the right context you just laugh it off, you know, it's fine. I think most viola player jokes are made up by violists actually ...

Second, stereotyping of others generally concentrates on negatively perceived attributes rather than positive ones. From a cross-cultural perspective, Apte (1985:127) observes that 'some traits have been found to evoke universal negative reactions, and these tend to be assigned to any group that is to be ridiculed and mocked'. It is therefore unsurprising that, in describing other instrumentalists, musicians are more prone to use words such as 'arrogant', 'neurotic', 'loud' or 'insensitive', whereas, when describing themselves words such as 'sensitive', 'friendly' or 'fun' become more apparent (see Lipton, 1987:89).

Finally, whereas much work has been done on the perceived differences between different groups of instrumentalists, this has not been further pursued to discover whether comparable traits persist among similar instrumentalists drawn to different musical styles. I have already shown that musicians in London evolve their self-conception not only according to the instrument they play but also according to the musical style(s) in which they prefer to participate. It is likely that I know a number of trumpet players who do not conveniently fit the stereotypical image because many of my contacts are within the field of contemporary music, which requires, I believe, a different type of commitment to that needed to play in a show. Most studies have concentrated on orchestras, perhaps because these present a convenient bounded unit within which to work. But stereotypes of musicians do exist, based on the musical genre in which they are perceived to specialize; those in early music are sometimes referred to as the 'open-toed sandal brigade' or the 'wholemeal bread lot'. I well remember being privy to a backstage conversation between the classical music critic of a national newspaper and a clarinet player with whom I was doing an opera. On hearing that my colleague most enjoyed working with a particular, largely self-taught composer, the critic, both surprised and dismissive, responded: 'Well, yes ... but that's *jazz* isn't it?' Similarly the show-musician/jazz-musician joke I introduced in Chapter Three depends for its effect on perceived notions of the qualities possessed by musicians working in these fields. Musical stereotyping, therefore, is not confined only to instrumental groups but can arise from perceptions, again with negative connotations, of musicians heavily engaged in one or other of the various areas of the musical marketplace.

Myth and humour can be seen as being related in another way because they are both significant identity referents. By this I mean that they can both be regarded as components through which individuals, groups, cultures and/or societies construct identities for themselves. In the case of myths we can see that, for example, subscribing to the Islamic faith and the belief system this implies clearly distinguishes a person from their Christian neighbour, notwithstanding that geographically and culturally they may in other ways be similar, as is the case, for example, between Greek and Turkish Cypriots. Even among those professing the same broad faith we can often discern enough differences of religious belief to form the basis of serious disagreements, as in Northern Ireland. Humour, too, is a great 'identifier'. The ability to get a joke relies on a number of factors, such as linguistic competence, cultural proficiency and shared experience, all of which quickly contribute to group identities. Broadly speaking, if you get the joke you're potentially 'in'; if you don't, you may well be 'out'.

Furthermore, possessing a sense of humour can be a significant component of the stereotypes we construct both of ourselves and of others. English people see themselves as having a strong (if idiosyncratic) sense of humour; they are less willing to invest this quality in their stereotypical images of Scots or Germans, for example. Similarly, several musicians noted that they felt having a sense of humour was an important part of being a musician and, on the few occasions when I mentioned my studies of humour among musicians, they frequently agreed that it played a notable role.

I shall consider some of this in more detail below, but I shall begin examining the use of humour among musicians with a brief overview of certain theoretical concepts.

Humour

The study of humour has perhaps been rather neglected in the anthropological literature. While some studies have been made on joking relationships (Radcliffe-Brown, 1940, 1949; Reynolds, 1958) and clowns or tricksters (Evans-Pritchard, 1967; Carroll, 1981), much of the academic research in this area has again come from psychologists, who tend to approach the subject from the perspective of the individual rather than the group. Only one account (Apte, 1985) attempts a broad anthropological overview, synthesizing information culled from disparate sources.[5] I have been drawn to the subject here, however, since my professional experience suggested to me that jokes, humour generally, and an individual sense of humour, were very important for myself and the musicians I work with. Reflecting upon it now I realize that it is indeed a significant element in the socialization of musicians, and is inherent within many of the other areas I have covered in this study: it is used in constructing both group and individual identities, in the assessment of musicianship and musicality, and it is directly related to the arena of play in which I shall position music performance events in Chapter Seven.

Analysing humour, however, can be problematic. General humour, playing about, light-hearted banter, are all to some extent liminal activities. Being themselves frequently unstructured they exist in the margins of conventional social behaviour, and can be difficult to pinpoint. Certain types of humour, formal joke patterns for example, can be found by asking informants, in books, and from other sources such as the Internet, although, being part of an oral tradition, they are best appreciated in context. But spontaneous humour, frequently more revealing, has to be experienced. You have to be there to get the joke, and once the moment is passed it is often forgotten by everybody. Humour functions as a social lubricant and, like most lubricants, we notice its absence rather more than its presence. There can also be the problem of 'getting the joke'. Observing something that others find funny is not at all the same as being amused by the joke yourself, and this is perhaps another perspective on the advantages and disadvantages of being a native anthropologist. For this reason many of the examples I shall give here are drawn directly from my own experience, although I have tried to incorporate the experience of others where I can.

The most comprehensive and influential theory of humour is that put forward early in the twentieth century by Sigmund Freud, who suggested that jokes[6] function in a similar way to dreams, in that both rely on three techniques:

transformation, in which thought-material is transformed from the optative (Oh! if only ...) to the present indicative (it is); condensation, in which material is extensively compressed so that elements within it may carry multiple meanings; and displacement, whereby 'things that lie on the periphery of the dream-thoughts and are of minor importance occupy a central position and appear with great sensory intensity in the manifest dream, and vice versa' (Freud, 1960:163–4). But whereas dreams remain in the unconscious, evoked later only by a recollection of the dream itself, jokes confront the inhibitions our consciousness seeks to impose upon them. In Freud's own words:

> Jokes do not, like dreams, create compromises; they do not evade the inhibition, but they insist on maintaining play with words or with nonsense unaltered. They restrict themselves, however, to a choice of occasions in which this play or this nonsense can at the same time appear allowable ... thanks to the ambiguity of words and the multiplicity of conceptual relations. (Ibid.:172)

This brief *résumé* does little credit to Freud's complex argument,[7] but the significant point is that humour represents a clash between the conscious and the unconscious, with the consequence that conscious control fails to dominate unconscious will. Mary Douglas (1975:96) neatly summarizes this as 'the juxtaposition of a control against that which is controlled, this juxtaposition being such that the latter triumphs'. Douglas further points out that this resonates comfortably with Henri Bergson's (1950:29) definition of humour as 'something mechanical encrusted on something living'. In both cases, she suggests, 'the essence of the joke is that something formal is attacked by something informal, something organized and controlled, by something vital, energetic, an upsurge of life for Bergson, of libido for Freud' (Douglas, 1975:95).

Like Douglas, I find Freud's definition of humour very satisfying, and although he intended it as an explanation of the way humour works in the individual rather than in groups, it provides a neat model to explain one widespread and popular genre of musicians' jokes and stories, those which involve 'conductor-baiting'. Musicians are notoriously ambivalent in their attitude to conductors, respectful of very few, hating many, merely grudging towards others. One eminent, mild-mannered and in many ways very gentlemanly wind player, who had recently retired from a major orchestra in which for many years he was a permanent fixture, suggested to me that, when the internationally renowned Musical Director of the orchestra died, he would happily 'dance on his grave'. As I noted previously, the control exerted by conductors over musicians can lead to significant frustrations for the individuals involved; these are partially relieved through the creation and dissemination of stories in which the authority of the conductor is undermined.

And there's a story about, I think it was the third horn player in the Covent Garden orchestra with Bernard Haitink, I think it was Bernard Haitink. He was coming to the end of a rehearsal and he put his hand up and said, 'Maestro, in the third act [he mimes taking up a large and heavy score] *scene 5* [mimes looking through many pages] *bar 678* [more miming] *third note in ... it's a wonderful moment, isn't it?'*

We were doing an opera in Germany once, and the director insisted that all questions were to be asked in German. We weren't allowed to speak English. And so the horn players, bless their hearts, they're fantastic, as soon as they wanted to ask a question they'd go [he mimics a Hitler moustache and a Nazi salute] *'Entschuldigen!' You just find little ways, it's a kind of resistance.*

The pattern of the controlling conductor triumphed over by that which is controlled, the musicians themselves, is blatant. And of course in this case the conductor does not just control musical dimensions but is also superior in terms of recognition, rank and economic reward, making the musician's victory taste doubly sweet.

Conductor-baiting is not only practised by hard-pressed London orchestras but seems a world-wide phenomenon and, thanks to the technology of the Internet, such jokes can be widely disseminated. The following few lines, taken from a collection covering several pages, are attributed to Eugene Ormandy, for many years musical director of the Philadelphia Orchestra in the USA, and were presumably collected (or, conceivably, fabricated) by musicians in that orchestra. They appear, however, on a website maintained by the New Zealand Symphony Orchestra:[8]

I'm conducting slowly because I don't know the tempo.
I guess you thought I was conducting, but I wasn't.
Did you play? It sounded very good.
That's the way Stravinsky was – Bup, bup, bup – The poor guy's dead now: play it legato.
This is a very democratic organisation, so let's take a vote. All those who disagree with me, raise their hands.

One final conductor story takes in an important component of humour: language. I had heard this story several times over the years, although until it occurred in an interview I had never heard any names attributed to it:

I'll tell you a really good true story which I like, which is Celibidache [a Romanian] *conducting the LSO. They were totally messing around and it was really starting to wind him up. And in the end he'd just had enough, and he put his baton down and said, 'You lot think I know fuck nothing, but I know fuck all!'*

In order to get the joke, of course, one needs to know that the English expression 'fuck all' actually means 'nothing', quite the opposite of what was intended. The linguistic competence which in this case Celibidache seems to have lacked is one of two, or perhaps three, components necessarily prerequisite for the appreciation of all verbal humour. I say perhaps three, because Delia Chiaro (1992:13) suggests that another component, in addition to linguistic competence, is the ability to understand the poetic use of language, which she defines as 'the ways in which linguistic options can be maneuvered in order to create a desired effect'. I would not take issue with a linguist on such matters, but for my purposes I am prepared to see them as different aspects of language expertise. However I would agree with her that, in addition to such expertise, the remaining component needed to appreciate jokes is sociocultural competence; in order to understand humour one needs to be conversant with the social and cultural concepts or issues contained within or implied by the word-play. The following viola joke, a significant category of musician's humour to which I shall return below, seems to exemplify this:

Q: How do you keep your violin from being stolen?
A: Put it in a viola case.

For this to be funny one has to know that violin and viola cases are similar, that violinists and violists have a traditional rivalry in which violinists and their instruments are portrayed as superior to violists and violas, and that violas and their players are the target of a large number of jokes, in which they are continually portrayed as worthless, stupid or ignorant. Change the instruments (clarinet/oboe, trumpet/horn) and the joke is lost. A considerable amount of sociocultural decoding is required to appreciate the content, and unless one has acquired the knowledge or experience necessary for this decoding the joke remains meaningless. It is only through this shared knowledge and experience that humour can be appreciated, and it is this which makes humour such an effective identity referent and why I think it plays an important role in the socialization of musicians.

Humour appears to underpin identities at many different levels, not least of which is the fundamental concept of *being* a musician, and the image musicians have of themselves as a group.

You know the saying that all dogs are like their owners? Well, there's a professor who wants to put this to the test and try and prove this theory, so he gets together an architect and his dog, a bank manager and his dog, and a musician and his dog. There's this little room set up with a pile of bones in the middle of the room. And the first dog is led into the room, and the first dog to go in is the architect's dog. The architect's dog builds a nice little kennel and sits in it. Experiment successful, led to the corner of the room, and told to sit

and stay. The next dog to go in is the bank manager's dog. The bank manager's
dog goes in and stacks all the bones in neat piles of ten around the room.
Experiment successful, led to the corner of the room and told to sit and stay.
The last dog to go in is the musician's dog. And the musician's dog goes in,
eats all the bones, fucks the other two dogs, and then says, 'How much am I
getting paid for this gig in any case?' I quite like that joke.

The self-image presented here appears to resonate comfortably with that part of
Merriam's paradigm which suggests that musicians have licence to deviate
from behavioural norms (Merriam, 1964:140). Whereas architects build houses
and bank managers deal with accounting, musicians are presented as being
concerned with eating, sex and getting paid. Stereotypes, as I mentioned above,
exaggerate the truth, but the joke reveals traits seen as belonging to musicians:
'this is us'; this is the subjective reality of being a member of this particular
group, regardless of whether or not this reality is supported empirically. Equally
revealing is that the musician who told me this joke was rather surprised when
I pointed out its self-deprecatory nature, as he had not considered it in that way.
But to me it does reveal a low self-esteem which is not necessarily apparent in
answers to direct questions such as 'Do you think our society values the role of
the musician?', when musicians generally try and present themselves in a rather
better light. So again we might read into this a clash between the conscious and
the unconscious; between, on the one hand, a surface representation which
argues that the work musicians do is important and valued, and, on the other, a
subconscious assessment of the musician's role, manifested through humour,
which appears to contradict or undermine this image.

Self-deprecation, however, is a recurring theme in musicians' humour,
particularly when it occurs spontaneously rather than in jokes contained within
formal patterns. And it seems often used to reinforce identities, not only in the
large-scale sense mentioned above, but also in sustaining sociomusical
identities on a smaller scale. For example, most saxophone players, because of
the work available to them in shows, will normally also play either clarinet or
flute. In fact, many will play all three but will generally consider themselves
stronger on one or the other of the second instruments. This can lead to some
disparagement of their own abilities on the third instrument. Among my own
colleagues, most of whom are saxophone/clarinet players, we make gentle fun
of our abilities on the flute through statements such as 'which end do I blow?',
'a fully paid-up member of the flute-owner's club', 'the flute's not a real
instrument, anyway', and so forth. There are several purposes to this self-
ridicule; firstly, we acknowledge our shared experiences as non-expert flute
players, strengthening the social bonds between us; secondly, we reinforce
both to ourselves and to others our own perceptions of our musical strengths
and weaknesses; and thirdly, by ridiculing our abilities before anybody else
does we provide a measure of self-protection in the event of being asked to

play difficult music on an instrument we feel least proficient on: 'it won't hurt if you laugh at me because I laughed at myself first'. This kind of self-deprecation is soon learned by those attempting careers as professional musicians. Gentle self-mocking is a widespread characteristic of musicians, and those who practise it are more quickly accepted into the various sociomusical groupings than those who are boastful or overconfident.

Both the linguistic and the sociocultural components of humour can be utilized to underpin identities of musical subgroups, which may in turn provide social and musical commentaries on both the group undertaking the joking and other groups, musical and non-musical. By this I mean that groups develop humorous anecdotes and witty comments which are meaningful only to the members of that group, either because other musicians did not share the experience giving rise to the anecdote or because the verbal construction may appear nonsensical to those unable to decode it; all these shared experiences contribute to the group's idioculture, as I noted at the end of Chapter Four. For example, in my quartet we continue to refer to one of our earliest rehearsals, undertaken while we were still students. It was somebody's birthday, and to celebrate this another of us had brought along a large bottle of whisky. As the rehearsal progressed, the amount of merriment increased in inverse proportion to the whisky left in the bottle. Eventually the charade of rehearsing was abandoned, with all of us in paroxysms of laughter, completely unable to play. Even now, fifteen years later, quips will be made in rehearsals about 'being on the whisky again' or 'bringing a bottle next time', reinforcing the identity of the group through the collective recollection of shared experience, expressed as humour.

As an example of a verbal construction contributing to group identity while also providing a musical commentary on others, I shall explain a term which again has arisen within the quartet, the origins of which also lie somewhere back in the deep mists of our shared history and which I no longer recall. The term in question is 'quasi fairer'. The first word, 'quasi', is a standard musical expression meaning 'like', 'as if' or 'approximately', and is generally found in conjunction with a noun or adjective to indicate a manner of playing: 'quasi allegro' would mean 'almost fast'; 'quasi arpa', 'play like a harp' and so on. However, allied to the word 'fairer', it means nothing outside our group and would be taken as nonsense not only by the world at large but also by other musicians. The second word in fact alludes to the name of another saxophone group whose collective sound and style of playing we would describe as 'very straight', 'bland' or 'without edge', whereas our subjective perception of our own playing would use words like 'gritty', 'focused' or, rather more colloquially, 'ballsy'. So the joking use of the term 'quasi fairer' clearly exemplifies Freud's condensation leading to multiple meanings; it again reinforces the social bonds existing within the group, since only we are likely to get the joke; it underpins our sense of group identity by differentiating this musical group from another which, having the same instrumentation, is superficially similar; and, simultaneously, it implies a musical judgment of both groups which says 'they play and sound like that, but we play and sound like this', and which also relates to our internalized conceptions of how we think the group should sound.

It is to be expected, of course, that any group of people working frequently and closely together share experiences which develop into linguistic idiosyncrasies and which in turn are incorporated as part of a general verbal repertoire; and the longer and more intense the relationships, the more extensive the intra-group language code is likely to be. This is over and above the technical language arising from occupational situations which are referred to as 'registers' by sociolinguists, and which are as applicable to musicians as they are to lawyers or doctors.[9] For freelance musicians, however, these shared experiences, condensed into witty remarks, reinforce identities among semi-permanent groups such as my quartet; furthermore, within the ever-shifting network of connections that make up freelance musical life in London, where musicians are frequently called upon to perform together in ad hoc groups but may not then see each other for some time, such expressions and similar anecdotes serve to create a temporary bond by illuminating a shared past, as well as lubricating the process of social interaction which is such an important part of professional musical life.

Having digressed momentarily into the world of sociolinguistics it is worth noting the occasional incidence of 'code switching', whereby people move between different forms of language (for example, informal as opposed to formal) according to social context. Most musicians converse in relatively familiar terms most of the time, and such behaviour is reinforced by the frequent use of humour, which is universally expressed in less formal speech (see Apte, 1985:193–6). Certain situations reveal more formal patterns of speech, however, such as initial teacher–pupil relationships, although these generally become less formal as familiarity increases. One notable exception is the frequent use of the word 'maestro' by orchestral musicians speaking to conductors of significant rank. The use of this word (literally 'master' in Italian) is not only a convenient universal term by which to address conductors of various nationalities, but also, naturally, underlines the differing social and musical ranks between musicians and conductors, which is perhaps why certain conductors insist on the term being used. Having this association the term does occasionally surface between musicians themselves, imbued with sarcasm, for the purpose of humorously deflating swelling egos.

Another perspective on the conversational familiarity that occurs between musicians is provided by the idea of joking relationships. In some pre-industrial societies institutionalized joking relationships are established which arise from kin-based relationships within the social structure, for example between a man and his wife's sisters, or between opposite sexes of different generations.[10] In industrial societies, however, joking relationships may arise, as I have already suggested, as expressions of various types of group identity, and admittance to these diverse social groups is subject to negotiations which may partly be pursued through joking. Apte summarizes this as follows:

> Acceptance of a person's joking is an indication that he or she is part of the social group. When any new person is introduced to a social group, the members generally maintain some distance and evaluate the new individual ... A newcomer may be only gradually accepted in the group, and an individual who makes an attempt to join in by self-deprecatory joking has better chances of being included. On the other hand, the exclusion of newcomers despite their persistent attempts to participate in the joking behavior may indicate that they are being denied entry into the group and the group identity that comes with it. In other words, joking relationships and joking itself serve as screening procedures for membership, especially in small groups, and also help define and redefine the boundaries of differentiated social groups. (Apte, 1985:54–55).

Such non-institutionalized joking relationships, which inevitably become more established between people who have known one another for some time, are an important part of the socialization of musicians. Not only do they create identities among certain subgroups of the community in the way I have already described, but they also reinforce in a more general way the bonds existing between community members so as to illuminate the shared experiences they have undergone, and particularly the experience of musical performance. Apte (51) notes that wars often produce 'war buddies', groups of people who become close because of their shared traumatic experiences. I suggest this is analogous to musical performance. In Western society, professional musical performance is acknowledged as a particularly stressful event.[11] Standards are very exacting and, for freelance players, which most musicians are, there is always the underlying fear that too many mistakes may result in lost work, reduced reputation and, therefore, diminished income. The result of these collective fears is that groups of musicians who go through these kinds of stressful occasions together do form bonds which become reinforced through shared jokes. I have noticed this during many shared car journeys back to London after concerts elsewhere. In the immediate aftermath of the concert there is a sense of group relief – 'we did it, we came through unscathed, we survived' – which manifests itself in light-hearted banter and joke telling. And these bonds become stronger in the case of musicians who are continually performing together, rather than those assembled ad hoc for freelance engagements. As another musician puts it: 'if musicians were not able to laugh at themselves ... then the strain of the job would be too much to bear' (Brearley, 1991:19–20).

It's amazing what a bit of adrenalin and fear can do [laughs]. *It's one of those dates that they say you have to wear bicycle clips for* [laughs again]. *Yeah, I'll be scared stiff.*

To some extent it is often regarded as unprofessional to admit in detail to one's nerves or fears; such problems are, by and large, regarded as part of the job. But the shared relief becomes evident in the humorous exchanges following the performance; and, inevitably, the sense of relief felt is proportional to the perceived importance or difficulty of the performance event.

It is this socializing aspect of humour which I see as being particularly significant among musicians. Several writers have written of humour as a social lubricant, oiling the social machine,[12] and the metaphor seems particularly apt to describe certain types of joking among musicians – not only in the sense of 'letting off steam' that I have just outlined, but also in enabling the social bonding and hence teamwork that is necessary for musical production.

The most important thing is to have a sense of humour. I think if you haven't got humour you're never going to get through these things. And most of our [difficult] situations have been diffused by humour, by having a good laugh together, and then letting it go away.

It is also the case that certain individuals will seek to ingratiate themselves with particular social groups in the hope of receiving work and, as Apte notes above, they may use humour and self-deprecation to effect this; if not done carefully, however, the humour may not be shared or may feel forced, causing the whole plan to backfire.

Significantly, humour can also be used to convey judgments on the musical abilities of others, normally when they are not present. Two examples will illustrate this. In one rehearsal a number of us were entertained by one of the group mimicking the playing of another player, known to us all, with whom he was doing a show. This involved him playing the saxophone in a loud, honking fashion, with fingers and tongue deliberately and excessively uncoordinated. The victim's competence, or adjudged lack of it, was of course being exaggerated for the purposes of the joke, and we were suitably amused. But it is clear that musical judgments were being expressed through this ridicule, which no doubt played some part in our subsequent perception of the victim's suitability for certain types of employment, and which informed the mental picture of another musician which all musicians necessarily cultivate. On another occasion I was discussing with a musician a particular flute player we knew in common who, somewhat to my surprise, I discovered was also having to play saxophone in a West End show they were doing together. I was surprised because I had not suspected that she played the saxophone and this was not part of the identity I had constructed for her. I said to the other musician, 'I've never heard her play the saxophone', to which he immediately replied, 'No, neither have I!' Thus his assertions on the musical abilities of the butt of the joke were expressed through humour, and show quite distinctly how musical judgments can be communicated between musicians in this way, and how such judgments become incorporated into the cognitive image one musician constructs of another.

Humour also has its place in controlling behaviour, that is, it can be used to reinforce behavioural norms and values existing within a society or group; ridiculing socially inappropriate behaviour promotes social control because it emphasizes social conformity. Patterns of behaviour acceptable to those who are already established in the professional music world are sometimes violated by those within it, or those attempting to find a place for themselves; such mishaps may subsequently be turned into jokes or anecdotes which in turn reinforce what is seen as appropriate behaviour to the rest of the group. During a break in one rehearsal a colleague told me that he had recently been doing a touring show in which another of the players had invited one of his students to sit next to him during the show, to 'learn the ropes'. The student, previously unknown to my informant but no doubt keen to get work, turned to him at the end and gave him a business card, saying: 'Now that I've seen the show, if you ever need a dep do give me a call.' My informant retold the story with some contempt: 'I knew it was coming! I'd seen it coming all evening! And I'd never even met the kid before, let alone know what his playing was like!' The delicate conventions governing the giving and taking of work had been breached, and in his humorous ridiculing of the student's behaviour my colleague unconsciously reinforced the idea both to myself and to others listening that this was inappropriate, and *not* the way to try and get depping work on a show.

While this particular example can be seen as promoting social behaviour, humour is also used to validate accepted musical behaviour. The 'quasi fairer' joke which I referred to above can also be read as implying a style of musical performance to which the members of this particular group (the quartet) should conform. The implied message is, 'this group plays and sounds like this, so let's make sure we all do it like that'. Even jokes contained within formal patterns may be said to conserve or promote desirable musical qualities. Consider the following rather blatant example:

Q. What is the difference between the first and last desk of a viola section?
A. 1. Half a bar.
A. 2. A semitone.

Here the obviously undesirable characteristics of being out of time or tune are invested in the viola players, frequently the group portrayed as possessing those qualities least desirable in competent musicians. Again the metamessage is not hard to discern.

Major practical jokes are not commonplace in professional music-making but they do occur, particularly in rehearsals or peripheral activities rather than the performance events themselves, although they are more frequent in shows, partially to alleviate the boredom and because in general the band cannot be seen. Given their relative insecurity and the stresses already inherent in the job, musicians are seldom likely to do things which deliberately jeopardize the performance. They do arise in music colleges, however, where students, who in part develop images of musicians' behaviour based on stereotypes, believe that practical jokes are 'all part of the game'. A small piece of polythene film stretched across the inside of a wind instrument, or a screw undone during the interval, seems hugely amusing during college years but is generally considered inappropriate in the professional music world, although this is not to suggest such things never occur. Most musicians do not take kindly to somebody sabotaging the performance they have, in general, worked hard to create. These kinds of college practical jokes could perhaps be read as being in some ways analogous to initiation rites; once you are in the business they are generally, but not entirely, left behind.

Although I have suggested that joking behaviour is widespread among musicians it is still the case that certain individuals demonstrate these behaviour patterns more frequently than others; that is, some people become known for their jokes and clowning around. This is the case with college practical joking, which is likely to be undertaken by those individuals with more extrovert, exuberant personalities. But even with verbal humour certain musicians are known for their stock of jokes, funny stories or joking behaviour. These people are not 'fools' in the sense Klapp (1950) suggests. They do not themselves serve as scapegoat, butt of humour, or cathartic symbols for aggression (see Klapp, 1950:161). But they do become recognized conservators of the group's 'jokelore' and, by their recitation of humorous anecdotes, the channels through which noteworthy deeds become transformed into models for stereotypical behaviour, and hence a type of myth. They provide more than their share of the social lubricant of humour and, as in the case of the two conductor-baiting stories above, they may sometimes be the focal point through which group humour is collected and expressed.

It is worth noting in passing that Klapp's representation of the fool-type has much in common with Merriam's assessment of the musician. Klapp suggests that, although the fool's status[13] is low, he is 'a symbol of fundamental importance, representing a role especially valued by the group' and further that fools are distinguished from the group 'by a deviation in person or conduct which is regarded as ludicrous and improper … His sole privilege is his "license"' (159–61). This is extraordinarily similar to Merriam's paradigm in which musicians are described as having 'low status ... high importance [and] deviant behavior' (Merriam, 1964:140). Douglas also suggests that the joker is 'a privileged person who can say certain things in a certain way which confers immunity' (Douglas, 1975:107) and again this resonates with Merriam's suggestion that song texts can 'express deep-seated feelings not permissibly verbalized in other contexts' (Merriam 1964:190). The close relationship between these two social types perhaps explains why humour is so prevalent and important among London musicians at least, and no doubt elsewhere, and also provides further evidence of the connections between music, myth and humour.

Viola jokes

Finally I wish to consider a category of jokes which are so widespread and popular they demand individual attention, and these are jokes about violas and their players. I have already given some examples of viola jokes and there are many hundreds more which could be presented. Indeed, in the early 1990s, *Classical Music*, a trade magazine for the music business in Britain, ran an occasional but continuing series of viola jokes with a new selection printed in each issue, from which the following three examples are taken:

Q: What's the difference between Grade V viola and Grade VIII viola?
A: For Grade VIII you have to tune up from memory.[14]

Q: Which is the best recording of the Walton Viola Concerto?
A: Music Minus One.[15]

Q: What's the definition of a viola player?
A: Someone who hangs around with musicians.[16]

The denigration of violas and their players, I am led to believe,[17] is a hangover from the eighteenth century, when viola lines were frequently filler parts,[18] demanding the least competence or application from the players involved and therefore supposedly attracting those with rather less ability or intelligence. Such stereotyping has been long established within the Western art music tradition, as the following extract from Richard Wagner's 1869 conducting treatise reveals:

> The viola is commonly (with rare exceptions indeed) played by infirm violinists, or by decrepit players of wind instruments who happen to have been acquainted with a stringed instrument once upon a time; at best a competent viola player occupies a first desk, so that he may play the occasional solos for that instrument; but I have even seen this function performed by the leader of the first violins. It was pointed out to me that in a large orchestra which contained eight violas, there was only one player who could deal with the rather difficult passages in one of my later scores! (Wagner, 1972:4)

Whatever the origins of the genre it is noticeable that those social and musical characteristics deemed by musicians to be least desirable are frequently invested in this group, even though few musicians would, objectively, see their colleagues in these terms. Suspension of disbelief is therefore an important component in the appreciation of jokes such as these; for the joke to work, subjective acceptance of the stereotype portrayed must not be spoiled by the objective perception of real viola players encountered. Thus to some extent 'viola players' fulfil the role of certain ethnic groups (the Irish in Britain, Poles in the USA) in different societies, who become the targets of a particular category of jokes. Apte (1985:127) notes that 'such traits as stupidity, dirtiness, brute force, and excessive sexuality are generally viewed negatively and can be linked to any target group'. To which list one might add, in the case of 'viola players', the musically undesirable attributes of bad intonation and timing, lack of technical competence, the possession of cheap or worthless instruments, and so on.

It seems likely that this allocation of undesirable characteristics to a component of the group itself is a social defence mechanism. Elliott Jaques has argued that the creation of such defence mechanisms against psychotic anxiety is a significant element in institutionalized human association. He suggests that one such mechanism arises from the projection of bad internal objects and impulses onto particular members of a group who, regardless of their function, are selected for that purpose:

> Societies provide institutionalised roles whose occupants are sanctioned, or required, to take into themselves the projected objects of impulses of other members. The occupants of such roles may absorb the objects and impulses – take them into themselves and become either the good or bad object with corresponding impulses. (Jaques, 1955:497)

He further suggests that this projection of bad impulses is accompanied by introjective identification, which we might describe as a form of unconscious social bonding. He writes:

> The persecuting group's belief in its own good is preserved by heaping contempt upon and attacking the scapegoated group. The internal splitting mechanisms and preservation of the internal good objects of individuals, and the attack upon, and contempt for, internal, bad persecutory objects, are reinforced by introjective identification of individuals with other members taking part in the group-sanctioned attack upon the scapegoat. (485)

These phantasy[19] social mechanisms not only afford protection against anxiety for the individual but contribute to the survival of the group as a whole.

I suggest that this, ultimately, is the function of viola jokes, to allow the ascription of undesirable characteristics to a particular group of people contained within the larger social group. Although the community of musicians is not quite institutionalized in the way Jaques suggests, many of the groups in which it operates, particularly the orchestras who gave rise to the viola joke phenomenon, can be considered in this way. It is also notable that in the world of jazz and big bands the viola player is replaced by the banjo player as the institutional scapegoat, implying a similar defensive process. So this projection of undesirable characteristics is part of a social defence mechanism which allows the group to function effectively; and, for anthropological purposes, we may turn the equation around and say that, *because* musicians feel it necessary to create this mechanism, this tells us that they do indeed conceive of themselves as a group, a community both sharing and rejecting certain identifiable characteristics which requires defence mechanisms for its protection.

I particularly choose the word 'community' not only because it provides a connection with some of my observations in other chapters, but also because it allows us an overview of the place of humour in professional musical life. Mary Douglas, following Turner, has written on the difference between 'community' and 'structure', and she suggests:

> Whereas 'structure' is differentiated and channels authority through the system, in the context of 'community', roles are ambiguous, lacking hierarchy, disorganised. 'Community' in this sense has positive values associated with it; good fellowship, spontaneity, warm contact. (Douglas, 1975:104)

Musicians, as I have suggested, do see themselves as a community and would generally agree with Douglas's description of its positive values, and I would concur with her that such values arise without reference to prevailing musical or social rank. Humour and jokes confront these rigid hierarchies of social structure, unconsciously creating a more egalitarian, undifferentiated field, wherein musicians disregard their social and musical roles to create both a sense of communal identity and, within this, smaller group identities, all sustained in part by the social lubricant of laughter.

Notes

1   This argument runs through much of Frith's writings. See particularly Frith (1978:203–9; 1989:71; 1991: 280–87).

2   Cited in *The Guardian*, 23 November 2002, p.3.

3   In his novel, *The Trial*, Kafka refers to the protagonist only as Joseph K.

4   'Pathemia' is defined by Cattell (upon whose work much of Kemp's is based) as 'a tendency towards living at the hypothalamic level'. The hypothalamus is found in the lower regions of the brain, neurologically speaking, and appears more active in those who choose to operate principally through emotions and feelings, as opposed to those who are described as more rational or logical, who are said to be more 'cortically alert'; see Kemp (1996:30).

5   Apte's book does contain an extensive bibliography, listing many papers and books by psychologists, sociologists and others, as well as those by anthropologists. For this reason alone it is a valuable resource.

6   Freud uses the term 'joke' to distinguish three different amusement types: 'comic', 'wit' and 'humour', each relating to different forms of psychic energy. Such distinctions, while significant elsewhere, are not important here and so, following Wilson (1979:2), I use the terms 'joke' and 'humour' interchangeably.

7   It may be pursued more extensively in Chapter VI ('Jokes, Dreams and the Unconscious') of Freud (1960).

8   *http://www.nzso.co.nz/fun/index.html*

9   For a fuller explanation of language registers and register switching, see Trudgill (1974:103ff).

10   For a comprehensive review of kin-based and non-kin joking relationships, see Apte (1985:29–66).

11   See, for example, Piperek (1981) and Salmon (1992).

12   For example, Martineau (1972:103) and Wilson (1979:228).

13   Klapp uses the term 'status' in the same way as Merriam, so I have retained it with this meaning here.

14   *Classical Music*, 21 July 1990, p.50.

15   *Ibid.*

16   *Classical Music*, 12 January 1991, p.38.

17   This explanation was given to me by a viola player when I asked him why violas and their players should have become the targets of so many jokes.

18   By which I mean they provided the missing notes to fill out the harmony, rather than having any of the importance attached to the bass or melody lines.

19   I deliberately use this spelling in accordance with the convention in which 'phantasy' implies unconscious phantasy, while 'fantasy' implies conscious fantasy.

CHAPTER SEVEN

The Performance Event:
Ritual, Theatre, Play

Introduction

In this chapter I shall consider how the performance events in which London musicians take part might be approached from an ethnomusicological perspective. As will be evident from earlier chapters, such events may occur in a variety of different contexts, including solo instrumental recitals, song recitals, chamber music, orchestral performances, operas and so on. Many of these events share, at a performative level, similar characteristics, although I have chosen to take a hypothetical orchestral concert as a paradigm of this class of events. This is partly because such concerts are, for many people, both audience and musicians, among the most important occasions within the Western music spectrum, imbued with a significance which is not always found elsewhere, and partly because the nature of such concerts makes them particularly suitable to the approach I have taken here. I will, however, refer to other types of events where appropriate.

Furthermore, I shall not provide a detailed description of any one particular concert; patterns of behaviour become increasingly meaningful only through repetition and are considered valid here only if readily observable at most, if not all, concerts. Nor will I present a synthetic example of an orchestral concert, amalgamated from a number of different events. This would be important if such concerts were largely unfamiliar to those most likely to be holding this book, but many readers will have direct experience of these events and most others will have some more or less accurately conceived notion or image of what occurs in them. For these reasons I shall recall only those points which seem most apposite for the discussion to follow, although this will, in fact, cover much of what occurs in an average London orchestral concert. The ethnographic editorializing to which I referred previously inevitably extends beyond the mere selection of interview quotations.

A problem arising from this, however, is that assertions made here cannot necessarily be extrapolated and applied elsewhere. Western art music at the beginning of the twenty-first century is no longer Western in any geographical sense, but is a world-wide phenomenon. As I noted in the previous chapter, it resembles Frith's description of music which is globally shared but locally adapted. For these reasons we must beware of transferring conclusions across cultural or societal boundaries. Concerts given during an orchestral tour of, say, London, Dresden, Delhi and Hong Kong may appear superficially similar at each performance, but the implications of these events are likely to be fundamentally different. This is true regardless of the actual music performed, but even more so when this is taken into account; a programme which includes, perhaps, one of Elgar's 'Pomp and Circumstance' marches, would have a very different cultural and historic resonance in each of these four cities. Here, then, I am dealing with orchestral concerts as they occur on a regular basis in London, specifically, and Britain generally. It is for others to decide to what extent my analysis may be applied elsewhere.

The basis of the analysis is that Western art music concerts in general, and orchestral concerts in particular, contain elements of both theatre and ritual, and the complementary coexistence of these two interrelated ideas is fundamental to these occasions. I shall begin by examining different aspects of these performance events, viewed from a variety of anthropological perspectives, to determine to what extent such events may accurately be described as rituals. I shall then attempt to distinguish 'theatre' from 'ritual' before examining those elements of a concert which seem to me to be more accurately described as theatrical. Finally I shall suggest how all these things can be located within the wider arena of play.

Ritual and ritualizing

One does not have to peruse the ethnomusicological literature to any significant degree before realizing that in many different cultures across the globe musicians are frequently cast in the role of ritual specialists. Norma McLeod (1964:287) has shown that on Madagascar, for example, musicians are particularly involved in both music for ceremony and funerary music, with their remuneration considerably enhanced for the latter because of the 'ritual danger' (their proximity to the spirit world) inherent in the event. Barbara Hampton (1982:101) has also demonstrated how the *Adowafoi*, female singers among the Ga of south-eastern Ghana, rank above secular leaders and elders in the community, because ritual authority is considered to be superior to secular authority in Ga society, and also because 'ritual specialists are responsible for maintaining harmonious relations between the gods and humans'. Similarly Fremont Besmer (1983) has shown the fundamental importance of specialist musicians in the *bori* possession-trance of the Nigerian Hausa, and there are numerous other studies which could be cited to show the ever-present connections between musical specialists and ritual occasions.

This inevitably invites the question, to what extent are urban Western musicians ritual specialists, and can the events in which they participate be considered as rituals in this way? For one writer at least, the issue is clear. Christopher Small's (1987) paper 'Performance as ritual' has as its basic tenet the idea that 'a symphony concert partakes of the nature of a ritual' (6) and is 'an important ritual of the powerholding class in our society' (7). Given that in the mid-1980s such approaches to Western art music practice were even less common than they are today, both the author's fortitude and his foresight are to be commended. But I have some reservations about the approach Small has taken, and I will come back to his work several times in the next few pages, as a means of adding a counterpoint to my own views on similar issues.

Before we can assert with confidence that an orchestral concert is indeed a ritual it is important to consider what we mean by this often (ab)used word. Small's definition is clear enough; for him a ritual is 'an act which dramatizes and re-enacts the shared mythology of a culture or social group, the mythology which unifies and, for its members, justifies that culture or group' (7). But this rather Durkheimian interpretation, in which rituals are seen as somehow crystallizing cultural beliefs and, by extension, social structures, is by no means universally accepted among anthropologists, and the notion of what constitutes a ritual, and what rituals might mean or do, has been argued about at some length. Even in common usage the word carries a degree of ambiguity: in the *Oxford English Dictionary*, for example, ritual is defined as '1. A prescribed order of performing rites'; rites being variously defined as 'religious or solemn observances' or 'a body of customary observances characteristic of a Church' (Allen, 1990:1040). This may seem relatively straightforward, but the next definition offered suggests that the situation is more complicated: '2. A procedure regularly followed', an interpretation which clearly widens the field beyond association only with sacred – another difficult word – activities.

This conceptual malleability has been carried into the world of academe, where scholars have approached the study of ritual from numerous directions. Some of these have been neatly summarized by Richard Schechner, who suggests:

> Rituals have been considered: 1) as part of the evolutionary development of animals; 2) as structures with formal qualities and definable relationships; 3) as symbolic systems of meaning; 4) as performative actions or processes; 5) as experiences. (Schechner, 1993:228)

Most anthropologists have considered ritual behaviour to be associated with some form of religion or, at least, underpinned by a mythically enhanced collection of beliefs. But some have asserted that such behaviour can occur in other, non-sacred settings, as evidenced by the title of Moore and Myerhoff's book, *Secular Ritual* (1977). Here various writers approach 'everyday' meetings and gatherings (sports events, political meetings and so on) with the same formal rigour and exactitude as might be expected in an analysis of overtly sacred rituals, in order to answer the question posed in the book's introduction: 'what new material becomes visible if the supernatural element is stripped away and this-worldly ceremonies and their outcomes are considered?' (4). It is this shift into a 'this-worldly' arena of ritual which is most relevant here, since it allows us to conceive orchestra concerts as quasi-rituals; there is no obvious association with a formally constituted collection of sacred ideas here, what might be described as a belief system proper. Yet, as I argued in the previous chapter, there is a connection with a particular type of mythology based on our perceptions of the value and importance of certain historical figures, and on this point at least I am in agreement with Small (1987:19) when he suggests that 'the lives and personalities of the "great composers" ... are paradigms for this belief, which is rehearsed every time their music is played ... in a concert hall'.

But the danger with broadening a field of enquiry in this way is that the term 'ritual' begins to cover so many activities that information becomes difficult to organize; in short, by potentially meaning so much the word in fact means very little. However a change of perspective is offered by a consideration of the act of 'ritualizing'. Rather than attempt to designate events as rituals or non-rituals it is perhaps more profitable to consider how patterns of behaviour differentiate certain significant events from other events in the same cultural sphere. Implicit within this is the idea that ritualization is dependent upon context for its efficacy. Catherine Bell suggests that, 'just as a sign or a text derives its significance by virtue of its relationship to other signs and texts, basic to ritualization is the inherent significance it derives from its interplay and contrast with other practices' (Bell, 1992:90). For her, ritualization is 'a way of acting that specifically establishes a privileged contrast, differentiating itself as more important or powerful. Such privileged distinctions may be drawn in a variety of culturally specific ways that render the ritualized acts dominant in status' (90). Thus certain events, despite their non-sacred nature, are distinguished within their own cultural context by the ritualized patterns of behaviour to which they give rise, and which differentiate them both from unritualized activities and from other events characterized by different patterns of ritualized behaviour. From this perspective we can begin to look at orchestral concerts in a rather different way, seeking out those behaviour patterns which seem to be particularly significant for these events and which thus contribute to the idea that they are somehow 'dominant in status'.

One of the earliest writers on ritual behaviour was Arnold van Gennep, who in 1909 published *Les Rites de Passage* in which he analysed those rituals associated with progress through the human life cycle, such as birth, circumcision, marriage and death. His assessment of these 'life crises' has greatly influenced a number of subsequent anthropologists. One of his principal contentions was that all these rituals consist of three essential stages: rites of separation (preliminal); transition rites (liminal – 'limen' being the Latin for 'threshold'); and rites of incorporation (postliminal). While all rites of passage can theoretically be reduced to these three stages they are not always equally important or equally elaborated (van Gennep, 1960:11). The first phase comprises symbolic behaviour denoting the detachment of groups or individuals from their previous position or state within the society. The liminal phase is ambiguous, during which the ritual subject displays none of the attributes of the previous or following states. In the final phase, which might be more clearly thought of as *re*incorporation, the passage is complete and the subject is once again in a relatively stable, but new, state, taking their place within a reconstituted social order.

Of these three stages it is the middle, liminal, phase which has provoked the most interest because of its inherent ambiguity. At this point the status of all participants, and particularly the main protagonists, cannot be categorized according to the accepted classificatory systems prevailing within their society. As Turner famously puts it:

> Liminal entities are neither here nor there; they are betwixt and between the positions assigned and arrayed by law, custom, convention, and ceremonial. As such, their ambiguous and indeterminate attributes are expressed by a rich variety of symbols in the many societies that ritualize social and cultural transitions. (Turner, 1969:95)

Turner is himself an important theorist on ritual behaviour, and elsewhere he makes a distinction between 'liminal', as outlined above, and 'liminoid' – 'liminal-like' – similar to the ritually liminal but not identical to it. In Turner's view limin*al* phenomena tend to be collective, concerned with calendrical, meteorological, biological or social–structural cycles and rhythms, and appear at what may be called 'natural breaks' in the flow of natural or sociocultural processes. By contrast, limin*oid* phenomena are more characteristically produced and consumed by known, named (that is, identifiable) individuals, though they may of course have collective or mass effects. They are not cyclical but continuously generated. Liminal phenomena are centrally integrated into the total social process whereas liminoid phenomena develop most characteristically outside the central economic and political processes (see Turner, 1977:44).

Much of this clearly resonates with the procedures and conventions of orchestral concerts. Such concerts are not seasonal but continuously generated; in London there is often a concert in one hall or another every night, frequently several. As Turner asserts, these concerts are not central to the political or economic structure of society, although they may well have political and economic structures within themselves. But there are more telling analogies with the theoretical positions I have described above, and particularly with van Gennep's tripartite model, which can be convincingly applied to such performance events.

Orchestral concerts can be said to have a preliminal stage. Before the actual music begins the various participants are separated from the rest of society by the physical act of congregation in their respective antechambers: for the audience and critics this is the foyer of the concert hall; for the musicians this will be a particular area backstage (often known as the 'green room') or in larger halls they will have dressing rooms, one of which will always be allocated to the conductor – his own private antechamber reflecting the significance of his rank. All individuals carry a symbol of their eligibility to take part in the event; each member of the audience has a ticket they have purchased on the night or in advance; the critics have either press passes or, more likely, complimentary tickets provided by the promoter; the musicians, soloists and conductor sometimes have backstage passes. Further symbols may be identified: programmes for the audience, music and instruments for the musicians, a baton for the conductor. All of these serve to distinguish the participants from the continuing social structures they have just left.

Once everyone is seated in the auditorium the event enters its liminoid phase. The participants are now 'betwixt and between', with none of the attributes of the state they have left or of the one to come. The social hierarchies existing outside the hall have been nullified or transformed within it. In the massed ranks of the audience one cannot tell the professional from the 'blue-collar' worker, the rich and famous from the *hoi polloi*, except, perhaps, for some easily misinterpreted clues given by the hierarchy of seat prices. The critics, who are important outside the hall because their reports give publicity and credence both to the orchestra and to the event itself, become anonymous figures within it, unknown to most of the rest of the audience and recognized, if at all, only by a few musicians, the promoter, or each other. The orchestra's uniform, of course, immediately suggests a different station from their life outside, at the same time implying that within the hall they are all equal; only when the music starts does it become apparent that certain individuals who play particular instruments have a more significant role within the performance event than others.

The final, postliminal or reincorporative, stage is the least emphasized in this event. After the concert there is no obvious reordering of the pre-existing social system and all participants return to the same social rank and position as before. However there are certain subtle changes which can best be explained by recalling Bourdieu's ideas on symbolic and economic capitals (see Chapter Three). Economic capital has been accrued in small amounts by the individual musicians, who are paid to play, by critics, who will be paid for their review, and in larger amounts by the soloists and conductor; the price of admission, programme, travel and so on means that most of the audience have paid out money, reducing their economic capital. But symbolic capital may be said to have been accrued by all participants. Orchestras, venue, conductors and soloists all contribute to the perception of certain events as being less or more prestigious, with varying amounts of symbolic capital gained through their participation, and by their association with these events audience members also accrue symbolic capital. Unlike a society where all members take part in a particular ritual, these 'industrial/liminoid' societies are now divided into two parts: those who attended the occasion and those who did not. In certain circles of Western society, where attendance at these high cultural events is regarded as desirable but not obligatory, those who are involved may be considered rather differently from those who are not. The accumulation of symbolic capital creates a subtle but perceptible social hierarchy, reflected in conversations that begin: 'Did you see so-and-so at The Albert Hall/Covent Garden/The South Bank last week/month?' Those who regularly take part in these events become recognized among their acquaintances and see themselves, as being significant imbibers of cultural production ('culture vultures'); over time this can become an important part of both their self-conception and their individual identity.

This application of van Gennep's model appears (to me at least) to be such a comfortable fit that I am bemused by Small's attempt to apply it, not to the event, but to the music itself. He argues that 'all the most popular orchestral works ... follow [a] dramatic progression from doubt and turbulence to triumph and even apotheosis of the soul', and he suggests that Turner's observation that a ritual contains 'a dialectic that passes from life through death to renewed life' is 'an excellent characterization of the symphonic progress at work' (Small, 1987:16). I am not convinced, however, that the middle (often the development) section of an individual work represents a structural dissolution compared to the outer sections in the way that van Gennep (and Turner) would require, even though there may be within it a great deal of 'turbulence', as Small puts it. There are still a considerable number of grammatical rules underpinning these musical structures (functional harmony, motivic development, cadential construction) which continue to apply throughout the work. While the surface material may change – and many ears would hear connective musical relationships anyway – the hierarchically determined structural relationships between notes and chords remain. And the return to the tonic at the end of these works does not imply that the musical structure has changed; in fact we return, not only to the same key, but back to an identical set of key and note relationships from where we started; there is nothing new about the reconstituted order. Of course, I would agree that many of these works play on the necessity to resolve an inherent musical tension, but this tension/resolution interplay is a feature of many different musical traditions and may, I suspect, fulfil some neurobiological function, a point for discussion which lies far outside this work.[1]

Naturally, I prefer to apply van Gennep's model in the way I suggested previously, if only because it emphasizes the most important part of these events, the musical performance itself, and this in turn underlines the shared nature of the experience: 'we were in it together'. Turner suggests that in such contexts people who share similar aspirations or characteristics 'withdraw symbolically ... from the total system ... to seek the glow of communitas among those with whom they share some cultural or biological feature they take to be their most signal mark of identity' (Turner, 1977:47). The dissolution of existing social structures, which Turner describes as 'social antistructure', heightens this feeling of shared experience and leads to what can be described as, again borrowing Turner's terminology, 'ideological communitas' (46). Communitas, which I use to mean not only a sense of shared experience and transitory communal identity but also the temporary subversion of the extant social structure, is an important feature of the liminal/liminoid stages of ritualized events. This communitas is sought during the course of an orchestral concert by a small, self-selecting group of people who share similar cultural aspirations, and whose participation in the event suggests a desire to withdraw, temporarily, from the highly ordered society they have left. Furthermore, I would argue that such communitas is generated most intensely at certain very specific points during concerts: at the ends of musical works or particular sections of them. At these points there is usually no movement and complete silence throughout the auditorium. This momentary stasis may be very short in the case of dramatic or virtuosic works, before being dissipated by enthusiastic applause, although the latter could also be described as engendering communitas. But in slower works, perhaps taken to be more 'beautiful' or 'emotional', this stasis may last many seconds before being disturbed, perhaps by a movement from the conductor or orchestra, leading to a general relaxation – 'the moment has passed' – and perhaps applause.

Turner has written of the nature of communitas in the theatre, but his words, and his apposite metaphors, would seem to be at least as relevant for musical performance events. He suggests:

> In a performance, there may be produced in audience and actors alike what d'Aquili and Laughlin (1979:11) call ... a 'brief ecstatic state and sense of union (often lasting only a few seconds) and may often be described as no more than a shiver running down the back at a certain point' ... This shiver has to be won, achieved ... after working through a tangle of conflicts and disharmonies. (Turner, 1990:13)

Clearly this 'ecstatic state and sense of union' represents something more than simply *ideological* communitas; it demonstrates also the *emotional* nature of the shared experience. Musical performance events not only bring together those who are culturally predisposed to participate in them, they also provide an emotionally satisfying episode for such participants. Yet it is important to note that, while this communitas is a shared, group experience, it also has an individual dimension; in this sense it is not 'communion', where individual 'I's are fused into a collective 'we', but an aggregate of collective individual responses which have both mass effect and individual significance. Elsewhere Turner argues that 'communitas preserves individual distinctiveness'

(1982:45). This is a significant dimension of the concept of communitas as I use it, and one to which I shall return below; for the moment I shall offer a number of concrete examples which I hope will demonstrate these rather abstract principles more clearly.

Some time ago I attended a concert at the Barbican Hall which included a performance of *Der Wein*, a concert aria for soprano and orchestra by Alban Berg, a member of the so-called 'Second Viennese School'. Although some audiences find this music difficult, Berg's pieces are among the most approachable within this musical genre, and many of the audience would have known this piece in advance, particularly as this concert, consisting only of Berg's works, was part of a larger festival devoted to his music and therefore likely to attract aficionados. The piece ends very quietly, the music seeming to drift upwards into nothingness, and at the end of the performance, after much excellent playing and singing, I sensed the audience ready for this moment of stasis. However, as the last note was played one member of the audience immediately began to applaud, and he or she continued for what seemed like 10 or 15 seconds before other members of the audience, almost grudgingly, joined in. The spell had been broken, disturbed by one individual, over-eager to show either their appreciation of the performance or their knowledge of the piece. I remember saying, rather tartly, to my companion, 'someone who knows all the notes and none of the music'. Once the general applause was established many of the musicians and the soloist looked up into the balcony to see if they could identify the individual who had deviated from the normal pattern of behaviour in this way. I was unable to see the reaction of the audience closest to the perpetrator, but my own reaction, and my companion's, was that this special moment had been violated in some way. Some months later, purely by coincidence, I happened to hear a recording of exactly the same concert on my car radio. I tuned in towards the end of *Der Wein* and must confess that it seemed only vaguely familiar *until* the applause began. The unusual behaviour allowed me immediately to recognize the piece and the event which I had previously attended. Now my situation was different: driving in urban traffic, having only heard one small part of the concert and divorced from the ritualized nature of concert-giving, I did not have the same feeling of violation as before, or the same irritation; the radio broadcast did not engender any feeling of communitas or shared experience. I also noticed that there was in fact very little time between the first applause and the rest of the audience joining, maybe three or four seconds at most. In the auditorium, as a participant in the performance event, time, for me at least, had slowed at this important moment of stasis, again indicating the intensity of this short period of time.[2]

A similar perspective is implied in the following newspaper cutting, which suggests that for a particular series of London concerts (the BBC Proms) this momentary stasis is a notable and characteristic feature:

But let's hear it for – let's listen breathlessly and gratefully for – the best moment
of every Promenade concert. It'll take less than a second of your time. It's that
moment when the audience takes in the last sound from the platform, knows the
end of its rapture, and only then lets it explode in a shout of pleasure and
partnership in the making and taking of music. That speck of time provides an
essential airlock between the music and the rest of experience.[3]

Reviewing my own experience as a soloist and teacher I realize that I
consciously attempt both to develop and to control these intense moments of
transfigured time. I make sure that loud or virtuosic pieces are delivered in such
a way that there is a drive, what I think of as a 'directed motion', towards the
finish; a performative statement which says, 'we have arrived'. In more modern
pieces, where the musical language may be so complex as to make it difficult for
the audience to follow the musical logic, this statement may need reinforcing by
particular actions or gestures: putting down my instrument, moving away from
the music stand or directly acknowledging the audience. In orchestral concerts
similar problems are circumvented by the conductor laying down his baton –
symbolic behaviour *par excellence* – or closing his score. In my quartet I am
aware that we do much the same, collectively freezing at the end of a piece, until
we indicate, by means of obvious relaxation or by removing the instruments
from our mouths, that the moment has passed. I encourage the same
performance behaviour in my pupils, showing them how, at the end of a slower,
reflective piece, they should remain completely still, keep the instrument in
place and breathe through their noses – 'don't spoil the moment'.

The idea that musical performance in some way transforms or manipulates
our perceptions of time is a recurring theme in the work of John Blacking. For
example, in his critical response to Rodney Needham's article on 'Percussion
and Transition' (Needham, 1967), he writes that 'music's special world of
virtual time has the power to awaken "the other mind", to transport us away
from the world of culturally regulated, *actual time*' (Blacking, 1968:314). In
his influential monograph, *How Musical is Man?* (1976), he cites Mahler's
observation that music may lead to 'the "other world" – the world in which
things are no longer subject to time and space' (51) and there are many other
examples which might be cited to demonstrate Blacking's belief in the
different quality of time engendered within musical performance events.
Blacking's ideas on this subject, and in particular his conceptual duality
between real time and virtual time, appear to owe something to Alfred Schutz,
a theorist whose work underpins Blacking's own perhaps more often than is
made explicit.[4] Schutz ([1951] 1977), for example, argues that it is the
'pluridimensionality of time' (116) which is felt by those who make music
together; that is, they experience simultaneously both outer time (the 'real'
time within which the music is performed) and inner time, a different quality
of perception provoked by their mutual involvement in the musical
performance. Schutz writes:

> Making music together is an event in outer time, presupposing also a face-to-face relationship, that is, a community of space, and it is this dimension which unifies the fluxes of inner time and warrants their synchronization into a vivid present. (117–18)

Schutz describes this sharing of a 'community of space', and the heightened sensitivity to the behaviour of others which it provokes, as a 'mutual tuning-in relationship' (108), a theoretical posture which is strongly resonant with the notion of communitas I advanced previously. Although Schutz was primarily concerned with the actions and relationships of the performers themselves, I suggest that such empathetic responses are equally significant in the audience's perception of the event, and in their relationship with the performers on stage.

So, by way of summary at this point, I am suggesting that the quasi-ritual of an orchestral concert is clearly analogous to van Gennep's rite of passage, albeit that it is only partially scaffolded by a mythologically enhanced belief system which might render it properly sacred; and its most important component, the liminoid stage during which the music is actually played, is distinguished by certain ritualized patterns of behaviour, which include the ushers guiding the audience and critics to their seats, the arrival of orchestra and conductor, the playing of various pieces of music, and the applause which accompanies them; and, paradoxically, it is often in those moments when nothing happens that communitas, the sense of shared experience – mutual tuning in – and social antistructure, is at its most intense.

In discussing these performance events I have been conscious always to include not only the active performers – the musicians, soloists and conductor – but also those with a more passive role, the audience, critics, ushers (who are both active and passive), promoters, and so on. I regard the participation of all these different groups as being fundamental to the event, and this more holistic view is to some degree influenced by Howard Becker's (1982) analysis of *Art Worlds*. Becker suggests that works of art are shaped by the actions and involvement of a large number of people, and are not just the product of a single creator, who in this case would naturally be the composer; each of these groups, even if represented only by a single individual, exerts its own influence on the resulting artwork. In his own words:

> Various groups and subgroups share knowledge of the conventions current in a medium, having acquired that knowledge in various ways. Those who share such knowledge can, when the occasion demands or permits, act together in ways that are part of the co-operative web of activity making that world possible and characterizing its existence. To speak of the organization of the art world – its division into audiences of various kinds, and the producers and support personnel of various kinds – is another way of talking about who knows what and uses it to act together. (Becker, 1982:67)

In Becker's terms, of course, there are many people contributing to the musical art work who may not be at the performance: instrument makers, union officials, music publishers, not to mention several perhaps long-dead composers. Schechner, working a similar canvas to Becker albeit with a broader brush, suggests that the actual participants in a ritual can be categorized into four basic groups: the group or individual that stages (or creates) the event; the group that receives this communication (the audience); the group that directs or oversees; and those who comment (critics and scholars) upon the event (Schechner, 1993:43).

Schechner's analysis, however, does not differentiate between those people who may nominally be considered in the same category but whose participation in the event is grounded upon very different expectations or terms of reference. Becker provides a perfect example:

> Orchestral musicians, for instance, are notoriously more concerned with how they sound in performance than with the success of a particular work; with good reason, for their own success depends in part on impressing those who hire them with their competence ... They may sabotage a new work which can make them sound bad because of its difficulty, their career interests lying at cross-purposes to the composer's. (Becker, 1982:25)

I can support this hypothesis with a well documented example. In 1988, the principal cellist of the BBC Symphony Orchestra publicly smashed his cello into the floor after the performance of a very avant-garde piece by a contemporary German composer, because he felt the piece made a mockery of his musical skills and training. The incident provided many column inches in the national newspapers[5] and clearly demonstrates the conflicting interests that may exist between individuals, in this case producer and reproducer, nominally assigned by Schechner to the same group. Another example from my own performing experience illustrates the same idea. In the late 1980s I was involved in a tour of Prokofiev's ballet *Romeo and Juliet*. This very dramatic score requires a large orchestra including tenor saxophone, my own part. The saxophone is used soloistically but sparingly, and during the course of what is a three-hour ballet there were long breaks when I was not playing. At these times I could withdraw from my obligations as a performer and simply sit back and enjoy the music, temporarily aligned with the audience, unlike those musicians still playing (particularly the string players) who were more or less continually employed. Once I got to know the music well I would look forward to these points, which served to heighten my enjoyment of the performance, in contrast I am sure to those who were required to work considerably harder than I was. Although in Schechner's terms we would be nominally assigned to the same group our experience of, and therefore relationship to, the event itself were noticeably different.

I think this is a significant point. It is too easy to observe an orchestra and, given the uniformity of dress, the teamwork involved and the unified musical product which emerges, assume that the experience of creating this is the same for everybody; but this is not the case. While members of the audience might be thrilled by a particular performance or become immersed in the musical event itself, an individual musician's perception of the event can be very different:

You could be sitting in front of the brass doing a Shostakovitch symphony and think you were going to die. Well that's not conducive to anything other than trying to escape the noise. You've got to sit there, you break into a sweat because you can't put your fingers in your ears, you can't move your head to get out the way, and someone, because it's their job, is blowing the balls off something. They have to, it sounds bloody marvellous, but if you sit in front of a noise like that for too long your hearing starts to go, or you think it's going to go. It's not a good working environment.

The position I sit in, right in the middle of the orchestra, it must be rather like the way the composer hears it. He's in the middle of it, and I feel I am. It's all around you. Marvellous.

It is also the case that the musicians' perceptions of the quality of the performance or the overall success of the concert can be very different from that of the audience:

Some people may sit there closing their eyes and listening, some people might look very sternly at you and you think, 'Gosh they're really not enjoying this are they?' But actually if it's somebody you know you might go up to them and say, 'You didn't like that did you?' and he'll go 'Yeah, course I did, it was great.' And it has happened quite a lot, actually, that I've thought somebody's really not liked it at all, and they've said 'Yeah, I thought it was great.'

These examples illustrate that the different groups who come together in musical performance events should not necessarily be regarded as homogenous, since individuals within them may have their own, potentially conflicting, agendas, or the nature of their experience may be substantially different from those around them. This is not to suggest that communitas does not occur, but rather that it is experienced differently by different people; experience is necessarily subjective, but the subjective 'I' is never completely subsumed within the communal 'we'. To some extent this is common sense. We know through our conversations with companions that we do not always react to certain pieces or performances in the same way as they did, yet we all enjoyed the event and the feeling of sharing something with others.

Furthermore, there may well be individuals or groups involved in these events who fall outside, or fit only uncomfortably within, the categories outlined by Schechner, yet whose presence (or absence) also helps define the event. Gerd Baumann has argued that rituals should be viewed, not as 'crystallizations of basic values uniformly endorsed by communities that perform them', but as collections of competing constituencies, allowing us 'to distinguish participation according to a variety of possible modes' (Baumann, 1992:113). Fundamental to Baumann's argument is the presence of 'others' at ritual occasions who, either as visible participants or as invisible categorical referents, help to define the event. He lists five possible categories of participation: disinterested bystanders; spectators participating as interested parties, either by appreciation or depreciation of the event; invited guests, who enhance recognition and status of the event; witnesses, who confer validity; and outside beneficiaries (110). Baumann's model is designed to account for rituals occurring in plural societies, where different ethnic groups, for example, may find themselves thrown together in rituals which were originally meaningful only to one or perhaps none of them; an Asian birthday party which also involved Afro-Caribbean and white European guests would be a hypothetical example. His approach necessitates a slight change of perspective from the one I have pursued so far, but it allows us to include a number of 'participants' at an orchestral concert who might otherwise be missed.

As Baumann notes (110), where any event involves only a subsection of a society, like an orchestral concert, there are likely to be disinterested bystanders. Many concert halls are part of larger complexes which house bars, restaurants, cinemas and/or other amenities, which would attract people not attending the concert; the building itself may also be culturally significant, thus generating tourist traffic. These people may be aware of the concert taking place but they do not become involved in it. In their transitory passage through the concert hall they do not acquire any of the symbols (tickets, programmes) conferring their right to participate, but their presence in the building emphasizes the 'otherness' of the event itself, as well as perhaps confirming the importance of the venue in which it takes place.

I have argued that all those in the hall – musicians, audience, critics – should be regarded as participants in the event, and, given the essentially closed physical environment of a concert hall, it is unlikely to attract spectators participating as Baumann's 'interested parties'. Only by purchasing tickets would individuals be allowed into the auditorium itself, at which point they would become participants. However, in our technologically complex society, the recording and broadcasting of the event, often simultaneously (live), means that large numbers of people may in fact become interested spectators. They cannot be said to be true participants, since again they do not acquire the necessary symbols required for this and their physical absence prevents their being so described; but their interest in the event, even from a distance, certainly helps to define it.

Invited guests are sometimes found at these concerts. They might be notable personalities, for example the Royal Family, visiting politicians or local civic dignitaries, whose presence endows the occasion with increased significance.

Witnesses, who confer validity, are also evident. Into this category I would put the music critic who, having been admitted on the strength of a press pass or complimentary ticket, has a different status from the majority of the audience. His or her report to the newspaper lends authority to the event and places it both within the context of other similar events and in a wider context of differing social phenomena. Outside beneficiaries can also be identified, particularly the promoter of a concert who might not attend the event, or the record company whose sales may increase because of the increased profile of a soloist or orchestra; and of course the families of those participants who are being paid for their work will benefit economically. Baumann's approach thus reinforces a view of the orchestral concert, not as an isomorphic entity reflecting one fixed set of ideas, but as a polymorphic one encompassing a number of different agendas. It comprises not only the 'us' of the active participants in the event but also those 'others' whose symbiotic association with the event simultaneously defines both it and their relationship to it.

Within the event itself, however, the different approaches of these competing constituencies may result in conflict, if there is a difference of opinion about exactly how the event should proceed. David Parkin has suggested that

> Participants in a ritual may well contest the proper conduct of the ceremony or may acknowledge their ignorance and ask others what to do or what some action or object means. But that the ritual *is* a ritual and supposed to follow some time-hallowed precedent in order to be effective or simply to be a proper performance is not in question. (Parkin, 1992:14–15)

Any conflict, then, is subject to a ruling on exactly what should happen, or who should be where at a particular moment; thus the participants in the event, while disagreeing about details of procedure, are 'united by a sense of the occasion as being in some way rule-governed and as necessarily so in order to be complete, efficacious, and proper' (15). Parkin's arguments are supported by examples of rituals where there is physical movement between certain fixed points, and he suggests that such directionality frequently represents a journey or passage. For him, ritual is 'formulaic spatiality carried out by groups of people who are conscious of its imperative or compulsory nature and who may or may not further inform this spatiality with spoken words' (18). While orchestral concerts are essentially static events, there is a great deal of what might be described as 'formulaic spatiality', where rulings of one sort or another may well be required, even though the event itself does not have the 'imperative or compulsory nature' by which it might accurately be described as a ritual under Parkin's definition.

To begin with, rulings are made by those responsible for planning and executing the event: the orchestral manager determines the correct dress for the concert; the promoter determines what time the event will start; the house manager decides when the doors will open; ushers arbitrate on any dispute about seating or ticket arrangements. More revealing, but perhaps less obvious, are the rulings made governing the positions of players within the orchestra. Here there is a very clear hierarchical structure, involving implied performance capabilities and reflected in the scale of economic reward. This is particularly noticeable in the strings. Players in each section (violins, violas, cellos, basses) are divided into pairs known as desks, hierarchically arranged from least prestigious at the back to most prestigious at the front. Each desk is further divided into an outside and inside player, the outside having a higher rank than the inside, with the latter thus being designated to turn the pages of the music. In professional orchestras these rules are clear: you are appointed to your particular desk and there you must sit at every performance.[6] But these positions can be a source of friction and jealousy in ad hoc orchestras, assembled from freelance players for one particular concert, where one player might consider him or herself deserving a more prestigious seat than that allocated. In the event of a dispute the orchestral manager, or sometimes the section leader, is required to make a ruling on which player should sit where.

The wind and brass sections are also hierarchically structured, each having a principal player, a sub-principal, and a number of other players according to the needs of the music. In permanent orchestras these are again designated positions ('chairs') to which you are appointed when you join, but in freelance groups somebody must decide who will play which part, a procedure normally undertaken when the musicians are booked. The percussion section is less rigidly structured than the others, with a less clear hierarchy, perhaps because of the greater variety of instruments to be played. The timpanist is usually a fixed position, while the principal percussionist will allocate players to those instruments required, again making a ruling.

These various theoretical approaches illustrate, I hope, that orchestral concerts contain considerable amounts of ritualized behaviour, and while one might argue that any one concert is not 'a ritual' as such, it is in many ways 'of ritual'. Furthermore, while I have necessarily concentrated on orchestral concerts, I would suggest that these ritualizing patterns, or analogues to them, exist in some shape or form in all Western art music performances. But this is not to suggest that everything which occurs in such performance events must necessarily be described as 'ritualizing', and in the next section I shall consider other parameters of musical performance which might better be described as 'theatrical'.

The theatre of musical performance

Theatre and ritual are not always easily distinguished. In one sense they are interdependent bedfellows since much ritual involves elements of theatre and much theatre contains ritualized behaviour; in another sense they can be seen as two poles of a continuum, along which we may posit particular events according to how we perceive them. In some instances the distinctions may become blurred, as in certain highly ritualized forms of Asian theatre such as the Japanese *noh*. In other cases we feel on firmer ground: West End musicals are theatre, baptisms are rituals. But no performance is entirely one or the other; musicals as performance events have elements of ritualized behaviour within them just as concerts do, and many participants at baptisms seem to find the screams of the half-drowned child highly entertaining.

Schechner suggests that the difference between ritual and theatre lies in who is performing what, where, and under what circumstances, and that distinctions between the two should be made according to whether the performance is intended primarily for entertainment, as in the case of theatre, or whether its purpose is to effect some kind of transformation, to be efficacious, as rituals should. He writes that 'the basic polarity is between efficacy and entertainment, not between ritual and theater. Whether one calls a specific performance "ritual" or "theatre" depends mostly on context and function' (Schechner, 1988:120).

As with any continuum, then, there will always be those events which seem to mix elements of one pole or the other in roughly equal quantities, making classification difficult. I have suggested *noh* theatre as an example of this and I would also argue that musical performance events lie somewhere between these two worlds of efficacious ritual and theatrical entertainment, having elements of both while belonging entirely to neither. One by-product of this situation is that certain patterns of behaviour can be seen as having both theatrical and ritual attributes, and an example of this would be the use of applause.

Applause features in many different social and cultural events in Western society (and elsewhere), and in general its application is both socially understood and communally executed. But the fact that its use is both widespread and yet specific to particular moments within certain occasions would seem to suggest that it is perhaps more meaningful than it first appears. I suggest that in an orchestral concert applause delineates the structure of the event in a highly formalized fashion, and is a significant part of both the theatrical and ritualizing aspects of the proceedings. In considering this applause we might recall Merriam's differentiation between use and function, wherein he suggests that "Use" ... refers to the situation in which music is employed in human action; "function" concerns the reasons for its employment and particularly the broader purpose which it serves' (Merriam, 1964:210). Merriam's definition is intended to refer to the various applications of music itself but his distinction can be applied to other phenomena, and using this differentiation we can consider the role of applause with regard both to its use and function: put simply, the 'when?' and 'why?' of its application.

In the context of an orchestral concert the audience first applauds when the leader, symbolizing the whole orchestra, takes the stage. This applause, although provoked by his arrival, is not specifically *for* him; he has, after all, done little at this point, he is probably unknown to most of the audience, and he seeks no congratulation simply for navigating his way through the chairs on the platform. Likewise the applause for the conductor, although he may indeed be more familiar to the audience. Thus the applause at this stage is being used to show the audience's awareness of the arrival of these two figures and the beginning of the concert. It has several functions, however. It marks the completion of the transfer from preliminoid to liminoid stage, with the participants acknowledging the beginning of the most formalized part of the proceedings; it signifies the audience's approval that the event is proceeding in the correct fashion, that 'things are being done as they should', according to a general perception of how this quasi-ritual should be executed; and it serves as a means of communication between audience and orchestra, unifying them from disparate groups into one larger group of participants in a particular shared environment and contributing to the social antistructure discussed above.

As the concert proceeds applause occurs at various preordained moments throughout the event. It marks the completion of each piece of music performed, at which point the audience apparently shows its appreciation of the performance. Yet the applause will occur regardless of the perceived calibre of the performance, and indeed musicians will often argue that many of the audience cannot distinguish between an excellent performance and a poor one.

Most of your audience won't know. They just won't notice when it goes wrong and as long as you just keep smiling they keep being fooled.

But they will applaud nonetheless, as the same musicians would expect, again demonstrating both parties' awareness of the correct ritualizing procedure and their perpetuation of it.

A similar procedure to that employed at the opening of the concert marks the beginning of the second half, if there is an interval, and a generally more sustained round of applause occurs at the end of the whole event. In the same way as the opening applause marks the transition from preliminoid to liminoid, so this last applause marks the change from liminoid to postliminoid. It also continues to demonstrate approval of procedure and to be a means of communication. Applause therefore delineates the whole structure of the event and provides a framework around which it may be said to hang. While its use may change according to context its function remains largely constant. Its presence in specific, conventional places is fundamental to the correct procedure of the event and its absence would be unthinkable to the various participants.

Although I have suggested that applause may be considered as straddling the two domains of ritual and theatre there are, inevitably, various components of orchestral concerts which may be thought of as being largely theatrical, a word I use in the sense of 'something provided for entertainment'. These elements – lighting, costumes, stage management – I conceive as the theatre of music; that is, certain features which are consciously manipulated or elaborated for the purposes of 'putting on a good show'; and within this there is a particularly important subgroup which I shall call 'music theatre';[7] that is, the natural theatrical parameters of any musical performance, which may or may not be consciously extended or manipulated.

Those who are responsible for the planning and execution of orchestra concerts are very conscious of the theatrical parameters of musical performance and the impact their decisions have on the reception of a particular event. In recent years the London orchestras particularly, in a bid to halt the decline in audience numbers for their London concerts, have examined various ways in which these concerts might be made more attractive, as the following newspaper cuttings show:

> The Royal Philharmonic and the London Philharmonic Orchestra plan to change to more colourful outfits. Both are attempting to win younger audiences by shedding their stuffy images ... 'Young people associate the tails with music and it all seems very heavy,' said Gareth Wood, double bass player and chairman of the Royal Philharmonic. 'We want to break down those barriers and if that means dressing in multi-coloured shirts and creating a rainbow we will do it.'[8]

> Concert-going is about to change. The Royal Philharmonic has big plans, which include training a camera on individual musicians and the conductor's face to magnify their images on to a screen; taking the orchestra out of evening dress for some concerts; holding concerts in the round, and as a spokesman says, 'have drama, lasers and maybe a camera right down the clarinet.'[9]

> Judy Grahame, spokeswoman for the Philharmonia Orchestra, was ambivalent about the other two orchestras' plans, however. 'The ambience in the hall is much more important than what people wear,' she said.[10]

> Gavin Henderson, chairman of the Arts Council music panel, said: 'Orchestras that decide to dress differently or introduce video screens to concerts might put off as many existing customers as they attract new ones.'[11]

I think a lot of people are put off by the stuffiness of classical music, and the fact that it is all so old and it's about things that happened 200 years ago and people wear silly tails. Some people think we wear wigs. People have a lot of misconceptions about what it is actually like, and I've always felt that if we got rid of a lot of that stuffiness a lot of people would come back to it.

It is not only performers' costumes that have been the subject of scrutiny. The question of lighting arrangements within the hall has been the subject of some debate in the magazine *Classical Music,* with one correspondent noting,

Surely the days are passing when a remote and poker-faced group of performers display their art to an equally remote audience separated, as if TV viewers, by dimness and gloom.[12]

This was part of a series of contributions from other correspondents as to whether such a move would be a good thing.[13]

A number of issues become apparent here. First, we can see that there is no consensus either on whether changing the musician's dress or the format of orchestral concerts is necessarily a good thing, or on what changes might best achieve the required end, which is to attract larger audiences. Such concerts are, by their nature, relatively static events, leaving only certain aspects that can be manipulated in any meaningful way; the musician's costume and the lighting are perhaps the most obvious of these. In fact, few of these changes have come about, and the vast majority of orchestral concerts still adhere to the same format and dress as they had in the nineteenth century. It is also noticeable that it was the Royal Philharmonic Orchestra who were at the forefront of these suggestions, since at this time (the mid-1990s) the RPO were deemed by various funding organizations to have gone rather down-market or 'populist', suggesting some correlation with the traditional image of evening dress and the serious presentation of art music.[14] While this remains the case for most orchestral concerts, different dress codes and different patterns of behaviour have become more noticeable elsewhere, and it is worth considering for a moment how the orchestral concert I have used as my paradigm fits within the larger panorama of Western art music performance.

It is apparent that this particular type of concert is only one of many different but related events that together constitute this tradition. These include chamber music concerts, which involve smaller groups and fewer musicians; solo recitals by just one performer; choir concerts, semi-staged operas, jazz and pop 'crossover' concerts, and so forth: a range of different performance events corresponding to different musical genres. Many of these share similar patterns of behaviour to those I have described for an orchestral concert. They often occur in similar environments with parallel procedures and expectations, and much of what I have described above as ritualizing behaviour is equally relevant. In all the events sharing these characteristics there is what might be considered a 'prescribed formality', that is behaviour patterns corresponding to what the participants regard as formal: traditional, conventional, even ceremonial.

Equally, there are noticeably different behaviour patterns in other events. Some digress from such highly formal behaviour, often claiming that they wish to 'break down the barriers' of formal concert performance, as was the case with the group 'Saxploitation' (see p. 94). They attempt to modify certain aspects of the event, perhaps by changing the musician's uniform, or the relationship between performers and audience, or by asking the conductor or composer to introduce certain pieces so as to give a more educational veneer to the performance. Yet these moves away from perceived convention only succeed in creating different, but still standardized, patterns of behaviour. For example, many contemporary music groups in London will stipulate black trousers with a coloured shirt as their dress code; musicals, where the band is in a theatre pit, require only black clothes, and so on. This relaxation of the traditional formal rules, as the participants no doubt see it, might be described as 'prescribed informality'. The extreme versions of these two approaches may be considered as two poles of an axis: the prescribed formality of the very traditional concert at one end, and the prescribed informality of certain other types of concert behaviour at the opposite end.

Furthermore, these performance events may be plotted upon another axis, according to whether their musical content tends towards the traditional or the innovative. Some orchestral and chamber concerts seek to uphold and reinforce the conventional aspirations of the Western art music tradition, playing indeed only tonal music from the most significant composers between *c*.1700 and 1940. Others seek to be more innovative, playing older or newer music, music by less familiar composers, or incorporating music from other traditions.

Putting these two axes together gives a map (see Figure 2) upon which various performance events may be located to understand how they relate to one another, and to the tradition of Western art music as a whole.

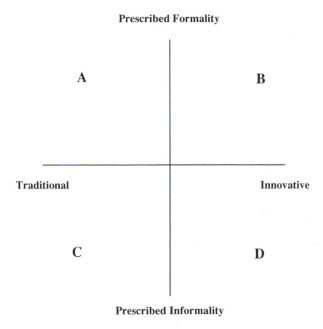

Prescribed Formality

A   B

Traditional   Innovative

C   D

Prescribed Informality

Figure 2: Mapping performance events

A, B, C and D are given as examples of where specific performance events may be mapped.

- Event A might be what I have called a traditional orchestral concert. It has a high level of prescribed formality – dress, etiquette, format – and seeks to present the more conventional musical repertoire associated with this type of event.

- Event B could be a concert involving a high degree of new or unfamiliar music. It still has the same outward symbolism as event A, and many of the same patterns of ritualized behaviour, but it seeks, musically speaking, to move the tradition forward or to expand or change it in some way; thus its meaning may be seen as rather different.

- Event C again seeks to reinforce traditional musical values of the event but to present these values using less traditional behaviour. Here might be placed the educational concert or certain one-off events such as 'The Last Night of the Proms'.

- Finally, event D is diametrically opposite A, seeking not only to introduce innovative musical ideas but also less conventional patterns of behaviour. Here we might find a 'crossover' concert, in which music by a jazz or pop composer has been brought into the concert hall, where some of the behaviour from these fields has also been transferred: applause during the piece, perhaps, or less conventional attire.

Although the four examples I have given are all orchestral concerts they might equally have been drawn from other musical fields. Traditional string quartet concerts would be closer to event A, whereas one involving modern music in a community centre or hospital would be nearer event D, and so on. Such a map also allows for certain anomalies. For example, a 1970s performance of mainstream repertoire on period instruments would, paradoxically, be in the top right quadrant, since these events were initially musically innovative, expanding the musical tradition while preserving the formal behaviour of conventional concerts. Over time, however, some of these innovations have become absorbed into the mainstream tradition itself, and so their position moves slowly backwards along the horizontal axis. Of course, an assessment of exactly what *is* musically innovative can be a matter of considerable dispute among the participants of these events, particularly among critics and academics, one of whose functions, it might reasonably be argued, is to make just these kinds of judgments. Such assertions are necessarily subjective and will not detain us here. But the map I have outlined above suggests how we might relate the outward forms of these performance events in some way, while at the same time allowing us to see that while they may be superficially related, the meaning inherent within them can change according to both context and content. The flexibility this model affords also shows how this class of events, these quasi-rituals, do in fact have the capacity for change, and that they can be efficacious, as Turner and Schechner suggest. They can be read as providing vehicles for change, certainly within the musical tradition itself, and possibly, by extension, within the wider social and cultural environment from which such events are drawn, a point to which I shall return below.[15]

And there is one final but important area to be considered within the sphere of the theatre of music and that is what I referred to above as music theatre. All musical performance is inherently theatrical; there is no genre of Western music performance that does not have some element of theatre about it, even if devoid of many of the traits I have discussed above. Virtually all music requires at least one performer, and even those few that do not, such as electro-acoustic music, are performed in such a way, normally within a hall or an installation, that a performance space is implied, with the attendant necessity to sell tickets, applaud and so forth; the mere act of listening both implies and is itself a type of a performance.[16] Within this broad spectrum, however, we can note various manipulations of the theatrical parameter of musical performance, which might conceivably be organized along a continuum. At one end lie those musical genres where the theatrical element is almost (but not entirely) absent, particularly if no obvious performer is present. Moving along from this we have events where a single performer plays a solo instrument, perhaps a cellist performing an unaccompanied Bach Suite. A little further along would be a traditional orchestral performance, inherently more theatrical because of the greater number of players, with the orchestra, conductor and perhaps soloists providing more of a spectacle. Further still we might again have a solo performer, but now the theatrical parameters of the performance have been deliberately extended by a composer who asks the performer perhaps to speak or move or perform obviously theatrical gestures; Berio's *Sequenzas* for voice or trombone or Stockhausen's *Harlequin* for a clarinet-playing dancer would provide examples. Just past this we would find similar approaches to ensemble or orchestral works, where the format of the traditional concert has been subverted in some way. Stockhausen's *Gruppen* splits the orchestra into three smaller orchestras placed around the audience; Tan Dun's *Circle with Four Trios* also has the orchestra placed around the audience with the conductor directing both musicians and audience. Further again we would come to the area where music and theatre have been given more or less equal roles. Here we would find a number of works by composers such as Peter Maxwell Davies (for example) *Eight Songs for a Mad King*) or Harrison Birtwistle (for example) *Punch and Judy*), and any number of operettas and large-scale operas. Finally, moving towards the other end of the continuum, we would observe those works where music – a difficult word to define when we reach this part of the spectrum – seems subordinate to theatre, or at least to theatre about music. Certain works by Mauricio Kagel or Vinko Globokar would furnish some examples here.

This listing is easily represented in diagrammatic form (Figure 3).

| MUSIC | | | | | | THEATRE |

| theatre largely absent – electronic music | unaccompanied instrumentalist | 'traditional' symphony orchestra concert | solo performance theatrically extended | group performance theatrically extended | music and theatre tend towards equality | theatre begins to dominate music |

Figure 3: Music–theatre continuum

While some might quibble with the musicological distinctions I have suggested, the important point is that some kind of distinction, some sort of taxonomy *can* be made; it is possible to conceive of these pieces in a way which quantifies the degree of theatricality inherent within a given musical performance. And since we generally find it easier to ascribe some kind of meaning to visual information rather than abstract musical sound, we feel we know at least what a piece is 'about', even if we are unsure what it 'means', when we are given some visual clues, when the theatrical parameter of the work is extended. Should we ever bump into Bruno Nettl's ethnomusicologist from Mars (Nettl, 1995:11) we would find it easier, at least in a relatively superficial way, to explain what Mozart's *Don Giovanni* is 'about' than we would a string quartet by the same composer.

The significance of this assertion will, I hope, become clear below. For the moment I would simply reiterate my various points, which are that these kinds of music performance events are separated from the normal social cycle by means of ritualized patterns of behaviour which endow such events with increased significance; that a form of ideological communitas is generated within them which is intensified at particular moments; that various aspects of the event can be manipulated in the service of what I have described as theatrical entertainment; and that the actual music in these events can be categorized in various ways, one of which quantifies the amount of theatre inherent in the musical performance itself.

Play

Finally, I would like to take a broader view of this whole area of theatre and ritual, and by extension the musical performance events with which I am primarily concerned, and locate it within the larger arena of play. Through this

I hope to provide a very general answer to the question, 'what do concerts do?'; that is, if concerts are in some way 'of' ritual, as I have suggested, in what ways might they be seen as efficacious, as providing models of or for change, as Schechner and Turner have suggested rituals should?

Like ritual itself, the concept of play is notoriously hard to pin down, and the search for a workable and satisfactory definition has provoked much debate in anthropology and related disciplines. In Western society we tend to regard play as something non-serious, the opposite of work, in much the same way as we oppose black to white or good to evil. Yet categorizing play in this binary fashion is too simplistic. We know from our own experience that play can occur during and as part of work, and can even aid work in certain contexts. Similarly, John Bowman (1987), drawing on a number of different ethnographic studies, has illustrated how a variety of pranks, acts of horseplay, joking relationships and so on can be observed in different employment situations. We also know that other activities which *ought* to be construed as play, such as competitive professional sports, can be taken very seriously indeed, not only by the participants themselves but also by those fans and followers who may have invested emotionally (and perhaps financially) in the outcome.

A review of anthropological literature demonstrates the wide range of perspectives employed in the study of play. For example, the various contributors to *Meaningful Play, Playful Meaning* (Fine, 1987a) demonstrate how play can be used to reinforce group or ethnic identities, and how patterns of play change as a consequence of social change. Contributors to a similar volume (Blanchard, 1986) show how children's play can be analysed from both psychological and ethnographic perspectives, and how games and sports can be exceptionally revealing of the cultural contexts in which they arise. More specifically, Don Handelman (1998:86–101) has shown how, in a sheltered workshop for the elderly in Jerusalem, what he describes as 'the donkey game', which involves surreptitiously hanging a make-believe donkey tail on an unwitting victim, could be read as a commentary on the participants' dissatisfaction with their lives and roles. As a sign the tail connoted the men's futility and impotence, ridiculing themselves and their position, in contradistinction to what, in their eyes, they might have or should have been. The participants were at best ambivalent about being in the workshop, but were obliged (for economic reasons) to remain there; they saw themselves as helpless persons controlled by hierarchy and authority, and this they found absurd. Handelman observes that, 'as their life-situations were absurd, so their play was serious commentary; but as their play was by definition unserious, that they played as they did was a commentary on the seriousness of their life-situations' (101). Thus play and what we take to be reality are symbiotically entwined, with the condition of one inevitably informing the other. Play may be fun, it may be funny, but it can also provide insights into 'real' life which are anything but unserious.

Yet if these various approaches give some flavour of the different directions from which anthropologists have latterly approached the subject of play, they are still to some degree indebted to an influential earlier work by Johan Huizinga, titled *Homo Ludens* ('Man the Player', [1944] 1955). Although much of what Huizinga has written has been subsequently recast by later writers, I am drawn to it here in part because of his characterization of both music-making and music itself as quintessential play activities.

There is much in Huizinga's work which resonates intriguingly with ideas I have introduced previously. He argues, for example, that play is not 'ordinary' or 'real' life, but demands that we find a separate cognitive space for it away from our more mundane concerns; play represents a 'stepping out of "real" life into a temporary sphere of activity with a disposition all of its own' (1955:8). Play is in the mind, it is ideational, a mental construct not reliant on material objects: 'we play and know that we play, so we must be more than merely rational beings, for play is irrational' (4). Play is also secluded or limited in some way, it is not limitless in time or space; it begins and then it is over. Much that Huizinga has observed in relation to play is equally true of rituals; indeed he argues that 'the ritual act, or an important part of it, will always remain within the play category' (27), notwithstanding that the recognition of its sacred nature remains. And, like ritual spaces, play areas are usually somehow marked out, delineated from 'ordinary' life either materially or ideally: 'just as there is no formal difference between play and ritual, so the "consecrated spot" cannot be formally distinguished from the play-ground. The arena ... the temple, the stage, the screen ... are all in form and function play-grounds, i.e. forbidden spots, isolated, hedged round, hallowed, within which special rules obtain. All are temporary worlds within the ordinary world, dedicated to the performance of an act apart' (10).

Such observations are equally applicable to orchestral concerts, which have just those qualities of fixedness and yet separation from real life which are at the core of Huizinga's observations. Indeed his characterization of those who play as generating a 'feeling of being "apart together" in an exceptional situation, of sharing something important, of mutually withdrawing from the rest of the world and rejecting the usual norms' (12) is remarkably consonant with the notion of communitas I described previously, and which I see as being particularly emphasized in these events. And his assertion that 'in play as we conceive it the distinction between belief and make-believe breaks down' (25) has further resonance with my remarks at the beginning of Chapter Six on the mythologizing of particular composers; such beliefs are reinforced within the play-frame of the concert hall, which is itself a magical world of make-believe.

However, it is Huizinga's observations on the nature of musical sound as 'the highest and purest' form of play (187) which are most intriguing in the present context. Such assertions stem from his belief that play is always in some way rule-bound. All play has its rules, and such rules, whether explicitly stated or intuitively understood, circumscribe the players' actions in the temporary world designated as play. As soon as the rules are transgressed the play-world is itself subverted; the game is over and 'real life' begins again (11). For Huizinga, music's dependence on a rigorous set of rules, a general understanding and acceptance of what is and what is not allowed in the way in which tones are organized in relation to one another, is one of two traits which leads him to characterize music as play. The second is that such tonal arrangements are not *in themselves* functional in any way – they serve no particular purpose (notwithstanding that they may, according to context, be socially construed as meaningful, or that the musical pieces may themselves be used functionally). It is this combination of the rule-based foundations of musical structure and music's essential functional redundancy that elevates it to the level of pure play. Furthermore, he observes the various distinctions between different musics, noting that 'no uniform acoustic principle connects Javanese or Chinese music and Western music, or mediaeval and modern music' (188). And it is this diversity of musical sound and structure which provides 'renewed proof that it is essentially a game, a contract valid within circumscribed limits, serving no purpose other than yielding pleasure, relaxation, and an elevation of spirit' (188) which, in Huizinga's eyes (and ears) defines music as play *par excellence*.

Huizinga is of course guilty of oversimplifying the nature of musical affect. The idea that music simply relaxes or elevates the spirit may well have appeared plausible in the mid-twentieth century to a writer responding largely to the masterworks of the Western art music canon, but the point is not universally valid and musical patterns in other traditions may provoke markedly different responses. Such responses are socially engineered and validated; there is nothing inherent in any particular musical structure which determines a universal response to it. However, his observation that music is in some way rule-bound, that those subscribing to a particular tradition have clearly formed ideas about what is musically acceptable within that tradition, obviously has a much broader cultural validity. Thus music is at one and the same time both completely arbitrary (since the ethnomusicologist in me believes that music systems are *social* constructs not necessarily related to natural acoustical laws) and intensively rule-bound (because work done on generative musical grammars around the world demonstrates this to be more than simply a Western phenomenon). And I find Huizinga's notion that this might be described as play, something by definition unserious or capricious yet with the capacity to be taken extremely seriously and to provide significant insights into other areas of social life, very satisfying.

Huizinga's observations on the differences between cheats and spoilsports are also intriguing in the present context:

> The spoil-sport is not the same as the false player, the cheat; for the latter pretends to be playing the game and, on the face of it, still acknowledges the magic circle … [but] the spoil-sport shatters the play-world itself. By withdrawing from the game he reveals the relativity and fragility of the play-world in which he had temporarily shut himself with others. He robs play of its *illusion*. (11)

In the context of musical performance the cheat is the person who enters the concert without a ticket. Although he breaks the rules for his own purposes, the conventions of the event itself are otherwise adhered to; the magical world remains intact. The spoilsport, on the other hand, undermines the event, destroying the play-frame: hence my irritation with the individual who clapped too soon after the end of Berg's *Der Wein*. For me the sense of violation had robbed the moment of its magic, its illusion; the moment was, literally, spoiled.

Huizinga's work, and that of the other anthropologists I have cited, demonstrates the interconnectedness of play and social reality; play both infuses and is itself informed by the wider social and cultural environments in which it arises. But while anthropologists have largely concentrated on these social dimensions, others, notably psychologists, have focused on the importance of play in contexts relating to the individual, particularly as evidenced in early learning and child development. Moreover, in keeping with my general perspective here that orchestral concerts impact upon participants not only as group members but also as individuals, I believe that some of the work done in this latter area can provide important insights into our experience of such concerts. And I take as my starting point ideas drawn from the work of the psychoanalyst D.W. Winnicott, particularly some of those expressed in one of his last works, *Playing and Reality* (1971).

Winnicott trained as a paediatrician but gradually became more interested in psychology, particularly the developmental psychology of babies and young children and the importance of play in healthy human development. He suggests that new-born babies are unable to differentiate between themselves and their mothers, or indeed any external object. Over time, however, babies develop, via the stimulation of the oral erotogenic zone by fingers, thumbs, fists and so on a perception of 'not-me' objects: a teddy, a doll, a cuddly toy. The intermediate experiences, before the perception of the first 'not-me' object, are stimulated by what Winnicott has called 'transitional phenomena' and 'transitional objects'; such experiences represent a fundamentally important stage of early human development. He writes:

> From birth therefore, the human being is concerned with the problem of the relationship between what is objectively perceived and what is subjectively conceived of, and in the solution of this problem there is no health for the human being who has not been started off well enough by the mother. *The intermediate area to which I am referring is the area that is allowed to the infant between primary creativity and objective perception based on reality-testing.* The transitional

phenomena represent the early stages of the use of illusion, without which there is no meaning for the human being in the idea of a relationship with an object that is perceived by others as external to that being. (Winnicott, 1971:11)

Winnicott goes on to suggest that this conflict, the struggle to relate inner and outer reality, not only applies to young children but continues throughout adult life (40), and that 'relief from this strain is provided by an intermediate area of experience which is not challenged (arts, religion, etc.). This intermediate area is in direct continuity with the play area of the small child who is "lost in play"'(13). Winnicott also suggests that there is a developmental line from these transitional phenomena to playing, from playing to shared playing, and then to cultural experience generally, and that such cultural experience is located in the potential space between the individual and the environment, between the subjective object and the object objectively perceived: 'cultural experience begins with creative living first manifested in play' (100).

Play for Winnicott, then, is in some senses a liminal entity, 'betwixt and between' external reality and inner psychic reality. It is that space where we begin to make sense of ourselves, of our surroundings, and of the relationship between the two. It again involves illusion, and perhaps dreaming. Winnicott suggests that, 'in playing, the child manipulates external phenomena in the service of the dream and invests chosen external phenomena with dream meaning and feeling' (51). Furthermore play is the basis for all cultural experience, which is 'the common pool of humanity, into which individuals and groups of people may contribute, and from which we may all draw *if we have somewhere to put what we find*' (99).

From Winnicott's perspective, then, all theatre and ritual, and music performance events which I have posited somewhere between, falls within this larger arena of play, of cultural experience, this space between the subjective object and the object objectively perceived. This is clearly congruent with Huizinga's assertion that play is ideational, and that play spaces are (or can be) mental constructs, not necessarily marked out materially. Perhaps play itself resists any more formal a definition than this, a more explicit terminological exactitude. Schechner (1993:43) suggests that 'it's much too limiting, too tight, too certain to build play theories around notions of play genres, identifiable "things"', while Turner, shifting his perspective from play to playfulness, writes:

Playfulness is a volatile, sometimes dangerously explosive essence, which cultural institutions seek to bottle or contain in the vials of games of competition, chance, and strength, in modes of simulation such as theater, and in controlled disorientation, from roller coasters to dervish dancing ... Yet although 'spinning loose' as it were, the wheel of play reveals to us ... the possibility of changing our goals and, therefore, the restructuring of what our culture states to be reality. (Turner, 1983:233–4)

In this final phrase we can once again see the link between, and hence Turner's interest in, play and ritual, and Schechner's (and Turner's) view that rituals do something, that they are in some way efficacious. Like play, rituals are also illusory. In the rarefied social antistructure of their liminal stage they provide us, not with real events or journeys undertaken by real people, but with symbolic behaviour which allows us to confront the social transactions which rituals seek to represent, while allowing us to avoid the conflicts and dilemmas such transactions present us with in the reality of our daily lives. Theatre is also illusory. Invented characters, whom we know to be 'not-real' as well as 'not-me', act out fictional events in predetermined environments, from which we infer – or, perhaps better, upon which we construe – meanings we take to be relevant for us in 'real' life.

Contextualizing ritual and theatre within the wider category of play in this way provides, I believe, some insight into the musical performance events which are the focus of this chapter. As I have shown, these events have elements of both ritual and theatre within them and, therefore, the elements of illusion these imply: the illusion of spectacle – penguin-suited musicians presumed to be equal yet somehow 'different from us', or at least 'different from those outside'; the illusion of equality – 'we're all equal now'; and so on. And of course the musical performance itself provokes certain types of illusion, most obviously in those works where the parameter of theatre is extended but also in other works; in programmatic music, for example, such as Berlioz's *Symphonie Fantastique* with its depiction of the *March to the Scaffold*; and even in music without any particular programme but which stimulates us to devise some sort of meaning to or representation of it, much as Miss Schlegel did for Beethoven's Fifth Symphony in *Howards End,* when she closed her eyes and saw 'a goblin walking quietly over the universe, from end to end. Others followed him. They observed in passing that there was no such thing as splendour or heroism in the world. After the interlude of elephants dancing, they returned and made the observation for a second time' (Forster, 1947:34).

So illusion, while perhaps not an obvious or dominant feature of these events, is certainly contained within them. And from illusion, via its Latin roots in *ludus*, we come back 'to play'; and by taking a slightly different linguistic track for a moment we realize that we knew we were playing all along. We speak of musicians *playing* their instruments, of orchestras *playing* particular works, just as we speak of 'going to see a play'. This revealing linguistic overlap is not only a feature of English but is found in many other languages also.[17] We are not at work, we are at play, however much the overlooked and overworked back-desk violinist may disagree with me. One musician described to me how he first discovered a violin in his parents' attic:

I think I might have played with it as a toy, and known it was a musical thing and tried to sort of figure out what you could do.

All of which leads me to concur with Huizinga (1955:162) when he observes that 'even if [the] primary fact that the essential nature of all musical activity is play is not always explicitly stated, it is implicitly understood everywhere'.

Within this arena of play we tend to lose ourselves, by which I mean that we become engrossed in the event and oblivious to the external reality around us. This is my perception of my own involvement in orchestral concerts as a member of the audience. In well-performed concerts of music which I identify with, I do not, even as a trained musician, follow the musical arguments of a particular work on a moment-by-moment basis (although others might). I am conscious of certain musical events: big tunes, recapitulations, dramatic moments. I am conscious also of the performers' activities, their work, so to speak. But I am also aware that my mind drifts away from these things and onto other completely unrelated ideas, thoughts, problems and so on. At times I drift back more consciously to the music and then away again in another direction, my thought processes existing side-by-side with the musical sounds presented to me. Nor am I alone in this behaviour. Edward Said (1992:86), for example, has written of his various thoughts while listening to a piano recital by Alfred Brendel, of the previous performances he was stimulated into recalling, as well as 'the fleeting, often banal non-musical associations that came to mind'. Even the musicians, who are under considerable pressure given the stresses of concert performance, may be said to be lost in their concentration. Winnicott writes:

> To get the idea of playing it is helpful to think of the preoccupation that characterizes the playing of a young child. The content does not matter. What matters is the near-withdrawn state, akin to the *concentration* of older children and adults. The playing child inhabits an area that cannot be easily left, nor can it easily admit intrusions. (Winnicott, 1971:51)

If I'm so in touch with the music and nothing to do with what I'm doing, or what's around me, but just listening so much to the music then something happens. When you've got rid of everything else ...

During the concert I was cut off from the rest of the world. No audience, no instruments, no everyday problems, nothing. A head full of music.

Once the thing's up and running I'm usually just in my own little world.

This is where the individual aspect of communitas becomes important. Although these performance events are in one sense shared cultural experiences, in another important sense they are individual experiences, personal adventures not shared by those around us, in which, by losing ourselves, we enter something similar to a dream world where various visual and aural objects mix with our own inner reality; a space between the subjective object and the object objectively perceived. Schechner's description of *noh* theatre provides a fitting analogy:

> The Japanese say that the proper way to 'watch' noh is in a state between waking and sleeping. Among the noh audience are many whose eyes are closed, or heavy-lidded. These experts are 'paying attention' by relaxing their consciousness, allowing material to stream upward from their unconscious to meet the images/sounds streaming outward from the stage. (Schechner, 1993:261)

It is this juxtaposition of conscious and unconscious behaviour, presented within the play frame of a concert which is in turn bounded by parameters both of theatre and of ritual, which best helps us to understand what such musical performance events 'mean' or 'do'. And it is here, finally, that we begin to see the broader efficacious effects of these musical quasi-rituals and how, to recall Turner's phrase, they contribute to the restructuring of 'what our culture takes to be reality' through the negotiation of musical meanings which we construe, at least in part, within the performance event. Such events provide us, not with a set of prefigured and unyielding cultural references, but with a domain in which such references can be reflected upon, reconsidered and, if necessary, cast anew. Susan McClary makes a similar observation:

> Music and other discourses do not simply reflect a social reality that exists immutably on the outside; rather, social reality itself is constituted within such discursive practices ... It is within the arena of these discourses that alternative models of organising the social world are submitted and negotiated. This is where the ongoing work of social formation occurs. (McClary, 1991:21)

Thus while musical performance events, as I observed previously, can clearly be seen as providing contexts for change within the musical tradition itself (because they create opportunities for the performance of new or unfamiliar works) they can also be seen as creating spaces, both material and ideational, in which our understanding of our world, inasmuch as it may be represented musically, is forged. I conceptualize the relationship between these various elements of ritual, theatre and play as given in Figure 4.

Furthermore, we might also note that there appear to be certain parallels between the place of music in our society, and that of humour. Here I am suggesting that we make sense of music in the space between the object objectively perceived and subjectively conceived of; in Chapter Six I put forward Freud's notion that humour occurs as a result of a clash between the unconscious and the conscious. In both cases we are at the interface of what we can control (subjectivity/consciousness) and what we cannot (object/unconscious), and both occur within the world of play; indeed, Freud suggests that 'a joke is developed play' (Freud, 1960:179). There are further parallels. Like humour, musical sound is essentially ephemeral; it is created, experienced, and then gone, existing only as a residue of memory until it is reconstituted and experienced once again.

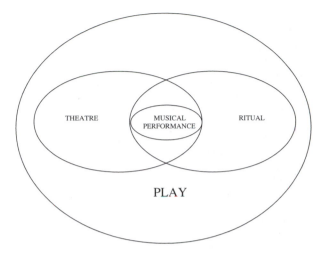

Figure 4: Musical performance as ritual, theatre, and play

Musical performance events also negate or challenge (by generating communitas) the extant social structure, just as humour does. And both humour and music require a great deal of sociocultural decoding; or rather, taken out of their original contexts their meanings may well be changed or lost. Perhaps the similarity which I observed previously between Merriam's paradigmatic musician and Klapp's fool type (see p. 143) is less remarkable after all.

So, by way of a conclusion, I am suggesting that all Western art music performance events have varying amounts of both theatrical and ritualized behaviour, and can therefore be posited in an intermediate area between these two, belonging entirely to neither but retaining elements of both. Furthermore, all these events exist within the world of play, where all cultural experience is located, and where we address the conflict between our subjective, inner realities, and the objective, external realities we designate as 'not-me'. It is in this space that we begin to construe meaning in music; 'patterns of humanly organised sound' (Blacking, 1976) which we take to be significant for ourselves and which we can share with others only if they construe similar, or at least sympathetic, meanings. But this shared experience, and the ideological communitas engendered within it, must not obscure the importance of the individual experience to which it gives rise. And, I suggest, it is in those areas where the theatrical parameters of music are most reduced, in the quintessentially playful environment of 'absolute' music perhaps, when we are given the fewest clues as to what the music is 'about', that this area of play is at its most complex and interesting, where we work hardest to make sense of what we experience in order that, paraphrasing Winnicott, we may somewhere put what we have found.

Notes

1   I find Small's alternative viewpoint reminiscent of Gerald Else's reworking of
     Aristotelian catharsis, a model which was and is usually applied to the feelings
     of the audience as they react to the drama, but which, Else argued, should be
     thought of as applying to the plot itself (see Else, 1967). In Small's case at least,
     the model seems to me less effective when considered in this way.
2   This would appear to underline Blacking's observation that 'music's special
     world of virtual time has the power ... to transport us away from the world of
     culturally regulated, actual time' (Blacking 1968:313).
3   *The Guardian*, 30 May 1997:2/24.
4   See Byron (1995:20) for further discussion on the often unattributed importance
     of Schutz in Blacking's thinking.
5   See, for example, *The Times*, 2 December 1988:1/3.
6   This is of course something of a generalised ideal. Changes do occur for reasons
     of illness or other absences, and a few orchestras (the London Symphony
     Orchestra being one) have a system of desk rotation, whereby string players
     change position on a weekly or monthly basis. The aim of this is to avoid
     staleness and to encourage competence in playing at both the front and the back
     of the section, seating positions which require rather different approaches.
     Such variations, however, still require rulings of one kind or another. The basic
     principle of string players being appointed to a particular desk is the norm in
     most professional orchestras.
7   I am aware that the term 'music theatre' is often used in mainstream musicology
     to denote a particular type of twentieth-century artwork which marries music
     and theatre in a similar fashion to opera, but on a much smaller scale and
     generally with a different underlying aesthetic. I hope my own rather more
     narrow use of this term can be read without confusion.
8   *The Sunday Times*, 15 May 1994:1/3.
9   *The Independent*, 8 August 1994:14.
10   *The Independent on Sunday*, 15 May 1994:3.
11   *The Independent*, 13 October 1994:5.
12   *Classical Music*, 17 May 1997:4.
13   See *Classical Music*, 5 April 1997:4; 19 April 1997:5.
14   An independent report into public funding of the orchestras at this time noted
     that 'The Royal Philharmonic ... has not in recent years pursued an adventurous
     programming policy. Its commercial strategy has been aimed at a market which
     wants to hear familiar music' (Hoffman, 1993:16).
15   Such a perspective again puts me at odds with Small, who argues that the fact
     that composers have continued to write works for orchestral concerts after 1920
     (his chosen endpoint for the Western art music canon) is to be regarded as
     'astonishing' (Small, 1987:14). That his model is unable to account for this
     would seem to diminish its value.
16   For more on the creative act of listening in the electro-acoustic environment, see
     Smalley (1992).
17   Huizinga (1955:42) notes Arabic and French, together with Germanic and some
     Slavonic languages. My own informal enquiries suggest Uzbek (a Turkic group
     language) and Tajik (allied to Persian) are similarly constructed.

... *da capo al fine* ...

Twists in the tale

In keeping with my intention to present my own role in this study as transparently as possible it is now appropriate to recount some more recent developments, and to reflect upon what has changed over the time it has taken to bring the work to fruition. In the process I need to outline further personal details, but I hope the usefulness of this brief supplementary biography, and the wider inferences which can be drawn from reflecting upon matters arising from it, will soon become apparent.

The early roots of this study can be traced back to the M.Mus. course I referred to at the beginning of Chapter One, when I first began to think about musical life in London, and my part in it, from an ethnomusicological perspective. Much of the text was then written for a subsequent doctoral dissertation, after which certain sections were added or amended in preparing the book manuscript. These chronological details are not in themselves particularly important, but what is significant is that, over this timescale, amounting to approximately a decade, my position within this community of freelance musicians has changed considerably; it would be disingenuous of me not to make this clear, and remiss of me not to include some of the insights which have arisen through this changing perspective.

When I initially reacquainted myself with the world of academe I saw myself as, and was seen to be, an integrated member of this community of musicians, in the manner I have already indicated in Chapter One. At this time my academic study was peripheral to my 'day' job, something akin to a hobby, in which I indulged for my own satisfaction rather than to earn money or because I thought it would advance my career in some way. After this first course was completed I then enrolled for a PhD, although this was, again, initially peripheral to the main thrust of my employment. As my doctoral studies proceeded, however, I became more involved in the world of higher education, earning money through teaching and lecturing, and eventually taking up a part-time position at a university on the outskirts of London. Over time my self-conception as 'a musician' became entwined with that of 'a lecturer', and for some time the two components were broadly equal. Eventually my academic activities translated into a full-time position at a different institution, a change of status which has notably curtailed my performing activities. Since then I have grown used to the delights of a regular salary appearing in my bank account at the end of each month, and my bank manager has grown accustomed to not being able to charge me as much as he had been used to, owing to the fact that I am no longer in the position of being continually advised by others that 'the cheque is in the post'.

This may appear a whimsical point but there are significant dimensions to it. First, it reinforces my previous assertions about the professional/amateur continuum. I do not now approach performances any differently than I did before, nor do I believe I play any worse, nor am I paid any differently. I am clearly no longer a 'professional' musician in the sense of my income being dependent on my performing activities, but I still perform in professional contexts and to professional standards. The same observations undoubtedly apply to other performers (and composers) who work from the relative financial sanctity of academic institutions. Therefore, and as I have already observed, our understanding of this term 'professional' arises from the manner in which it is used rather than through unambiguous definition, and it can describe many different points of engagement with the field of paid musical employment.

Furthermore, the comparative regularity of institutional life – the weekly timetable, the annual academic calendar – contrasts notably with the lack of regularity inherent in a freelance musical career, and this unfamiliar stability prompts me to reflect that this is another distinguishing characteristic between professional and amateur music-making. Ruth Finnegan (1989:318ff) draws attention to the regularity of local musical activities among amateur musicians in Milton Keynes, and the way the repeating schedules of musical participation contributed significantly to the framework of people's lives. These cycles of performances and rehearsals, whether weekly, monthly or annual, were not only characteristic of amateur music-making in a variety of different genres ('Monday, the Hogsty Folk Club, Tuesday, The Black Horse Folk Club ...' (319)) but also provided important signposts as people attempted to construct their own particular pathways through the complexities of urban life. By contrast, there is little that is regular or repeating in the lives of most professional musicians (the West End musical being an obvious exception). Most freelancers seldom if ever have one week just like any other, and many will cite this as one of the attractions of the job. Discharging their obligations on a variety of musical fronts will normally involve a pot-pourri of different times, travel arrangements, rehearsal spaces, concert venues, dress, even instruments for certain musicians. And this remains true even in the major orchestras, notwithstanding that they may be working to a schedule distributed a month or more in advance and will in fact revisit particular venues or studios more frequently than others. Thus it is not only the itinerant nature of a musician's life which in part characterizes it as professional, but its lack of cyclical regularity also, in contradistinction to some of Finnegan's observations on amateur musicians.

A further ramification of my new employed status is that, although my performing activities have been somewhat reduced, the monies I receive for playing are now in addition to salaried income. This point is not lost on some of those I work with, and has led in some cases, I think, to a different perception of my status as a musician. Little has been stated explicitly – although one colleague did remark: *I'm certainly not earning as much as you are these days* – and there may well be a degree of hypersensitivity on my part relating to this issue. But my suspicion is that those who know I also have a full-time job now view me differently, as though, because I no longer 'need' to play and my financial survival is not predicated on musical performance in the same way as others, my status in the community is qualitatively different. Moreover, this is a curious inversion of the 'What's your day job?' syndrome. Many musicians will have experienced an occasion when a stranger who encounters them as a musician will ask, in all seriousness, 'what's your day job?' or (worse) 'What's your real job?'; this has certainly happened to me and the point also arose during several interviews. That such questions are well meant and, from the point of view of the questioner, perfectly innocuous, does not lessen the sense of frustration or irritation they inevitably provoke. The reinforcement of the musician's social marginalization, or the perception that what they do does not count as a real job, is understandably galling to those who have usually worked very hard to attain their position, and who sustain themselves at great effort and for comparatively little financial reward. Now, however, the boot is on the other foot and I *have* a 'real' job (which, incidentally, I do not imagine will ever lead to a question such as 'what's your fake job?'). But the financial stability this provides may marginally colour the way some other musicians see me, since I no longer share their concerns to the same degree, particularly in relation to where the next work might be coming from, or how empty the diary might look for a particular week or month; indeed, an empty week or two now provokes quite the opposite reaction to that experienced previously.

I am not (of course) suggesting anything approaching ostracization or exclusion, merely a perception on my part of a different identity being constructed for me within this social world. This changed identity is further reinforced by the fact that I no longer trade engagements with musicians to the same degree, since I am now more selective about those engagements I accept or decline, and have fewer to offer in return. And the mapping of engagements which I constructed in Chapter Three would now look slightly different, since I can regard those jobs I have little wish to do as being even less desirable, and I am in the fortunate position of not necessarily needing the remuneration they provide. Retrospectively, I can see that this changing status progressed even during my doctoral studies. At one stage as I was finishing the dissertation a colleague rang me to discuss future work plans and said: *Ah! So you're ready to start taking on freelance work again now?*, although I had never suggested to anybody that this was not the case.

In moving more to the periphery of this community of musicians I have also become conscious of the particular mindset which goes with conceiving of oneself as a 'fully-engaged' performing musician, as opposed to one whose involvement is rather more 'semi-detached' (I resort to this unsatisfactory terminology in some desperation in an effort to overcome the professional/ amateur dichotomy). I was alerted to this in a recent discussion with one of my earlier saxophone teachers, who told me that, when I arrived in London from the provinces: *It took you a while to develop the mindset of being a musician.* I don't doubt that he was right, but even now I find it difficult to outline explicitly what this involves. Part of it is certainly to do with being adequately prepared for professional performance: knowing the notes, having the best reed on, being sufficiently rehearsed, giving a good presentation, and so on. But such qualities are not lost just because they are called upon less frequently, and once learned they are, or should be, retained. Rather it is the way in which one interacts with others in the community, valuing information about who is undertaking what job and when (connecting to the 'bush telegraph'), sharing concerns over work or lack of it, being in regular and direct contact with musicians through gigging with them, touring with them and in general just sharing the musician's lot in a way which engenders an attitude – as Margaret Thatcher might have put it – of being 'one of us' rather than 'one of them'. It is a cognitive space in which one confidently asserts to oneself that 'I *am* a musician; this is what I do, and these are the things I need to do in order to sustain myself at the required level.' It is in part through such mental constructs that one aligns oneself with the community of musicians, a community which, recalling Anthony Cohen's words, may lie largely in the mind.

Another biographical detail which might usefully be clarified at this stage is that, as the finishing touches are being put to this manuscript, I have resigned as leader of the quartet which I founded nearly two decades ago, and to which I refer frequently in Chapter Four. Obviously this was not an easy decision, and it has been to some degree prompted by my move into a full-time position, which has made it difficult for me to devote the necessary time and energy that leading a chamber group of this sort demands. But there were also other reasons: some concern on my part about what sort of musical challenges were still available to us after this length of time together, and a perception (rightly or wrongly) that the personal relationships between us were not working as smoothly as they once did. It is interesting to hear the other members now reflect on the differences made by a new player joining the group. For any group, the subtle differences in the playing of a replacement musician (or a deputy), no matter how excellent a musician they may be, can have a significant impact on what a performance *feels* like within the group; that is, on what Charles Keil and Steven Feld (1994) have described as 'the musical groove'. I doubt very much that an audience, in most cases, would be able to discern this, but for the musicians themselves any minute changes in tempo, flexibility, intonation and so on, can have a disproportionate effect on what might be described as the comfort zone in musical performance. In future years I hope to be able to discuss issues arising from this situation more fully, and there may be more insights from this period; at present I am too close to these events to dissect them, as well as being hesitant to discuss publicly details relating to a group which continues to perform.

Indeed this last point has been an issue throughout the writing of this work, since I have occasionally found it difficult to relate events in which I have been closely involved, for several reasons. For example, when incidents have occurred which I know provide interesting ethnographic insight but which I or others close to me have found difficult or painful, I have not yet felt sufficiently detached from these experiences to bring to them the necessary objectivity that this study requires. These will no doubt provide suitable data for future research, thus providing a clear example of the way in which, as I noted previously with regard to Hastrup's writings, the ethnographic present continues over time, as the ethnographer seeks to make sense of his or her experiences in the field. Furthermore, the proximity of 'the field' itself, being close at hand and not in some far-flung and relatively inaccessible corner of the globe, has obliged me to be ultra-cautious with regard to the dangers of implicating particular informants in my text, who may be recognizable to others despite my attempts at anonymity, for fear of disturbing delicate sociomusical relationships. This is an inevitable problem for the native anthropologist, who does not leave the field on completion of the fieldwork or who, particularly in my case, continues to live and work among the same people when material is published. In such cases the writer must endure the consequences of his or her work among those who have ready access to it, who may be interested to read it, yet who may disagree with its conclusions or its content. I am also aware through conversations with other anthropologists that similar concerns arise even decades after work has been published, when, perhaps through the coincidence of diasporic migration or for other reasons, groups or individuals who were previously thought to be unlikely to see certain ethnographic texts have established themselves in countries where such texts are readily available. The anthropologist treads ever more warily among such pitfalls in the context of increasing globalization and rapidly developing intercontinental communications.

Because I have drawn upon my own experience extensively and included my own voice in the writing of this work, the end result is undoubtedly influenced by my perspective on and position within this community; but I have attempted to make the potential bias this may produce as transparent as possible, allowing others to infer what they will from my words. I do not believe my involvement in this community makes this work any less 'real' or valid; it would be a perverse approach to anthropology which denied a platform for the individuals under observation, even if one of those is the ethnographer himself. While I believe this does not reduce whatever significance this study may have, it does inevitably colour the interpretation I have presented, in the same way as two ethnographers would present different pictures of the same group or culture even had they lived there contemporaneously. However, the defence for such 'self-centred' ethnography (if defence were needed) has already been articulated by Tim Rice in *May it Fill Your Soul*, a book about Bulgarian music and musicians in which the author's own experience of the tradition under observation plays a substantial role:

> The notion of reporting on one's own experience is sometimes criticized as irrelevant to an understanding of another tradition. However, I would argue that personal experience is neither free nor individual; it is constrained by interaction with the tradition. If I discover something 'true' in the experience, it is not because of a virtuosic subjectivity but because I have questioned the tradition and, in the process, opened myself to it. (Rice, 1994:308)

Rice is of course reflecting upon an engagement with a tradition other than his own, whereas my work has been on a tradition with which I was already intuitively, perhaps even unquestioningly, engaged; indeed the questioning I have undertaken has inevitably been as much of myself as it has been of others, an approach which, as I have already observed, undoubtedly lends a particularly personal dimension to this work. But if Rice and myself have come at the issue from different directions, the conviction that we have both generated meaningful insights through reflections on our own experience is, I believe, equally valid.

On another tack, Nettl (1983:278–89) argues that there is a plausible case for examining the biographical details of a given musician's life, because this can reveal much about changes in performance practice, for example, as well as in broader issues of cultural change inasmuch as they apply to music and music-making. He contrasts the ready use of biography in historical musicology, particularly when it shows the different stages into which composers' lives might be divided and how these resonate with or are exemplars of broader cultural currents, with the relative paucity of such approaches in ethnomusicology.[1] Nettl observes that 'the use of biography – essentially autobiography, gathered through interviews that must be corroborated and edited – is a major thrust in anthropological field method' (279); and while I doubt that he had the autobiography of the ethnographer in mind at this point, when the native ethnographer is himself part of the plot such inclusion, suitably reflexive and contextualized within the autobiographical reflections of others, has, I suggest, a validity beyond narcissistic literary impulse. The autobiographical elements of this study are not intended to be extensive, nor have I dealt with aspects of changing musical interpretation as such, in the way Nettl suggests; but I hope that in other issues related to the organization of musicians' lives, and in those conceptualizations which are tangential to but impact upon musical performance itself, the use of my own experience and views has been in some way meaningful.

Limitations of the ethnography

If giving myself a particular role in this work is useful in certain ways it is clearly unhelpful in others, and it is necessary at this point to consider some of the limitations of this study. One potential deficiency is its complete lack of consideration of gender issues; indeed, in some respects it may be seen as an 'asexual' ethnography, since the various theoretical constructs I have put forward have been presented as though they were equally applicable to musicians of either sex; and I have in general desexed the interview quotations I have presented, so that the gender of the informant is neither made explicit nor was it a consideration relevant to the reasons for the inclusion of that particular quotation. This is dangerous territory, however, and it would be wrong to think that simply androgynizing language in this way obviates gender bias. As Brian Morris (1994:169–91) has pointed out, the disciplines of philosophy and the various social sciences have all too often used ideas such as 'man', 'reason' and even 'person' in ways which, while appearing to be value-free, have in fact espoused a particularly androcentric orientation. Feminist critique of such usage has led to a realization that 'gender is not only important for epistemology but is inextricably bound up in conceptions of personhood' and thus 'the concept of person is gender-specific' (170). I realize that I may be equally guilty of the charge of adopting what I believe to be a gender-free stance, yet which is, by the very nature of the particular role I have ascribed to myself here, rather more gender-specific than I had intended. If so, I hope that the possibilities I have demonstrated here will encourage others to tackle similar issues from a more avowedly feminist or gender-oriented stance than the one I have adopted.

Notwithstanding the above, however, it is certainly useful to reflect on what little information is available in this area, particularly where it casts different shadows upon the supposedly asexual landscape I have outlined here. One particular area of Western musical practice, of course, has famously discriminated against women for some considerable time. In the male-dominated world of professional orchestras women have frequently been barred from entry, or suffered prejudice once in place, for several centuries. Orchestral music-making appears to have been, almost by definition, a chauvinist occupation, and the representation of women in the orchestras has, until very recently, been somewhat token, even where it is found at all (with the exception of the war years when, as elsewhere, women were drafted into the orchestras to replace men engaged on the battlefront). This is not simply a feature of London's musical demography but is a hallmark of orchestral life more widely, as Abbie Conant's experiences with the Munich Philharmonic graphically demonstrate.[2] Recently, however, the number of women playing in London's major orchestras has risen considerably, so that they comprise at least 25 per cent of most orchestras, and as much as 50 per cent of the BBC Symphony Orchestra.[3] Strategies such as blind auditions (with part or all of the audition panel unable to see who is performing) have contributed to this gradual erosion of inequality. It remains unlikely, however, that the female experience in this area is not qualitatively different from that of the male, although the one study I located on this particular issue (James, 1995) presents little evidence of blatant sexism.

However, with respect to the particular approaches I have concentrated on in this work, the ways in which notions of self and group identity are created and sustained, how such identities are reinforced through conceptualizing sound, deputizing strategies and so on, there is considerable justification for suggesting analogous patterns of behaviour between the two sexes. My own interviews have not alerted me to significant differences in these areas and, indeed, that I have been able to intersperse quotations from different sources (and sexes) without difficulty would suggest the verisimilitude of their approaches to these issues, notwithstanding the caveats I have outlined above.

On a different issue, it will also be noted that throughout this study there are few references to specific musical works and no musical examples. Nor have I dealt in any substantial way with music sound ('the actual music'), which is something rather different from the concepts of individual or group sounds which I considered in earlier chapters. Thus the anthropological bias of this work invites a description more as 'the anthropology of music' rather than one of 'ethnomusicology', which would in some quarters at least be considered as a more equal marriage between musicology and anthropology than that demonstrated here. This is not to suggest that ethnomusicology cannot contribute to a greater (or at least, broader) understanding of the musical structures of Western art music, since I firmly believe that it can. The rather more interpretive perspectives recently adopted elsewhere in musicology clearly show a desire to explain musical artworks, not so much as having meaning within themselves,[4] but from the ways in which they are used by those who seek to assign meaning to them.[5] This appears to me a profoundly ethnomusicological concern. But the approaches I have taken here with reference to the purveyors of this tradition, the musicians themselves, how their community is organized, the values and meanings they themselves ascribe to what they do, the manner in which they manipulate the symbolic nature of performance events and their influence upon the content of them, would seem to be of fundamental importance to the ways in which musical artworks are perceived and conceived by others in society at large and, therefore, a necessarily prerequisite step towards a better understanding of what such music can mean in Western society.

Musicians' lives and social rank: the urban musician-type

The rumination and introspection this study has provoked on my part has inevitably led me to evaluate critically the quality and 'value' of a career as a professional musician in London. And a further reflection prompted by my move into a full-time job is that it unarguably reveals a certain discontent with the life of a professional musician or, at least, my life as a professional musician; clearly, if I were so contented with things as they were, I would not have wanted to change them. Yet, rather than this demonstrating a particular idiosyncrasy (or shortcoming?) of my own position, I see it as being representative of a general level of dissatisfaction among many of my erstwhile colleagues. I have had long conversations with several other musicians in their late thirties and early forties, who have wondered what else they might do to provide some form of income, either in part or in whole turning their backs on a fully engaged musical career. I know of one orchestral wind player now retraining to be a teacher, with the expectation at some stage of taking a school teaching job in preference to his orchestral career of the last 14 years or so; an orchestral string player who has taken a position as Head of Strings in an independent school, and who now juggles this with reduced orchestral commitments; a freelance wind player who, in his late thirties, has retrained as a lawyer and now works in the City of London; another who has long moonlighted as a computer specialist. These are not, I believe, isolated examples, but represent a tangible sense of frustration among a certain proportion of musicians in mid-career, over and above, I suggest, the mid-life crises to which many are susceptible at this age. Some simply become frustrated with the itinerant lifestyle and the perpetual insecurity of freelance work; what can seem rather glamorous and exciting in one's independent twenties becomes considerably less so in one's forties, particularly if there is now a family to support and educate. Part of the problem can also be attributed simply to the relatively low incomes most musicians achieve, when set against their skill levels and the extensive training they undertake:

You can't actually earn much money, even in the LSO. It's very poorly paid. That is the biggest resentment of any orchestral musician I know, the fact that they're so poorly paid. You always quote how much it costs when you get a plumber or an electrician, and they wouldn't be going up to Watford for £65, or whatever the single classical recording session is now. You wouldn't get him going up there, when it takes you half a day.

Yet, set against this, it is very hard to give up being a musician. As I have already shown in Chapter Two, musicians do generate a very strong self-conception *as* musicians, something which is cultivated and internalized over many years, and which is reinforced by the sacrifices and commitments which must be made to be successful; simply to turn one's back on this significant investment and do something entirely different is not a decision taken lightly. And even those who become jaded with the trappings of a musician's life often continue to enjoy the musical performances themselves:

I think there is a big resentment. But the thing is, a lot of them wouldn't do anything else. People say, jokingly, 'I've got to supplement my income, I've got to do mini-cabbing' and all that sort of stuff. But I mean I do enjoy it, certainly, I wouldn't have stayed in it for this long. But for the level of skill, for the amount of hours you put in to actually reach that sort of standard, you know ...

Perhaps such resentment is also bound up with the broader difficulties which the Western art music tradition currently experiences, a topic recently identified by Nicholas Cook (1998b:40–51). Cook argues that some commentators (he cites Lawrence Kramer as an example) believe that there has been a long period of decline in this particular musical tradition, and that 'Western classical music is in a state of crisis' (45). Cook himself is more ambivalent about such assertions, noting the success of such things as *The Three Tenors*, the Polish composer Henryk Górecki's *Symphony No.3*, and the popularity of the London-based *Classic FM* radio station, notwithstanding the latter's habit of broadcasting single movements of larger works ('bleeding chunks') which so irritates those of a high-brow inclination. Yet I believe that many London musicians would feel very sympathetic to this description of the tradition in which they work as being in a state of crisis. Rightly or wrongly they perceive their roles to be continually devalued; funding to the orchestras and opera houses seems perpetually cut back,[6] and audiences appear increasingly difficult to attract for anything except the most popular events involving the most highly promoted (and expensive) conductors and soloists. The old certainties have been fractured: classical music is no longer by definition better or more worthy than other musics, but must compete against them for its slice of the ever-diminishing public subsidy pie; orchestras and other ensembles are no more perceived as having some unspoken but inalienable right to exist, but must justify their funding with educational or community outreach work and commitments to new music and/or touring to regional venues; London's pre-eminence in the European film score and classical music recording field has been significantly eroded by numerous cheaper orchestras from eastern Europe and elsewhere, which has a knock-on effect for freelance musicians in general (because the pool of available work diminishes); and so on.

There's a feeling that it's not highly regarded, the arts aren't highly regarded in this country, and you're constantly being told that you've got to justify your existence, you've got to do educational work.

Cook suggests that, 'if there is a crisis in classical music, it is not in the music itself, but in ways of *thinking* about it' (50). He may well be right. But for those who are charged with recreating and recording such music, and whose livelihoods depend on its continuing health, the cultural uncertainty about its role and its place in Western society translates into very pragmatic concerns about where their next work might be coming from, and how they might continue to put bread on the family table.

Furthermore, if it is true that 'the arts aren't highly regarded in this country', what does this tell us about the social position of artists in general, and musicians in particular? And how might such admittedly subjective impressions be objectively cross-referenced in order to address the question I posed at the end of Chapter One: to what extent do London's musicians conform to Alan Merriam's paradigmatic assessment of musicians across different cultures as sharing three particular traits: low social rank, high importance, and deviant behaviour subsequently capitalized upon? I suggest that they do appear to conform to this model, albeit with the proviso that within the context of a complex urban society such categorizations are perhaps less clear than Merriam makes them appear for societies such as the Basongye of Africa. There is both anecdotal and empirical evidence to support this, and many musicians have been forthcoming with their views.

One incident which made a particular impression on me with regard to this question concerned the future direction of an 18-year-old school student, with considerable but somewhat idiosyncratic musical skills, who was for many months weighing up the desirability of going to Oxford University to read Politics, Philosophy and Economics, or going to the Royal Academy of Music to enrol on their jazz course. His family, both wealthy and high-achieving, with one son already at Oxford, were clear about their similar aspirations for the second son. Eventually he was rejected by Oxford, much to the dismay of the parents, who subsequently told the school's Head of Music: 'Well, I suppose we're slowly coming to terms with the fact that we're going to have a musician in the family.' They may not have said this with quite as much irony as it was communicated to me, but their underlying perception of the social position of a musician seems clear enough.

There are certain concrete examples which also seem to support this view. Musicians generally pay more for car insurance, that is, they are considered a higher risk, than most other workers, leading many musicians to declare themselves (illegally, of course) as 'teachers' or occasionally 'company directors' or something similar on their insurance form. I was once refused home contents insurance on the grounds that I was a musician, and would therefore be keeping my instruments at home, despite having these covered by a separate insurance policy. Obtaining mortgages can also be a problem, although this is perhaps an issue more generally related to the self-employed. But there does seem to be something of a perception, in Britain at least, that musicians do not rank highly in terms of social hierarchy, and musicians themselves also generally see things this way.

You're just a musician, you're a necessary part of the jigsaw.

And such perceptions are reinforced when musicians are confronted with the 'what's your real job?' question to which I referred above, a question which, whatever the musician's response, is all too frequently accompanied by the observation that 'it must be wonderful making a living out of a hobby, something you do for enjoyment'. Such statements or, regardless of empirical accuracy, the perception that such sentiments are widely held, further illustrate the rather marginal position which musicians themselves feel they occupy:

It's not highly regarded at all. It's got this amateur status in this country. It's just the way orchestras have developed in this country. They're not professional outfits.

But it is equally true that neither are musicians right at the bottom of the social hierarchy, displaying the kind of undesirable characteristics noted by Merriam for musicians among the Basongye ('debtors, impotents, hemp smokers' and so on), although examples of heavy drinking can be found among musicians without too much difficulty, something that no doubt contributes to the insurance problem noted previously. Some of this is revealed through particular linguistic idiosyncrasies. In general, when musicians want to put the best possible spin on what they do, they will refer to being in 'the profession', no doubt subconsciously equating it with other professionals such as doctors or lawyers. At other times, particularly when conversing among themselves in more colloquial language patterns, this becomes 'the business', a description connoting an altogether less elevated plane.

This ambiguity is carried through into considerations of the significance of their work; in general, although musicians themselves feel that what they do is important, they also suspect that few other people feel this way:

They probably read things in the paper about the national lottery allotting huge funds to the Opera House, for instance, and they probably think 'Well, they're only musicians, do they need all that money? What about the nurses?' and things like that. So I think we're not generally looked at with a great deal of sympathy.

At the end of the day we are entertainers, that's all we're doing, so are footballers, so are rock musicians, so are film actors, and I'd say most people are interested in the latter ones rather than classical musicians.

I think there is a feeling of resentment. It is a very skilled profession, but it's not highly regarded, and it's not something that is highly rated in financial terms.

But the issue is not clear-cut. The following musician obviously did feel that his work was valued:

But what you have to hang on to are the people you know outside. Friends of mine are always very interested in what I've been up to, even if they're not going to buy anything I've done or played on, they're very interested in what you've been doing. No-one's ever said, 'I think you're a timewaster, what you're doing is just a waste of time, why don't you do something that's worthwhile.' Everyone has actually valued it.

The notion of other people being 'outside' is itself a significant assertion of the idea of musicians forming a distinct community. That society at large seems to find the work of this community important to some degree would seem evidenced by the continuing amounts of money that are made available through public subsidy, via various funding mechanisms of one sort and another. While musicians continue to complain that these sums are inadequate to sustain the musical fabric of the nation to the extent they would like, and although the orchestras in particular feel rather badly treated in comparison with other institutions, the mere fact that musicians – as part of 'the arts' – are sustained at all in this way obviously indicates that some kind of value or importance is placed on the work they do. Indeed, one only has to look at the many countries where there is no institutionalized music education, no music in school, conservatoires or university music departments, nor perhaps the extensive amateur music-making structures outlined by Finnegan, to realize how much music *is* valued both in Britain and in Western societies in general.

I have already alluded to certain stereotypical images of musicians, and the somewhat outlandish patterns of behaviour contained within these would appear to confirm the potential of musicians to deviate from social norms, as Merriam suggests, although I have found little evidence that they are more prone to sexual deviancy than any other subgroup of society. One hears stories, of course – the musician working on a cruise who took two girls to bed together because he was unable to choose between them; the English group touring Russia who had a collection to secure the services of a lady of the night for somebody's birthday – but while such things might arouse the interest of a tabloid subeditor they are hardly deviant in the sense of breaking clearly established social mores, and they certainly do not provide the necessary ethnographic accuracy to establish a consistent pattern of deviant sexual behaviour. However, it is intriguing to note Becker's (1951:137) observation that his professional dance musicians regarded themselves as sufficiently different and separate from the rest of society for some of them to hold the view, *in extremis,* that 'only musicians are sensitive and unconventional enough to be able to give real sexual satisfaction to a woman'.

Moreover, the following anecdote from Christianson does illustrate that musicians are sometimes allowed deviant patterns of behaviour in other ways:

> In another band one player was a social security inspector who also usually collected the band's earnings, while at least two other members of the band were drawing social security and were being handed their share – in cash – by the social security inspector. (Christianson, 1987:226)

A similar event was related to me by a musician who had been paid in cash ('forgetsies' is a euphemism often employed) after a prestigious ball in a top London hotel; the event was being organized by the Conservative Party, the payer was a notable administrative official within it, and there were several ex-prime ministers present plus the chancellor of the exchequer. I doubt very much whether the hotel or the caterers were paid in cash, but for the musicians it was presumably seen as acceptable.

There are also certain aspects of Kemp's work on the personality of Western musicians which appear to be relevant here. He suggests firstly that, in concentrating on the development of their inner selves and aspiring towards independence, musicians show 'a disregard for externally imposed rules combined with tendencies to be governed by personal urges' (1996:64); he also cites Chambers (1969) who, reviewing the literature on creativity in general, suggests that such types are 'independent non-conformers, relatively unconcerned with group approval of their actions ... On the whole they ... have chosen not to conform to a given mould but rather to express their sensitivities and other characteristics through their creative abilities' (cited in Kemp, 1996:64).

Kemp also notes that, in terms of personality characteristics, musicians have a tendency towards androgyny; that is, they 'minimize differences on gender-related traits or, in some cases, actually reverse them' (119),[7] and that these characteristics 'may well result in musicians appearing to be different from ordinary people, or even strange. This may, in turn, have the effect of marginalizing them socially, quite apart from their natural tendency to segregate themselves because of their introverted and individualistic interests' (120). Becker also observes that his dance musicians 'emphasised their isolation from the standards and interests of the conventional society' (1951:143). All this would seem to underline the point that, not only do musicians become seen as a (self-selecting) subgroup of society, which I have described as a community, but also that they do exhibit patterns of behaviour which can loosely be described as 'deviant'; and they are, perhaps, by the nature of their disposition, slightly less ready to conform to the legal and moral framework which binds most of the other members of the society in which they work. Taking all this into account, it would appear that Merriam's paradigm does indeed hold true for musicians in an urban Western context, although not perhaps with the exactitude or to the same degree as he suggests is the case elsewhere. For example, it is clear that particular musicians do achieve notably higher positions of social rank as a direct result of their musical endeavours: *Lord* Yehudi Menuhin or *Sir* Simon Rattle, to name but two. Even certain individuals without honorary titles bestowed upon them may achieve a higher social rank than others, although in the global market throughout which Western art music is now disseminated this is no doubt allied to the issue of fame, which is itself bound up with marketing expertise. However, such observations apply, not only to those from the Western traditions, but also to others such as Ravi Shankar, Nusrat Fateh Ali Khan or Salif Keïta, who have also benefited from increased global communications and technology, and who may equally be seen as having a higher social rank than other individuals within the communities of musicians from which they are drawn.

Thus there is something of a pyramid structure in the hierarchy prevailing among Western musicians, and perhaps elsewhere, and it is reasonable to suggest that Merriam's musician-type more accurately represents the experiences of the many in the lower parts of the pyramid than it does those of the fortunate few who inhabit the higher levels. It is my own experience within these lower reaches that, as I made clear at the outset, I have drawn on considerably in writing this ethnography, while at the same time attempting to frame this experience among the observations and assertions of others, thus retaining, I hope, sufficient analytical rigour for this work to have a wider validity than would a simple autobiography.

Through these different approaches I have tried to indicate something of the variety of professional musical life in London, a life so often associated with the prestigious London orchestras and opera houses, but which in fact extends far beyond these particular institutions, as indicated by the complexity of the strategies musicians must employ to sustain themselves within this world, and the sophistication of their conceptualizations which underpin these strategies. Sharing these mental constructs, however, does encourage a sense of camaraderie, and I have tried to show that London's musicians can be considered as a community in an analogous fashion to communities of musicians elsewhere, closely integrated within the wider social fabric yet separately identifiable from it by virtue of its members' specialisms. Moreover, this community can be conceived as an intricate web of sociomusical relationships which exist over and above the institutions often taken to represent it, notwithstanding that those institutions (by which I mean performance groups and others such as educational establishments) and the performance events in which the musicians' work occurs, may all be considered as nodal points within this complex matrix.

London musicians, I suggest, do have a sense of belonging to this community, but they also have a highly developed self-conception as individuals, formulated through the interaction of a variety of components, including instrumental specialism, educational background and teaching lineage, individual sound production, and preferred genres of musical performance; all of which encourages the development of their own individual voice – a form of musical self-expression – as well as providing them with an individual identity which situates them within the larger social whole. This identity is expressed in part through the deputy system, a system wherein musicians implicitly but inevitably make social and musical judgments on others; and through the discourse partially engendered by these judgments they bestow hierarchically differentiated levels of musicality upon others, which in turn also become components of such musicians' individual identity.

Yet this highly developed sense of self can create tensions within the necessarily social context in which musicians work, and the various performance opportunities which they undertake inevitably influence the degree to which they feel able to express their musical selves; thus within the context of musical performance an element of tension often inheres between the aspirations of the individual and the necessary compromise or refinement of those aspirations for the means of musical production. The ways in which individual skills are manipulated to achieve these ends I have described as musicianship, the craft of musical performance, which also entails the execution of particular social skills in order to interact competently with other musicians in the contexts of orchestras and other musical ensembles. These groups can themselves become powerful symbols of shared musical aspirations, leading to internalized conceptions of what the group represents which become reified through their choice of repertoire, publicity material, CD covers and so on.

I have also tried to demonstrate the importance of myth and humour in this community, and indeed I would argue that music, myth and humour demonstrate many parallels even within our technologically complex Western society. The entire Western art music tradition is predicated on the mythological status which we ascribe to its most significant creators; certain stellar performers attain something of a mythical status within their own lifetime; musicians themselves are presented with stereotypical patterns of behaviour to which they feel they should conform – patterns which may not be true but which they believe to be true. Humour has a particularly important role to play within this community: as an identifier of social groupings, as an indicator of shared experience, as a social defence mechanism, and to underpin social and musical judgments of others. Humour permeates the cracks and crevices of the larger social framework, confronting or subverting extant social structures and hierarchies, and in this quasi-liminality it shares something with musical performance itself. We use ritualizing patterns of behaviour to differentiate musical performance events from everyday activities, distinguishing them from our 'ordinary' lives and creating a more egalitarian space wherein we generate communitas, which itself confronts and subverts the social hierarchies existing outside of the performance space. These performance events I have located within the larger arena of play: we are not at work, we are at play, in that space between the object objectively perceived yet subjectively conceived of.

And throughout all of this, the 'ordinary' musicians who form the focus of this study would, I think, recognize something of themselves in Merriam's paradigmatic observations of them; whether they would like what they saw, however, is a different matter entirely.

I'm often asked if I would like my children to become musicians, and the answer is a categorical no. If I knew then what I know now, I wouldn't be doing it.

Notes

1 As Nettl himself notes, there are exceptions to this rule. Jonathan Stock's (1996) work centred upon the life of the Chinese musician Abing provides one obvious example of this approach, as well as supplying a brief résumé (17 fn.2) of those few other ethnomusicological texts taking a similar line.

2 Conant details the prejudice and difficulties she has experienced in Bavaria, and the many years of court proceedings she has endured to attain parity with her male colleagues, on the website *www.osborne-conant.org*. She also provides detailed statistics on the gender imbalance of other central European orchestras, including, of course, the Vienna Philharmonic, which was until very recently all male, and cussedly proud of it.

3 Figures relate to 1995, and are taken from James (1995).

4 What might be described as the 'absolutist' position: see Meyer (1956:3).

5 Cook and Everist (1999:v–xii) provide a good overview of some of these musicological directions.

6 Even as this is being written the chorus of English National Opera is beginning a series of strikes in protest at proposed redundancies for both the chorus and the orchestra.

7 It is perhaps worth making clear, as Kemp does, that there is little evidence to suggest that musicians' androgyny is a general manifestation of homosexual tendencies

Appendix

Attributed quotes

Although the majority of quotes which I have integrated within the text have been taken from my own interviews, a small number were extracted from television documentaries. Although these are 'in the public domain', as it were, I feel it desirable to list them below, so as to avoid any possible implication of plagiarism.

The following were taken from the Channel 4 series, *The Phil*, a documentary in three parts about the life of the Philharmonia Orchestra, broadcast on 24 January, 31 January and 7 February 1999:

The sound of the Philharmonia … (p.53).
When I was a student … (p.105).
The whole nature of being an orchestra musician … (p.107).
The whole job of a conductor … (p.108).
It's a two-way thing … (p.108).
We're artisans rather than artists … (p.119).
We were doing an opera in Germany … (p.135).
It's amazing what a bit of adrenalin … (p.140).
The position I sit in … (p.161).
I'm often asked if I would like my children … (p.199).

Those below were taken from a different documentary, also broadcast on Channel 4 as part of the *Sound Stuff* series, called 'The Private Life of an Orchestra'; I have been unable to establish the exact transmission date, but it was some time in 1991:

You hear an ideal sound within yourself … (p.48).
It's like putting colour … (p.106).
As a musician, even when you're young … (p.107).
During the concert I was cut off from the rest of the world … (p.179).

Bibliography

Abeles, Harold F. and Susan Yank Porter (1978), 'The Sex-stereotyping of Musical Instruments', *Journal of Research in Music Education*, **26**, 65–75.

Ablon, J. (1977), 'Field Method in Working with Middle-class Americans', *Human Organisation*, **36**, 69–72.

Agawu, V.K. (1984), 'The Impact of Language on Musical Composition in Ghana: An Introduction to the Musical Style of Ephraim Amu', *Ethnomusicology*, **28**, 37–74.

—— (1987), 'Tone and Tune: The Evidence for Northern Ewe Music', *Africa*, **58**, 127–46.

Allen, R.E. (ed.) (1990), *The Concise Oxford Dictionary of Current English*, Oxford: Clarendon Press.

Allmendinger, J., J.R. Hackman, and E.V. Lehman (1994), 'Life and Work in Symphony Orchestras: An Interim Report of Research Findings', report no.7, *Cross-national Study of Symphony Orchestras*, 95–107.

Apte, M.L. (1985), *Humor and Laughter: An Anthropological Approach*, Ithaca: Cornell University Press.

Baily, John (1979), 'Professional and Amateur Musicians in Afghanistan', *World of Music*, **21**, 46–61.

—— (1988), *Music of Afghanistan: Professional Musicians in the City of Herat*, Cambridge: Cambridge University Press.

Barthes, Roland (1977), *Image, Music, Text*, London: Fontana Press.

Baumann, Gerd (1992), 'Ritual Implicates "Others": Rereading Durkheim in a Plural Society', in D. de Coppet (ed.), *Understanding Rituals*, London: Routledge, 97–116.

Becker, Howard S. (1951), 'The Professional Dance Musician and his Audience', *American Journal of Sociology*, **57**, 136–44.

—— (1982), *Art Worlds*, Berkeley: University of California Press.

Bell, Catherine (1992), *Ritual Theory, Ritual Practice*, New York: Oxford University Press.

Bell, C.R. and A. Cresswell (1984), 'Personality Differences among Musical Instrumentalists', *The Psychology of Music*, **12**, 83–93.

Bergson, Henri (1950), *Le Rire: Essai sur la Signification du Comique*, Paris: Presses Universitaires de France.

Besmer, Fremont E. (1983), *Horses, Musicians, and Gods: The Hausa Cult of Possession Trance*, South Hadley, MA: Bergin and Garvey Publishers.

Blacking, John (1968), 'Percussion and Transition', *Man*, **3**, 313–14.

Blanchard, K. (ed.) (1986), *The Many Faces of Play*, Champaign, IL: Human Kinetics Publishers.

—— (1976), *How Musical is Man?*, London: Faber and Faber.

Bohman, J. (1999), 'Practical Reason and Cultural Constraint: Agency in Bourdieu's Theory of Practice', in R. Shusterman (ed.), *Bourdieu: A Critical Reader*, Oxford: Blackwell Publishers, pp.129–52.

Born, Georgina (1995), *Rationalizing Culture: IRCAM, Boulez and the Institutionalization of the Musical Avant-Garde*, Berkeley: University of California Press.

Bourdieu, Pierre (1977), *Outline of a Theory of Practice*, Cambridge: Cambridge University Press.

—— (1984), *Distinction: A Social Critique of the Judgement of Taste*, London: Routledge & Kegan Paul.

—— (1990a), *The Logic of Practice*, Cambridge: Polity Press.

—— (1990b), *In Other Words*, Cambridge: Polity Press.

—— (1991), *Language and Symbolic Power*, Cambridge: Polity Press.

—— (1993), *The Field of Cultural Production: Essays on Art and Literature*, Cambridge: Polity Press.

Bowen, José A. (1999), 'Finding the Music in Musicology: Performance History and Musical Works', in N. Cook and M. Everist (eds), *Rethinking Music*, Oxford: Oxford University Press, pp.424–51.

Bowman, John R. (1987), 'Making Work Play', in G.A. Fine (ed.), *Meaningful Play, Playful Meaning*, Champaign, IL: Human Kinetics Publishers, pp.61–71.

Brearley, John (1991), 'How Musical is the Band? Aspects of Musicians' Personalities with Regard to the Instrument They Play', unpublished MS, Goldsmiths College, University of London.

Buxton, David (1990), 'Rock Music, the Star System, and the Rise of Consumerism', in S. Frith and A. Goodwin (eds), *On Record: Rock, Pop, and the Written Word*, New York: Pantheon Books, pp.427–40.

Byron, Reginald (1995), 'The Ethnomusicology of John Blacking', in R. Byron (ed.), *Music, Culture and Experience: Selected Papers of John Blacking*, Chicago: University of Chicago Press, pp.1–28.

Carroll, M.P. (1981), 'Lévi-Strauss, Freud and the Trickster: A New Perspective upon an Old Problem', *American Ethnologist*, **8**, 301–13.

Chambers, J.A. (1969), 'Beginning a Multidimensional Theory of Creativity', *Psychological Reports*, **25**, 779–99.

Chanan, Michael (1994), *Musica Practica: The Social Practice of Western Music from Gregorian Chant to Postmodernism*, London: Verso.

Chiaro, D. (1992), *The Language of Jokes: Analysing Verbal Play*, London: Routledge.

Christianson, Harry (1987), 'Convention and Constraint among British Semi-professional Jazz Musicians', in A. Levine White (ed.), *Lost in Music: Culture, Style, and the Musical Event*, London and New York: Routledge & Kegan Paul, pp.220–40.

Clifford, James and George E. Marcus (eds) (1986), *Writing Culture: The Poetics and Politics of Ethnography*, Berkeley: University of California Press.

Cohen, Anthony (1985), *The Symbolic Construction of Community*, London: Tavistock.

—— (1994), *Self Consciousness*, London: Routledge.

Cook, Nicholas (1998a), 'The Domestic Gesamtkunstwerk, or Record Sleeves and Reception', in W. Thomas (ed.), *Composition, Performance, Reception: Studies in the Creative Process in Music*, Aldershot: Ashgate Publishing Limited, pp.105–17.

—— (1998b), *Music: A Very Short Introduction*, Oxford: Oxford University Press.

—— (2003), 'Music as Performance', in M. Clayton, T. Herbert and R. Middleton (eds), *The Cultural Study of Music*, London: Routledge, pp.204–14.

Cook, Nicholas and Mark Everist (eds) (1999), *Rethinking Music*, Oxford: Oxford University Press.

Cooper, Jilly (1996), *Appassionata*, London: Transworld Publishers.

Danziger, Danny (1995), *The Orchestra: The Lives Behind the Music*, London: Harper Collins.

D'Aquili, Eugene, Charles D. Laughlin and John McManus (eds) (1979), *The Spectrum of Ritual*, New York: Columbia University Press.

Davidson, Jane W., Michael J.A. Howe, and John A. Sloboda (1997), 'Environmental Factors in the Development of Musical Performance Skill over the Lifespan', in D.J. Hargreaves and A.C. North (eds), *The Social Psychology of Music*, Oxford: Oxford University Press, pp.188–206.

Davies, J.B. (1976), 'Orchestral Dischord', *New Society*, **35**, 46–7.

—— (1978), *The Psychology of Music*, London: Hutchinson.

Davis, John (1992), 'Tense in Ethnography: Some Practical Considerations', in J. Okely and H. Callaway (eds), *Anthropology and Autobiography*, London: Routledge, pp.205–20.

Douglas, Mary (1975), *Implicit Meanings*, London: Routledge & Kegan Paul.

Ehrlich, Cyril (1985), *The Music Profession in Britain since the Eighteenth Century: A Social History*, London: Clarendon Press.

Else, Gerald (1967), *Aristotle's Poetics: The Argument*, Ann Arbor: University of Michigan Press.

Evans-Pritchard, E.E. (1967), *The Zande Trickster*, London: Oxford University Press.

Fabian, J. (1983), *Time and the Other: How Anthropology Makes its Object*, New York: Columbia University Press.

Faulkner, R. (1971), *Hollywood Studio Musicians*, Chicago: Aldine Athertone.

—— (1973a), 'Orchestra Interaction', *Sociological Quarterly*, **14**, 147–57.

—— (1973b), 'Career Concerns and Mobility Motivations of Orchestral Musicians', *Sociological Quarterly*, **14**, 334–49.

Fine, Gary (1979), 'Small Groups and Culture Creation: The Idioculture of Little League Baseball Teams', *American Journal of Sociology*, **44**, 733–45.

—— (ed.) (1987a), *Meaningful Play, Playful Meaning. Proceedings of the 11th Annual Meeting of the Association for the Anthropological Study of Play (TAASP)*, Champaign, IL.: Human Kinetics Publishers.

—— (1987b), 'The Strains of Idioculture: External Threat and Internal Crisis in a Little League Baseball Team', in G. Fine (ed.), *Meaningful Play, Playful Meaning. Proceedings of the 11th Annual Meeting of the Association for the Anthropological Study of Play (TAASP)*, Champaign, IL.: Human Kinetics Publishers, pp.111–28.

Finnegan, Ruth (1989), *The Hidden Musicians: Music-Making in an English Town*, Cambridge: Cambridge University Press.

Forster, E.M. (1947), *Howards End*, Frome, Somerset: Butler and Tanner.

Freud, Sigmund (1960), *Jokes and their Relation to the Unconscious*, London: Routledge & Kegan Paul.

Frith, Simon (1978), *The Sociology of Rock*, London: Constable and Company.

—— (1989), 'Editor's Note', in S. Frith (ed.), *World Music, Politics and Social Change*, Manchester: Manchester University Press, pp.71–2.

—— (1991), 'Critical Response', in D.C. Robinson, E.B. Buck and M. Cuthbert (eds), *Music at the Margins; Popular Music and Global Cultural Diversity*, Newbury Park, CA: Sage Publications, 280–87.

Gamble, David P. (1957), *The Wolof of Senegambia*, Vol. XIV, London: International African Institute, Ethnographic Survey of Africa.

Garton-Ash, Timothy (1997), *The File: A Personal History*, London: HarperCollins.

Geertz, Clifford (1988), *Works and Lives: The Anthropologist as Author*, Stanford: Stanford University Press.

Gennep, Arnold van (1960), *The Rites of Passage*, London: Routledge & Kegan Paul.

Giddens, Anthony (1991), *Modernity and Self-identity*, Stanford: University of California Press.

Gillett, P. (2000), 'Ambivalent Friendships: Music-lovers, Amateurs, and Professional Musicians in the Late Nineteenth Century', in C. Bashford and L. Langley (eds), *Music and British Culture, 1785–1914: Essays in Honour of Cyril Ehrlich*, Oxford: Oxford University Press, pp.321–40.

Goffman, Erving (1959), *The Presentation of Self in Everyday Life*, New York: Doubleday.

Gould, J. and W.L. Kolb (eds) (1964), *A Dictionary of the Social Sciences*, London: Tavistock.

Green, Lucy (2001), *How Popular Musicians Learn: A Way Ahead for Music Education*, Aldershot: Ashgate Publishing Ltd.

Hampton, Barbara L. (1982), 'Music and Ritual Symbolism in the Ga Funeral', *Yearbook for Traditional Music*, **14** (1), 75–105.

Handelman, Don (1998), *Models and Mirrors: Towards an Anthropology of Public Events*, New York: Berghahn Books.

Hargreaves, David J. (1986), *The Developmental Psychology of Music*, Cambridge: Cambridge University Press.

Hargreaves, David J. and Adrian C. North (eds) (1997), *The Social Psychology of Music*, Oxford: Oxford University Press.

Harrison, Frank L. (1963), 'American Musicology and the European Tradition', in F.L. Harrison, M. Hood and C.V. Palisca (eds), *Musicology*, Englewood Cliffs, NJ: Prentice-Hall, pp.1–85.

Hastrup, Kirsten (1992), 'Writing Ethnography: State of the Art', in J. Okely and H. Callaway (eds), *Anthropology and Autobiography*, London: Routledge, pp.116–33.

Henry, Edward O. (1976), 'The Variety of Music in a North Indian Village: Reassessing Cantometrics', *Ethnomusicology*, **21**, 49–66.

Herndon, Marcia (1988), 'Cultural Engagement: The Case of the Oakland Symphony Orchestra', *Yearbook for Traditional Music*, **20**, 134–45.

Hoffman, The Rt Hon. Sir Leonard (1993), 'The Advisory Committee on the London Orchestras', Arts Council of Great Britain.

Holstein, James A. and Jaber F. Gubrium (2000), *The Self We Live By: Narrative Identity in a Postmodern World*, New York: Oxford University Press.

Howitt, Basil (1993), *Life in a Penguin Suit*, Manchester: Manchester Camarata Ltd.

Huizinga, J. (1955), *Homo Ludens: A Study of the Play-element in Culture*, Boston: Beacon Press.

Jackson, Anthony (1987), 'Reflections on Ethnography at Home and the ASA', in A. Jackson (ed.), *Anthropology at Home*, London: Tavistock, pp.1–15.

Jairazbhoy, N.A. (1971), *The Rags of North Indian Music*, London: Faber and Faber.

James, Eleanor (1995), 'A Study of the Women who Play in British Symphony Orchestras', unpublished M.Sc. thesis, University of Manchester Institute of Science and Technology.

Jaques, Elliott (1955), 'Social Systems as a Defence against Persecutory and Depressive Anxiety', in M. Klein, P. Heimann, and R.E. Money-Kyrle (eds), *New Directions in Psycho-Analysis*, London: Tavistock, pp.478–98.

—— (1990), *Creativity and Work*, Madison, CT: International Universities Press.

Jenkins, Richard (1992), *Pierre Bourdieu*, London: Routledge.

Jones, E.E. and H.B. Gerard (1967), *Foundations of Social Psychology*, New York: Wiley.

Jones, E.E. and T.S. Pittman (1982), 'Toward a General Theory of Strategic Self-presentation', in J. Suls (ed.), *Psychological Perspectives on the Self*, Hillsdale, NJ: Lawrence Erlbaum Associates, pp.231–62.

Keil, Charles and Steven Feld (1994), *Music Grooves: Essays and Dialogues*, Chicago: University of Chicago Press.

Kemp, A. (1981a), 'The Personality Structure of the Musician: I. Identifying Profile Traits for the Performer', *The Psychology of Music*, **9**, 3–14.

—— (1981b), 'The Personality Structure of the Musician: II. Identifying a Profile of Traits for the Composer', *The Psychology of Music*, **9**, 69–75.

—— (1996), *The Musical Temperament: Psychology and Personality of Musicians*, Oxford: Oxford University Press.

Kerman, Joseph (1985), *Contemplating Music: Challenges to Musicology*, Cambridge, MA: Harvard University Press.

Kingsbury, Henry (1988), *Music, Talent, and Performance: A Conservatory Cultural System*, Philadelphia: Temple University Press.

Kirton, Michael (1989), 'A Theory of Cognitive Style', in M. Kirton (ed.), *Adaptors and Innovators*, London: Routledge, pp.1–36.

Klapp, O. (1950), 'The Fool as a Social Type', *American Journal of Sociology*, **55**, 157–62.

L'Armand, Kathleen and Adrian L'Armand (1978), 'Music in Madras: The Urbanization of a Cultural Tradition', in B. Nettl (ed.), *Eight Urban Musical Cultures*, Urbana: University of Illinois Press, pp.115–45.

Lawson, Colin (ed.) (2003), *The Cambridge Companion to the Orchestra*, Cambridge: Cambridge University Press.

Lebrecht, Norman (1991), *The Maestro Myth*, London: Simon and Schuster.

Lévi-Strauss, Claude (1986), *The Raw and the Cooked*, London: Penguin Books.

Lipton, Jack P. (1987), 'Stereotypes Concerning Musicians within Symphony Orchestras', *The Journal of Psychology*, **121**, 85–93.

Lomax, Alan (1968), *Folk Song Style and Culture*, Washington, DC: American Association for the Advancement of Science.

—— (1976), *Cantometrics*, Berkeley: University of California Press.

Lortat-Jacob, Bernard (1995), *Sardinian Chronicles*, Chicago: University of Chicago Press.

Marcus, George E. and Michael M.J. Fischer (1986), *Anthropology as Cultural Critique: An Experimental Moment in the Human Sciences*, Chicago: University of Chicago Press.

Martineau, William H. (1972), 'A Model of the Social Functions of Humor', in J.H. Goldstein and P.E. McGhee (eds), *The Psychology of Humor*, London: Academic Press, pp.101–28.

Mascarenhas-Keyes, Stella (1979), *Goans in London: Portrait of a Catholic Asian Community*, London: Goan Association (UK).

—— (1987), 'The Native Anthropologist: Constraints and Strategies in Research', in A. Jackson (ed.), *Anthropology at Home*, London: Tavistock, pp.180–95.

Mauss, Marcel (1990), *The Gift: The Form and Reason for Exchange in Archaic Societies*, London: Routledge.

McClary, Susan (1987), 'The Blasphemy of Talking Politics During Bach Year', in R. Leppert and S. McClary (eds), *Music and Society: The Politics of Composition, Performance and Reception*, Cambridge: Cambridge University Press, pp.13–62.

—— (1991), *Feminine Endings: Music, Gender, and Sexuality*, Minneapolis, MN: University of Minnesota Press.

McLeod, Norma (1964), 'The Status of Musical Specialists in Madagascar', *Ethnomusicology*, **8**, 279–89.

Merriam, Alan (1977), 'Definitions of "Comparative Musicology" and "Ethnomusicology": An Historical–theoretical Perspective', *Ethnomusicology*, **4**, 189–204.

Merriam, Alan P. (1964), *The Anthropology of Music*, Evanston: Northwestern University Press.

Meyer, Leonard B. (1956), *Emotion and Meaning in Music*, Chicago: University of Chicago Press.

Moore, Sally F. and Barbara G. Myerhoff (eds) (1977), *Secular Ritual*, Assen/Amsterdam: Van Gorcum.

Morris, Brian (1994), *Anthropology of the Self: The Individual in Cultural Perspective,* London: Pluto Press.

Murnighan, J. Keith and Donald E. Conlon (1991), 'The Dynamics of Intense Work Groups: A Study of British String Quartets', *Administrative Science Quarterly*, **36**, 165–86.

Myers, I.B. (1993), *Gifts Differing: Understanding Personality Type*, Palo Alto, CA: Consulting Psychologists Press.

Needham, Rodney (1967), 'Percussion and Transition', *Man*, **2**, 606–14.

Nercessian, A. (2002), *Postmodernism and Globalization in Ethnomusicology: An Epistemological Problem*, Lanham, MD: Scarecrow Press.

Nettel, Reginald (1948), *The Orchestra in England: A Social History*, London: Jonathan Cape.

Nettl, Bruno (1963), 'A Technique of Ethnomusicology Applied to Western Culture', *Ethnomusicology*, **7**, 221–4.

—— (1983), *The Study of Ethnomusicology: 29 Issues and Concepts*, Urbana: University of Illinois Press.

—— (1995), *Heartland Excursions: Ethnomusicological Reflections on Schools of Music*, Urbana: University of Illinois Press.

Neuman, Daniel M. (1978), 'Gharanas: The Rise of Musical "Houses" in Delhi and Neighboring Cities', in B. Nettl (ed.), *Eight Urban Musical Cultures*, Urbana: University of Illinois Press, pp.186–222.

—— (1980), *The Life of Music in North India – The Organization of an Artistic Tradition*, Detroit: Wayne State University Press.

Newlin, Dika (1980), *Schoenberg Remembered: Diaries and Recollections (1938–76)*, New York: Pendragon Press.

Nketia, J.H.K. (1963), *Drumming in Akan Communities of Ghana*, London: Thomas Nelson.

—— (1974), *The Music of Africa*, New York: W.W. Norton and Co.

O'Connell, John Morgan (1998), 'The Sounds of Ethnomusicology: Ethno-musicology, Eth-No-Musicology and the Fragmented Condition of Music Studies', paper given at British Forum for Ethnomusicology annual conference, Cambridge.

Okely, Judith (1983), *The Traveller-Gypsies*, Cambridge: Cambridge University Press.

Parkin, David (1992), 'Ritual as Spatial Direction and Bodily Division', in D. de Coppet (ed.), *Understanding Rituals*, London: Routledge, pp.11–25.

Philip, R. (1992), *Early Recordings and Musical Style: Changing Tastes in Instrumental Performance*, Cambridge: Cambridge University Press.

Picken, Laurence (1998), address given to the British Forum for Ethnomusicology annual conference, Cambridge.

Piperek, Maximilian (ed.) (1981), *Stress and Music: Medical, Psychological, Sociological and Legal Strain Factors in a Symphony Orchestra Musician's Profession*, Vienna: Braumuller.

Radcliffe-Brown, A.R. (1940), 'On Joking Relationships', *Africa*, **13**, 195–210.

—— (1949), 'A Further Note on Joking Relationships', *Africa*, **19**, 133–40.

Reynolds, V. (1958), 'Joking Relationships in Africa', *Man*, **58**, 29–30.

Rice, Timothy (1994), *May It Fill Your Soul: Experiencing Bulgarian Music*, Chicago: University of Chicago Press.

Rogers, Carl R. (1970), 'Towards a Theory of Creativity', in P.E. Vernon (ed.), *Creativity: selected readings*, Harmondsworth: Penguin Books, pp.137–51.

Russell, Thomas (1953), *Philharmonic*, London: Penguin Books.

Sahlins, Marshall (1974), *Stone Age Economics*, London: Tavistock.

Said, Edward (1992), *Musical Elaborations*, London: Vintage.

Sakata, Hiromi Lorraine (1983), *Music in the Mind: The Concepts of Music and Musician in Afghanistan*, Kent, OH: Kent State University Press.

Salmon, Paul (1992), *Notes from the Green Room; Coping with Stress and Anxiety in Musical Performance*, New York: Lexington Books.

Schechner, Richard (1988), *Performance Theory*, London: Routledge.

—— (1993), *The Future of Ritual: Writings on Culture and Performance*, London: Routledge.

Schutz, Alfred (1977), 'Making Music Together: A Study in Social Relationships', in J.L. Dolgin, D.S. Kemnitzer and D.M. Schneider (eds), *Symbolic Anthropology: A Reader in the Study of Symbols and Meanings*, New York: Columbia University Press, pp.106–19.

Schwarz, David, Anahid Kassabian and Lawrence Siegel (eds) (1997), *Keeping Score: Music, Disciplinarity, Culture*, Charlottesville: University Press of Virginia.

Seeger, Anthony (1987), *Why Suyá Sing: A Musical Anthropology of an Amazonian People*, Cambridge: Cambridge University Press.

Shelemay, Kay Kaufman (1991), 'Recording Technology, the Record Industry, and Ethnomusicological Scholarship', in B. Nettl and P.V. Bohlman (eds),

Comparative Musicology and the Anthropology of Music, Chicago: University of Chicago Press, pp.277–92.

—— (1996), 'Crossing Boundaries in Music and Musical Scholarship: A Perspective from Ethnomusicology', *Musical Quarterly*, **80**, 13–30.

—— (2001), 'Toward an Ethnomusicology of the Early Music Movement: Thoughts on Bridging Disciplines and Musical Worlds', *Ethnomusicology*, **45**, 1–29.

Shepherd, John (1991), *Music as a Social Text*, Cambridge: Polity Press.

Slobin, M. (1993), *Subcultural Sounds: Micromusics of the West*, Hanover: Wesleyan University Press.

Sloboda, John (1985), *The Musical Mind: The Cognitive Psychology of Music*, Oxford: Oxford University Press.

Small, Christopher (1987), 'Performance as Ritual: Sketch for an Enquiry into the True Nature of a Symphony Concert', in A.L. White (ed.), *Lost in Music: Culture, Style and the Musical Event*, London: Routledge and Kegan Paul, pp.6–32.

Smalley, Denis (1992), 'The Listening Imagination: Listening in the Electro-acoustic Era', in J. Paynter and R. Orton (eds), *Companion to Contemporary Musical Thought*, London: Routledge, pp.514–54.

Stewart, Andrew (1994), *LSO at 90: From Queen's Hall to the Barbican Centre*, London: London Symphony Orchestra.

Stobart, Henry (1994), 'Flourishing Horns and Enchanted Tubers: Music and Potatoes in Highland Bolivia', *British Journal of Ethnomusicology*, **3**, 35–48.

Stock, Jonathan P.J. (1996), *Musical Creativity in Twentieth-century China: Abing, his Music and its Changing Meanings*, Rochester, NY: University of Rochester Press.

—— (1998), 'New Musicologies, Old Musicologies: Ethnomusicology and the Study of Western Music', *Current Musicology*, **62**, 40–68.

Stokes, Martin (1992), *The Arabesk Debate: Music and Musicians in Modern Turkey*, Oxford: Oxford University Press.

Stravinsky, Igor (1947), *Poetics of Music in the Form of Six Lessons*, Cambridge, MA: Harvard University Press.

Suls, J. (ed.) (1982), *Psychological Perspectives on the Self*, Hillsdale, NJ: Lawrence Erlbaum Associates.

Suls, J. and A.G. Greenwald (eds) (1983), *Psychological Perspectives on the Self*, vol. 2, Hillsdale, NJ: Lawrence Erlbaum Associates.

Tait, Simon (1996), 'Power Point', *Classical Music*, 3 February, 14–15.

Taruskin, Richard (1995), *Text and Act: Essays on Music and Performance*, Oxford: Oxford University Press.

Tomlinson, Gary (1984), 'The Web of Culture: A Context for Musicology', *19th-Century Music*, **7**, 350–62.

Toynbee, Jason (2003), 'Music, Culture, and Creativity', in M. Clayton, T. Herbert, and R. Middleton (eds), *The Cultural Study of Music*, New York: Routledge, pp.102–12.

Trudgill, Peter (1974), *Sociolinguistics: An Introduction*, Harmondsworth: Penguin Books.

Turino, Thomas (1993), *Moving Away from Silence: Music of the Peruvian Altiplano and the Experience of Urban Migration*, Chicago: University of Chicago Press.

Turner, Victor (1969), *The Ritual Process*, London: Routledge & Kegan Paul.

—— (1977), 'Variations on a Theme of Liminality', in S.F. Moore and B.G. Myerhoff (eds), *Secular Ritual*, Assen/Amsterdam: van Gorcum, pp.36–52.

—— (1982), *From Ritual to Theatre: The Human Seriousness of Play*, New York: PAJ Publications.

—— (1983), 'Body, Brain and Culture', *Zygon*, **18**, 221–45.

—— (1990), 'Are There Universals of Performance in Myth, Ritual, and Drama?', in R. Schechner and W. Appel (eds), *By Means of Performance: Intercultural Studies of Theatre and Ritual*, Cambridge: Cambridge University Press, pp.8–18.

Van Leewen, Theo (1999), *Speech, Music, Sound*, London: Macmillan Press.

Wachsmann, Klaus (1981), 'Applying Ethnomusicological Methods to Western Art Music', *World of Music*, **23**, 74–86.

Wagner, Richard (1972), *On Conducting: A Treatise on Style in the Execution of Classical Music*, London: William Reeves.

Westby, D.L. (1959), 'The Career Experience of the Symphony Musician', *Social Forces*, **38**, 223–30.

Wilson, Christopher P. (1979), *Jokes: Form, Content, Use and Function*, London: Academic Press.

Winnicott, D.W. (1971), *Playing and Reality*, London: Tavistock.

Wolf, Margery (1992), *A Thrice Told Tale: Feminism, Postmodernism and Ethnographic Responsibility*, Stanford, CA: Stanford University Press.

Index